D0482521

BOWING TO
BEIJING

BOWING TO BEIJING

How Barack Obama Is Hastening America's Decline and Ushering a Century of Chinese Domination

BRETT M. DECKER
Editorial Page Editor, the *Washington Times*

WILLIAM C. TRIPLETT II
New York Times Bestselling Author

Since 1947
REGNERY
PUBLISHING, INC.
An Eagle Publishing Company • Washington, DC

Copyright © 2011 by Brett M. Decker
Copyright © 2011 by William C. Triplett II

All rights reserved. No part of this publication may be reproduced or transmitted in any form or by any means electronic or mechanical, including photocopy, recording, or any information storage and retrieval system now known or to be invented, without permission in writing from the publisher, except by a reviewer who wishes to quote brief passages in connection with a review written for inclusion on a website or in a magazine, newspaper, or broadcast.

Library of Congress Cataloging-in-Publication Data

Decker, Brett M.
  Bowing to Beijing : how Barack Obama is hastening America's decline
and ushering a century of Chinese domination / by Brett M. Decker and
William C. Triplett II.
      p. cm.
  Includes bibliographical references and index.
  ISBN 978-1-59698-289-5 (alk. paper)
  1. United States--Relations--China. 2. China--Relations--United
States. 3. Obama, Barack. I. Triplett, William C. II. Title.
  E183.8.C5D43 2011
  327.73051--dc23
                        2011041235

Published in the United States by
Regnery Publishing, Inc.
One Massachusetts Avenue, NW
Washington, DC 20001
www.regnery.com

Manufactured in the United States of America
10 9 8 7 6 5 4 3 2 1

Books are available in quantity for promotional or premium use. Write to Director of Special Sales, Regnery Publishing, Inc., One Massachusetts Avenue NW, Washington, DC 20001, for information on discounts and terms or call (202) 216-0600.

Distributed to the trade by
Perseus Distribution
387 Park Avenue South
New York, NY 10016

DEDICATION

William C. Triplett II:
For Liu Xiaobo, one of the noble prisoners fighting for freedom for all of China.

Brett M. Decker:
For my parents, John Decker and Sharon Decker, who have made everything possible; and Anneke E. Green, for keeping my feet to the fire to make sure this book got done.

CONTENTS

CHAPTER ONE

OBAMA BOWS TO THE REDS

Some say the world will end in fire,
Some say in ice.
From what I've tasted of desire
I hold with those who favor fire.

—Robert Frost

It was a typically cold winter day in Washington, D.C. A strong gale whipped up whitecaps on the icy Potomac river and battered the marble monuments near the banks. The draft whistled through the trees and shot through the National Mall like a wind tunnel as a few snowflakes fluttered to the frozen ground. The thousands who came to watch the ceremony of the official changing of administrations huddled together in a vain attempt to keep warm. However, what cast the worst chill on America that blustery day was not the weather but the results of the recent election: the most left-wing politician in the history of presidential politics was moving into the White House.

At high noon on Wednesday, the 20th of January, 2009, the newly elected president walked out of the Capitol building and onto the steps of the west porch overlooking the crowd on the mall. He put his left hand on Abraham Lincoln's copy of the Bible, raised his right, and stated, "I, Barack Hussein Obama, do solemnly swear that I will execute the office of president of the United States faithfully, and will to the best of my ability preserve, protect and defend the Constitution of the United States."[1]

Since that moment, the forty-fourth president of the United States has spent every day undermining the power, economy, security, and prestige of America and making a mockery of his oath of office. Presaging the mistake-prone amateurishness of the Obama presidency, even the oath had to be repeated because of gaffes made during the official inauguration; some words were said out of order, so Chief Justice John Roberts trekked to the White House the next day to re-do the oath to allay any fears that Obama was not legally the chief executive of the government.[2] And so it has been: controversy and doubt about the direction of the country from day one.

The forty-fourth president of the United States has spent every day undermining the power, economy, security, and prestige of America.

There were signs foreshadowing trouble to come in Obama's inaugural address. Reflecting his radical roots as a community organizer who counted Weather Underground terrorist Bill Ayers as a mentor, the novice president intoned, "Every so often, the oath is taken amidst gathering clouds and raging storms."[3] As he uttered these words, a squall was indeed rising up to hammer America, and its origin was the People's Republic of China (PRC). Whether the new administration admitted it or not, America was facing down a red storm from a rising communist powerhouse.

For forty years, cadres in Beijing have been diligently building a more modern state. By the time Barack was unpacking pictures of Michelle for his Oval Office desk, the Chinese reds were within striking distance of becoming the largest economy in the world. While America was mired in recession, the PRC economy was growing at 10 percent per year, a feverish pace it had maintained for two decades. China's rulers had poured this massive wealth into hi-tech industries and weapons programs to arm an increasingly ferocious military. For America to maintain its position as the world's preeminent power, it needed to dramatically cut government spending to liberate private enterprise from the yoke of taxes and regulations so the economy could grow and create jobs. Obama was the wrong man at the wrong time, and the chief beneficiary of his profligacy has been our communist competitor in the Far East.

Under Obama's presidency, America is indisputably in decline—and Obama seems to welcome this outcome. During the 2008 presidential campaign, he declared, "We can't drive our SUVs and eat as much as we want and keep our homes on 72 degrees at all times … and then just expect that other countries are going to say OK." As a *Washington Times* editorial pointed out in exasperation, "He has yet to explain why he thinks the American people need to ask permission from other countries to maintain a high standard of living."[4]

Regardless, that standard of living is coming to an end, as is American independence. In Obama's view, the United States is simply one nation among many, and there is nothing particularly unique about it except for its special need to atone for its alleged historic arrogance. On his November 2010 state visit to India, the president complained that during his lifetime, "The U.S. was such an enormously dominant economic power … that we always met the rest of the world economically on our terms."[5] He has made sure that is no longer the case.

In 2008, gross U.S. public debt was 69 percent of the year's economic output. In 2011, it was poised to surpass 100 percent. This means the national debt will be bigger than everything built, bought, sold, leased, and serviced in the whole country for an entire year. We have dug a hole so deep that even the world's most productive economy can't get out of it. It's the excessive debt accumulated through Obama government spending that put the nation in this dire condition. As former Federal Reserve Chairman Alan Greenspan observed in early 2011, "I conclude that the current government activism is hampering what should be a broad-based robust economic recovery."[6] In other words, Big Government is keeping the economy down—and it's dragging with it America's predominant position in the world.

The government's unsustainable spending was bad enough under President George W. Bush, but Obama matched Bush's spending spree and then dramatically ramped it up, increasing the national debt by an astounding $4 trillion in just two-and-a-half years (compared to a rise of $4.9 trillion for the entire eight years of the Bush presidency).[7] And under Obama, this program of government profligacy and ruinous debt is by design, as is its result: a debilitated, humbled, and shackled America more dependent on foreign nations.

While running our own economy into the ground, the Obama administration has sucked up to the Chinese reds. Ignoring the precedent of the Bush White House protesting China's human rights record, Obama acquiesced to Chinese demands and honored President Hu with a full-fledged state dinner in January 2011. First Lady Michelle Obama wore a grotesquely modern, flashy red gown, apparently oblivious to—or maybe supportive of—the fact that the color red is symbolic of communism, and she was hosting the leader of the largest Communist nation in history. Regarding this red pandering by the administration during Hu's visit, the liberal *Washington Post* reported, the color was a prominent theme among Hu's hosts: "Mrs. Obama wore red gloves, President Obama wore a red tie, and [daughter] Sasha wore red pants for President Hu's arrival, and Hillary Clinton wore a red jacket to lunch."[8]

Of course, the red also could represent all the blood of innocents spilled at Hu Jintao's command, or the tens of millions murdered by the Maoist government during its sixty-plus years in power. Under either interpretation, it was completely inappropriate for the first family to honor such a dishonorable history by wearing the color of the Chinese Communist Party (CCP), but such callousness is par for the course for this crowd—as is unnecessary and outrageous public kowtowing to communist thugs.

Hu had come to expect such deference from the leader of the free world—at least, in this White House. The most embarrassing and telling sign of President Obama's obsequiousness toward the CCP leader was when Obama bent over and gave a full bow to Hu at the Nuclear Security Summit in Washington in 2010. Dr. Lillian Glass dissected Obama's gesture on her Body Language blog: "The Chinese leader's body language is in marked contrast to Obama's where Hu is leaning away from Obama and looking directly at him as a visible sign of personal power as Obama bows and gazes downward in a subservient gesture." Dr. Glass continued, "The Chinese leader does not return the bow. In fact the leader looks very superior to Obama as he doesn't bow back…. The Chinese leader does not bow back in the least as his posture is ramrod straight and appears in a completely upright body position. It clearly shows that the Chinese leader is the one in the power position."[9]

America is indisputably in decline—and Obama seems to welcome this outcome.

Obama has awkwardly bowed to numerous foreign leaders and officials, including the Emperor of Japan, the King of Saudi Arabia, the Queen of England and her husband Prince Philip, the president of Ukraine, and on and on, including some mid-level bureaucrats in China. In fact, Barack's navel inspection isn't limited to foreigners. He bowed to New Jersey Governor Chris Christie and, in a separate incident, to the blushing mayor of Tampa, Florida, who looked quite embarrassed by the president's show of fealty to a civic manager.

Although many liberals wave off Obama's penchant for bowing as a protocol mistake or a well-intentioned but badly executed attempt to be mannerly, these gestures have real consequences in the world of international diplomacy—they make the president look weak while unmistakably signaling U.S. national subservience. The president of the United States has plenty of experts to instruct him how to behave properly. It's obvious Obama is doing this on purpose, and it's a serious matter.

As Dr. Glass concluded, "The bottom line, perception wise, is that when a president of a powerful country bows to other heads of state or those in a lesser political position like the husband of a queen, a governor of a state or the mayor of a city, it makes him appear weak as a leader…. There is nothing humorous about a president of one of the most powerful countries in the world being perceived as weak, under any circumstances."[10]

U.S. weakness under the Obama presidency is not lost on the Chinese, who are pressing their political, economic, business, and military advantages in every conceivable way. The communists view their rivalry with us as a matter of survival; having witnessed America challenge and bury the Soviet Union, they worry that Washington has a similar end-game in store for them. "As seen from Beijing, Washington is a dangerous, crusading, liberal, quasi-imperialist power that will not rest until it imposes its views and its way of life on the entire planet," explains Princeton professor Aaron L. Friedberg, a former advisor to Vice President Dick Cheney.[11]

That's why the Chinese regime is hell-bent on rapidly building up the power of the People's Liberation Army—this is a life or death struggle against the Yankee imperialists. That's also why the Chinese are pursuing economic expansion and business competition with warlike zest—because for them, this is a real battle, a zero-sum game that one side will ultimately win and the other will lose. Viewing the Washington-Beijing relationship as a multi-front war, the PRC is dedicated to asserting its strength in every realm and to winning on all fronts. Consequently, the United States is confronted with the Chinese stealing technology, ripping off patents and trademarks, manipulating and even counterfeiting U.S. currency, breaking trade laws, misrepresenting military spending, selling toxic toys to American kids, dispatching armies of foreign agents to influence U.S. politicians, testing U.S. resolve on sensitive diplomatic issues, purchasing stakes in our banks, nurturing U.S. commercial dependency on Chinese business, building a blue-water navy, expanding its nuclear arsenal, and hacking our computer networks. All is fair in love and war, and this is war. And China is winning.

The cadres in Beijing must have enjoyed a particularly good chuckle when Obama officials talked optimistically about future collaboration in a joint U.S.–China space program. "Many of us, including the president, including myself, including [NASA Administrator Charles] Bolden, believe that it's not too soon to have preliminary conversations about what involving China in that sort of cooperation might entail," White House science advisor John Holdren said while addressing the prospect of a joint U.S.–China mission to Mars. "If China is going to be, by 2030, the biggest economy in the world … it could certainly be to our benefit to share the costs of such an expensive venture with them and with others."[12]

China is winning.

What Holdren conveniently left unsaid is that America is so broke it can no longer afford a space program and that, since the shuttle program was scuttled in July 2011, the United States cannot even send astronauts into space unless they hitch a ride with another country. Notice as well that Holdren accepted the supposed inevitability of America's decline, implying there is nothing we can do to prevent the PRC's economy from surpassing our own.

Washington being lost in space is a fitting metaphor for our entire relationship with Beijing: America is becoming meeker, China is becoming stronger, and if we don't radically change course, in the future the United States will rely on the communists for everything from purchasing our debt to putting men in space. The Obama administration looks at this as a fait accompli—and a deserving one at that, given all our supposed past sins.

President Obama is placing us in a dangerous position vis-à-vis China, but not everyone in official Washington is blind to the threat. For example, spread around the capital city is a network of anti-Beijing hardliners called the Blue Team, which refers to the code name PRC officials give to their enemies in war games.[13] This group is not an official organ of government but an informal collection of conservative policy experts, government aides, and scholars—many of whom prefer their identities remain secret—who advocate through both official and unofficial channels a tough stance against China.[14]

The team's general outlook is that the PRC is not a benign giant simply trying to develop its economy and mind its own business; it is, instead, a new Evil Empire that must be challenged on every front. This view doesn't sit well with many Democratic politicos as well as a large chunk of the GOP, which opposes a strident position because it will impede trade and business dealings. For the Blue Team, though, making the Middle Kingdom wealthier is just pouring fuel on the fire that could consume us. Confrontation is inevitable; the world isn't big enough for both powers to be on top, the team believes, so America must employ every course of action to contain Beijing.

The Blue Team's influence peaked early in the George W. Bush administration, when Republicans controlled the presidency and both houses of Congress, and the number of hawks in town was at an all-time high. However, Democrats taking over Capitol Hill and the White House clipped the Blue Team's wings, and they haven't been heard from recently. Beijing's manhandling of the Obama administration indicates the Blue Team needs to ramp up its operation again. Although China is successfully challenging the United States across the board, its ultimate victory is by no means assured. But at a time when our nation's leaders refuse to even put up a fight, it's crucial to have a battle-ready team waiting in the wings. As the line of the old Simon and Garfunkle tune puts it, "Where have you gone, Joe DiMaggio, our nation turns its lonely eyes to you."

Ronald Reagan, the greatest president of the twentieth century, liked to refer to the United States as "the shining city upon a hill." That's because, as George W. Bush explained when he was running for president, "Our nation is chosen by God and commissioned by history to be a model to the world."[15] America is great because it is good, and our best days and greatest glories always lie ahead. That's the belief of an optimistic, hopeful nation. Or at least it used to be.

In his inaugural address, President Obama broached the subject of American decline. In a rebuke to the ostensible militarism of the George W. Bush administration, Obama lectured that "our security emanates from the justness of our cause, the force of our example, the tempering qualities of humility and restraint." Or put another way, U.S. security depends not on boldness and power but on servility and reserve. That's fitting because Obama's policies have tempered our security by restraining our power through—if not humility—national humiliation, particularly through crippling indebtedness. Every major policy pursued by the forty-fourth president has made the United States weaker and in so doing has strengthened those aiming to do us harm.

This book will investigate the evil of the Maoist regime in Beijing and expose how Barack Obama has accelerated American decline and hastened Chinese global ascendency by genuflecting to the policy priorities—and physically bowing to the blood-soaked leader—of the People's Republic of China.

CHAPTER TWO

"THE NEW CHINA"

*Communism is not love. Communism is a hammer which
we use to crush the enemy.*

—Mao Zedong

On Christmas Day 2009, Liu Xiaobo was shackled, thrown into a windowless van at gunpoint, and carted away to serve out an eleven-year sentence in a dank Chinese prison. Today his health is failing, and he has been denied family visits that are common to inmates even in the People's Republic. He is not heard from for months at a time, sparking persistent rumors that he may be dead.[1] His crime? Subversion of state power.

To be found guilty of this serious charge, the frail, bookish, bespectacled literature professor didn't release poisonous gas on a Beijing subway car, blow up a military recruiting center, or plot to fly an airliner into a government office building. Instead, he committed the crime of speaking out for freedom in a communist land where dissent is considered treasonous. As George Orwell wrote, "In times of universal deceit, telling the truth will be a revolutionary act." It's a lesson Liu is learning the hard way while doing hard time.

There's nothing too out of the ordinary about this wretched plight in the Middle Kingdom. In fact, there would be no reason for anybody in the outside world to know about Liu except that the Nobel Committee in Oslo, Norway, awarded him the 2010 Nobel Peace Prize for his non-violent activism on behalf of Chinese political reform. The Chinese Communist Party took this honor for one of its citizens badly. "Liu Xiaobo is a criminal who has been sentenced by Chinese judicial departments for violating Chinese law," fumed the PRC's Foreign Ministry.[2]

That's incendiary rhetoric directed at a man whose chief act of disloyalty to the regime was co-authoring a manifesto, "Charter 08," that advocates an independent judiciary, the popular vote, and the historic American principle of no taxation without representation. "It was released on December 10, 2008, the anniversary of the [United Nations'] Universal Declaration of Human Rights, and emulates the Charter 77 written by Czech dissidents including Vaclav Havel, that called for an end to Soviet repression," explains Peter Foster of the London *Daily Telegraph*. "Originally the document was signed by 302 academics, lawyers and prominent people, but now has more than 12,000 signatures."[3]

China's Nobel Laureate had spent plenty of time behind prison walls before his 2009 sentence, including three years of hard labor for demanding the release of imprisoned protesters after the 1989 Tiananmen Square crackdown and a couple more years for supporting the democracy movement. Most recently, authorities put his wife under house arrest and full-time surveillance. The Nobel awards ceremony in Oslo brought an onslaught of repressive actions from Beijing, with communist cadres rounding up dozens of dissidents and enforcing a blackout of foreign news inside China, while the Foreign Ministry exerted a full-court diplomatic press that convinced eighteen other nations to boycott the occasion. The paragons of national virtue that caved in to Beijing's demand and boycotted the Nobel festivities were Afghanistan, Colombia, Cuba, Egypt, Iran,

Iraq, Kazakhstan, Morocco, Pakistan, the Philippines, Russia, Saudi Arabia, Serbia, Sudan, Tunisia, Ukraine, Venezuela, and Vietnam.

Hoping to rally its people behind the red flag, Beijing has used Liu's Nobel prize as an excuse to pump out propaganda warning Chinese citizens about a U.S.-led Western plot to embarrass and humiliate China. "Awarding the Nobel Peace Prize to Liu Xiaobo once again reflects the strong attempts of Western countries to intervene in the political process in China," complained an editorial in *People's Daily*, an official newspaper of the communist government. "It is a well-planned event, premeditated and long organized by Western countries, and is part of a series of actions by the U.S., its allies and companies to undermine China."[4]

Our president has nary a bad word to say about the butchers in Beijing.

If only that were true. Unfortunately, our president has nary a bad word to say about the butchers in Beijing. Barack Obama—himself one of the most undeserving recipients of the Nobel Peace Prize ever—has stubbornly and repeatedly refused to meet with prominent Chinese dissidents and human rights leaders. With Secretary of State Hillary Clinton more concerned about protecting the U.S.–China trade relationship than about protecting human rights, the Obama administration has barely made a peep about the plight of the president's fellow Nobel Laureate as he suffers in his Chinese prison cell.

The "New China" Myth

According to a fashionable theory, what we see in Beijing today is "the New China"—a gradually emerging, modern, progressive society that will eventually bring the communist state in line with the rest of the civilized world. Give it time, and everything in China will be all right, the logic goes. There are some challenges (mostly economic) and occasionally a setback (usually a violent crackdown on peaceful protesters, but the authorities had no choice, wink, wink), but today's Communist Party leaders are not really communists at all. They have to talk the talk occasionally for the sake of tradition and to keep the old hardliners on board, but behind the scenes, they want to be just like us. That's the line.

This convenient dogma has been central to America's engagement with Beijing since President Richard Nixon flew there in 1972 to toast mass murderer Mao Zedong and officially open U.S. relations with communist China after two decades of isolation. "We both realized that a bridge of understanding that spans almost 12,000 miles and 22 years of hostility can't be built in one week of discussions," Nixon said shortly after meeting with Chinese leaders. "But we have agreed to begin to build that bridge, recognizing that our work will require years of patient effort."[5]

This perspective still motivates U.S. policy toward the PRC today. Supposedly, we need to "engage" China to keep it moving in the right direction. By trading with the communists and making them rich, we'll eventually convince them of the virtues of a free capitalist society. So long as we help the Chinese people become wealthier and acquire more economic rights, they eventually will demand more political rights from their government. That's the basic reasoning—and it's an expensive gamble because if the dice come up snake eyes, we will have enriched our enemy, increased a brutal regime's power to persecute its own people, and underwritten the expansion of a belligerent military force.

For the past half-century, U.S. foreign policy has focused on bribing rather than isolating our rivals. Trade is the central component of this effort to purchase lasting and meaningful relationships, especially with communist China. And trade we have—American consumers buy more stuff from China than any other nation. In fact, in 2010 alone, we imported $365 billion worth of products from the PRC.[6] Since 1985, we have paid more than a whopping $3 trillion for Chinese imports. In 2010, the trade imbalance with Beijing was $273 billion in the communists' favor. Over the 26-year period between 1985 and 2010, America's trade imbalance with Red China was $2.4 trillion.

The supposed political payoff for this trade hasn't materialized, as the Chinese government is more authoritarian than ever. The Marxists know the Land of the Free is hooked on their cheap goods, and that we'll ignore a lot of ugliness on their side of the Pacific so long as the junk keeps flowing here.

Despite increased trade with the West, China's government is more authoritarian than ever.

The bridge to China envisioned by Nixon forty years ago has turned out to be more like an underground tunnel dug right into America's bank vault. Of course, U.S.–China ties do bring some benefits for American consumers, who can save money on their shopping trips to K-Mart. However, these ties weren't supposed to be about commerce, but about building a relationship that would spread our political ideas to the Chinese people and ultimately to the communist authorities. That hasn't worked as planned. The Chinese people are less free and more shackled by the communist yoke now than at any time in the past twenty years.

"The Chinese use two brush strokes to write the word crisis. One brush stroke stands for danger; the other for opportunity. In a crisis, be aware of the danger—but recognize the opportunity," Nixon once said. American policymakers have embraced the opportunity of engaging with the PRC but gotten into the comfortable habit of forgetting there is any danger involved. The big question about our multi-trillion dollar engagement with China is whether it's achieving the original goal of establishing a trustworthy alliance and helping to build a better society for the Chinese people trapped behind the Bamboo Curtain. Across the board, on every meaningful indicator, the answer is no. By every measure, as we make China richer, it is becoming correspondingly less free.

Consider for example:

- *Has freedom of religion or freedom of conscience taken root? No.*
  Communist authorities arrest and torture bishops, priests, and believers of all stripes for following dictates of faith that are antithetical to Marxist atheism.
- *Has the Chinese regime allowed for freedom of the press? No.*
  There were more journalists under arrest in PRC prisons in 2010 than at any time in recent memory. Communist China is the second least free nation in the world when it comes to reporters' freedom to cover news without fear of violent reprisal.
- *Does the regime respect freedom of speech and allow the Chinese people to voice their aspirations and concerns about the direction of their country? No.*
  Police detain teachers and arrest bloggers, while everyday Chinese workers simply disappear for expressing opinions that contradict the Communist Party line.
- *Does the regime respect freedom of assembly? No.*
  Farmers, students, factory workers, and white-collar professionals alike are rounded up or mowed down if they dare to join together in mass movements to protest the regime's policies. Authorities today typically rely on less obvious methods than rolling over protesters with tanks as they did in Tiananmen Square in 1989, but their basic modus operandi for dealing with dissidents has not changed: might is still right. If the head of a nail is sticking up, they beat it down with Mao's hammer.
- *Does the regime recognize property rights? No.*
  Beijing uses China's billionaires and growing middle class as props to show the outside world that the PRC is nourishing an opportunity society, but the reality is much grimmer. The government picks the nation's winners and losers; no one thrives without the tacit approval—and

usually the active backing—of their communist overlords. Authorities can confiscate wealth in the blink of an eye without pretext. Millions of farmers have been tossed off their land to make way for development projects with little or no compensation, and forced evictions of urban dwellers leave countless everyday people without permanent homes.

- *Does the regime respect the right to life? No.*
  This most fundamental human right is perhaps the most precarious of all. China still enforces the barbarous One Child Policy, meaning communist bureaucrats force pregnant mothers to have abortions if they have exceeded their allotted one child or if women get pregnant outside the government's reproduction schedule. The state coerces other women into undergoing sterilization to prevent "unlawful" reproduction. Life outside the womb isn't any safer. Thousands of Chinese are executed every year for transgressions as minor as stealing food to survive. As described later in this chapter, the organs of executed inmates are harvested for transplants in the lucrative global market. Refusing to recognize the most basic right to life, the communist regime unsurprisingly tramples upon every other right as well.

All these rights—which are guaranteed by the U.S. Constitution and largely taken for granted in the Western world—are suppressed with violence by the Chinese Communist Party. Traditionally, Americans have believed these rights are not granted by the government but are held in common by all people as a natural condition of existence. Refusing to recognize them or abusing them nullifies the social contract between the government and the governed. By definition, a regime that suppresses the rights of the people and rules without the consent of the governed is a tyranny.

If America's relationship with the PRC is indeed geared toward making China more like America, the experiment is failing spectacularly.

Rather than becoming a benevolent empire that uses its power and influence to safeguard life, liberty, property, and the pursuit of happiness among its own people and around the world, Red China begets national policies based on lying, cheating, stealing, and killing for the sake of the regime's self-aggrandizement. The adage "better dead then red" was popular during the Cold War; today's cadres in Beijing are more than willing to oblige, copiously doling out death to their own dissidents.

The Bamboo Prison

Dissent is not allowed in the PRC, period. The most innocuous of murmurs or innocent complaints about the system can get the most harmless Chinese citizen into life-threatening trouble. Complain about unreliable electricity in your apartment building and you could be out of a job. Try to get your little emperor moved to a different school and you could be out of your apartment. Sign a student petition demanding more say in school administration and you could get kicked out of university. Speak up for better working conditions and you might disappear to an undisclosed location, never to be seen again. Write essays on the need for political reform—God forbid on a foreign website—and you will likely be jailed and even tortured. Join a protest march calling for freedom for Tibet or democracy in China and you could be shot down in the streets.

From the smallest detail of everyday home life to the most fundamental questions about the proper role and function of government, the Communist Party violently rejects criticism no matter how constructive or humbly delivered. The regime views a gripe as inherently unpatriotic because it suggests something is wrong with the nation founded by the great Mao Zedong.

One particularly painful example involves a human rights lawyer who was beaten so badly by police in 2002 that she is permanently crippled and wheelchair-bound. Ni Yulan made the unforgivable mistake of offering legal aid to the persecuted Falun Gong spiritual movement and documenting the forced evictions and demolition of homes in Beijing.

For Ni's efforts, the government destroyed her family's home and looted all their possessions. She and her husband were forcibly confined to a hotel for months with no electricity or water until they were rearrested on April 7, 2011.[7] Ni's jailers won't let her use a wheelchair or crutches, so she's forced to drag herself around on the dirty, concrete prison floor.

Dissent is not allowed in the PRC, period.

The same week Ni and her husband were arrested, authorities took into custody the father of a baby poisoned by contaminated milk formula. Zhao Lianhai, a former health inspector, had previously been sentenced to two years in prison for helping expose—and leading a parents' justice group related to—a melamine chemical poisoning outbreak that sickened at least 300,000 children and killed numerous infants. His conviction was for the vague, treasonous act of "provoking quarrels and making trouble."[8]

Also in April 2011, police at the Beijing airport arrested Ai Weiwei, an internationally renowned avant-garde artist and outspoken critic of China's censorship policies, for "surprising speech," "surprising behavior," being "stubborn and unruly," and for unspecified financial irregularities.[9] The last of these is common code used when the communists want to detain a so-called troublemaker but don't have enough to hold him even by the PRC's loose legal standards.[10] "Ai Weiwei chooses to have a different attitude from ordinary people toward the law," an editorial in a communist newspaper ominously stated. "However, the law will not concede before 'mavericks' just because of Western media criticism."[11]

Like many other oppressive regimes, Beijing became particularly nervous during the people power uprisings that began in early 2011 and overthrew Zine El Abidine Ben Ali in Tunisia, Hosni Mubarak in Egypt, and threatened to topple other authoritarian governments across the Middle East and beyond. With Chinese activists calling for a "Jasmine Revolution" at home, the regime arrested dozens of human rights lawyers and advocates in a desperate attempt to snuff out any incipient unrest. When public demonstrations were planned in thirteen Chinese cities in

February 2011, police set up a dragnet to catch anyone who might take to the streets, whether they were civil rights lawyers, students, homemakers, or dispossessed farmers. Communist leaders were so paranoid over any concentration of people that they cancelled Shanghai's 2011 St. Patrick's Day Parade.[12]

The authorities apparently regard green beer as a threat, but not as much of a threat as the internet. Throughout 2011, Chinese censors blocked the word "jasmine" from search engines, chat rooms, and websites, and obstructed Twitter, Facebook, and other social networking sites deemed dangerous tools for spreading a counterrevolution.[13] In the Jasmine crackdowns, police arrested hundreds at organized protests and detained thousands as "precautionary measures," while an unknown number of citizens simply disappeared. "This shows just how nervous and how insecure the Chinese government is," explained Wang Songlian of the Hong Kong-based Chinese Human Rights Defenders.[14]

Keeping a lid on so much bubbling discontent requires a vast system of jails, gulags, and forced labor camps. China has a reported 1.5 to 2 million inmates in this system, which is a difficult number to verify given that it comes from Chinese government reports. These tend to be unreliable for many reasons, primarily because if no one knows how many prisoners there are, it's easier for communist authorities to launch a cover up when they die in custody. There are various causes of these deaths, including outright murder by the authorities. In Hunan province, for example, a detainee was beaten to death during questioning about a robbery in 2009. In March of that year, two police officers were prosecuted for torturing to death a 19-year-old while trying to force a confession for a murder the department was anxious to solve.

During preparations for the 2008 Beijing Olympics, police frequently rounded up the homeless, handicapped, and mentally disabled off the streets because the regime did not want foreigners to think Chinese people were weak. The body of one mentally retarded child was unceremoniously dumped at the front door of his mother's house after he had gone missing while walking home from school; it turns out police officers beat the boy to death after picking him up in a dragnet to clear the streets of undesirables before the arrival of the International Olympic Committee. Many of the defenseless innocents caught up in these police sweeps were never seen again. These unexplained disappearances, combined with the hushed-up deaths of numerous construction workers involved in the rushed building of Olympic sports facilities, led some PRC critics to dub the Beijing games the bloodiest Olympics ever.[15] Prison officials employ various excuses to escape blame, the most frequent being that a deceased or disappeared victim was never held at a particular facility even if witnesses saw the victim entering it. Even when a corpse is unaccounted for, there is no check on police power in the police state.

In a particularly offensive example of jailer callousness, authorities in Yunnan province claimed 24-year-old Li Qiaoming died while playing hide and seek (known as "eluding the cat" in China) with other inmates.[16] He was playfully blindfolded, they claimed, but amidst all the merriment he accidentally ran into a wall and died. It's all fun and games in PRC prisons, you see. The family of the deceased—a farmer who was arrested for illegally chopping down trees—took the story public when their son's body was released and showed multiple signs of abuse or torture.

After the scandal went viral, the prison backpedaled and insisted other prisoners had killed the young man, though there is no proof to back up this second version of events. Still, if true, it would not be a unique case, as prisoner-on-prisoner violence is an everyday fact of life in Chinese jails. In many instances, jail officials unofficially deputize the most brutish inmates as guards to forcefully keep the rest of the prison population in check. When the rough stuff goes too far, the corrections facility can deny involvement and wave it off as unavoidable friction among bored, frustrated jailbirds.

The official explanation of the "hide and seek" murder shows that communists regard the death of prisoners as, quite literally, a joke. Authorities further demonstrate their contempt for the dignity of the frightened and persecuted masses by the sugar-coated figure of speech police use to summon a citizen for an interrogation: "Why don't you come in for a cup of tea?"[17] How lovely.

The Penal Meat Market

Capitol punishment in the PRC is a uniquely dubious practice because the Chinese Communist Party leads the world in state-sanctioned executions. In 2009, 714 people were put to death in eighteen countries, according to Amnesty International.[18] The Iranian mullahs were responsible for more than half of this head count by executing 388 that year. Red China, however, is not even included in Amnesty International's report because the number of executions there is a state secret.

Estimates vary, but most human-rights activists put the number of Chinese officially put to death by the state every year at somewhere between 4,000 and 10,000, far surpassing the total from the rest of the world combined for many years. "China used the death penalty in 2010 against thousands of people for a wide range of crimes that include non-violent offenses and after proceedings that did not meet international fair trial standards," Amnesty International reported in March 2011.[19] "On average, China secretly executes around 22 prisoners every day," Amnesty International UK Director Kate Allen said in 2008. That works out to more than 8,000 executions per year. By comparison, the United States executed fifty-two inmates in 2009, all for violent crimes.

The PRC's zealous use of capital punishment appears even more barbaric when one considers the glaring defects of the Chinese judicial system: people are executed for minor offenses; there are no checks on the judiciary; there is typically no right to appeal; and the condemned are executed immediately following a verdict, usually by a single bullet shot to the back of the head while kneeling in a field.

The Chinese prefer the single-shot method of execution because it causes minimal tissue damage and preserves the condition of the person's organs. This is crucial because the butchers in Beijing make a tidy profit by carving up executed prisoners and selling their body parts for organ transplants. By some estimates, as many as two-thirds of the PRC's thousands of annually executed prisoners are used as involuntary organ donors. With prices for human organs skyrocketing amidst rising demand and static global supply, Chinese authorities face perverse economic incentives to escalate their use of capital punishment.

"If you want a heart, kidneys, unlined skin ... we will shoot a prisoner to order," said two Chinese organ traders.

According to an eye-opening exposé in the *Sunday Telegraph* of London, jail officials routinely inspect prisoners' physical attributes in conjunction with a list of patients willing to pay substantial amounts of money for organs. "If you want a heart, kidneys, unlined skin ... we will shoot a prisoner to order," two Chinese organ traders told dissident human rights activist Harry Wu during an undercover sting in New York's San Carlos Hotel in 1998.[20] The businessmen were carrying a body-parts price menu, contracts, and authorization papers from a PRC government prosecutor who was in a position to indict individuals to meet the demand for organs. "One prisoner, during his seven-year jail term, told how he saw numerous prisoners being medically prepared for organ removal," reported the *Telegraph*. "On the night before the execution, the prison staff would take blood samples."[21] The savage reality is that the Chinese Communist Party uses the state penal system as a profit-making meat market.

When the cadres don't kill you, they drive you crazy. In the PRC, authorities use mental institutions as jails for political dissidents, a tactic previously perfected in the Soviet Union. Hidden deep inside the Middle Kingdom are dozens of secret hospitals for the criminally insane called Ankang, which stands for "peace and health." Those who question the government or belong to suspicious organizations are considered unhealthy threats to national peace, so according to the communists, locking them away in Ankang furthers the cause of stability.

From the communist perspective, two of the most dangerous signs of mental illness are religious belief and political pluralism. "Thousands of political and religious dissenters—including urban dissidents, exposers of official corruption, persistent complainants and petitioners, and unconventional religious sectarians—have in recent decades been forcibly and unjustifiably incarcerated in mental asylums," explained Robin Munro in the *Asian Wall Street Journal*.[22] In the 1960s and 1970s, for example, as many as 70 percent of those given psychiatric evaluations for alleged criminal behavior were detained for political reasons. In many instances, after these politicized checkups, those deemed criminally insane and a danger to society were put on debilitating medicines and even given electric-shock therapy to "cure" them—in other words, their brains were medicated and zapped until the zombies could no longer think, let alone question authority.

The communist state doesn't bother to hide the system of using mental hospitals as penal institutions. These secret asylums for political prisoners are operated by the regime's main police power, the Ministry of Public Security.

Pandaroo Courts

The PRC, lacking any objective rule of law and maintaining a notoriously corrupt court system, is characterized by official lawlessness. There are no strict standards for what qualifies as admissible evidence, so anything goes in court, especially self-incriminating testimony. Even former PRC Vice Minister of Justice Duan Zhengkun has bemoaned the lack of checks and balances and absence of any independent oversight of the regime's courts and prisons. "Detention houses should not be managed by public-security departments," he told *China Daily*, "because they make the arrests and sometimes torture the accused to force them to confess."[23]

In March 2011, the Party Committee of the Ministry of Public Safety acknowledged the epidemic of police violence by issuing an order to clean up—or at least do a better job of covering up—savage interrogation techniques because of growing public attention to the "unnatural death of personnel involved in cases."[24] Merely issuing a bureaucratic press release, however, does not mean anything will change. As Hong Kong-based writer Kent Ewing summarized the systemic conflict of interest in Red China's penal system, "With security forces currently empowered to arrest, interrogate and imprison—as well as to investigate any alleged abuses that may occur during this multifaceted process—there should be little wonder that the system has failed to protect the rights of the accused." There is no transparency in the judicial process because it is not in the interests of the state, which is all that matters.

Because the courts' raison d'etre is to instill fear in the people and keep them in their place, there is institutional value in inequitable justice. Put another way, the charge is always bigger than the crime. Rejecting the Western ethical principle of the punishment fitting the crime, the Chinese regime believes if the authorities really throw the book at 'em, it will send a signal to others. That message was definitely received when a farmer in Henan province was sentenced to life in prison for evading highway tolls while driving a delivery truck.[25]

Breaking the law—no matter how minor that law is—is a threat to the state that must be handled harshly, as the toll evader discovered. The only value the state appreciates is stability, which is the single mission of the law—not justice, fairness, or due process. As Joshua Rosenzweig of the human-rights group the Duihua Foundation puts it, the law is not a shield that protects the people but a weapon wielded by the government.[26] There are no protections provided by the law, only fear of it. This is essential for imposing conformity and obedience.

The judiciary is a crucial component of the communists' grip on power. Simply put, the court system is the means by which the Communist Party achieves its primary goal, which is maintaining power. This is consistent with ancient Chinese practice under the emperors, when the law was always subsidiary to the political system that existed at that time. It's what University of Miami Professor June Teufel Dreyer calls rule *by* law rather than rule *of* law. "There is no effective way to enforce constitutional rights, since the courts are not empowered to do so, and the Standing Committee of the National People's Congress, which is empowered to do so, has thus far not chosen to exercise its authority," she explains.[27] This leaves the mass of 1.3 billion Chinese citizens officially voiceless in their own government.

China watchers generally agree that communist hardliners have been solidifying their power base in recent years, in part by using courts as an arm of the internal security apparatus. In the late 1990s, international legal scholars believed Beijing was taking steps in the right direction to develop a modern, independent judiciary and a more objective legal code that would offer the people some protections against government abuses. That positive outlook has eroded as the rule of law has moved in the opposite direction, with a rising number of compulsory detentions and forced confessions, long sentences to hard labor for crimes of conscience or political dissent, and a never-ending body count piled up by thousands of executions every year.

In hundreds of thousands of cases, the courts are circumvented altogether, as PRC law allows alleged troublemakers to be condemned for up to four years of "reeducation through labor" without going through the judiciary system. This means there is no public charge, no official prosecution, no open court deliberation, and no opportunity for an individual to defend himself; instead, he just disappears one day to some hellhole to be beaten into submission through back-breaking, around-the-clock manual labor. In April 2011, a retiree was carted off to two years of "reeducation through labor" with no trial for taking photos of a police crackdown at a pro-democracy rally. The same man had already spent thirty months at hard labor for protesting forced evictions.[28] Like organ harvesting, forced labor is a lucrative business, and many Chinese companies use prisoners to manufacture products for export.

Although not found guilty through the court system, untold masses of Chinese are sentenced to forced labor of a different kind. It is routine for children as young as nine years old and for the mentally handicapped to be sold to sweatshops where they work around the clock in slave-like conditions. Tragically, child labor is most common in toy factories. Other workers initially take jobs voluntarily but then are padlocked in dormitories and forced to work up to eighteen hours a day in a subhuman environment for as little as fifty cents an hour. Some common items found in Western homes that were made in such factories include Apple iPods, Bluetooth accessories, Ikea products, and Marks & Spencer clothing.[29] Some of the makers of these products have since cleaned up their act, but many have not. Irrespective of particular offenders, almost all Chinese merchandise sold to Americans is made in conditions that would be illegal here. Whether its people are surrounded by prison walls or not, the PRC's labor market is one giant gulag imprisoning millions of workers.

Child labor is most common in toy factories.

Rough justice is particularly prevalent in Xinjiang province, where the communist government is trying to suppress unrelenting ethnic unrest among the Muslim Uighurs who dominate the region. In March 2011, Bilik, the editor of a pro-Uighur website, was sentenced in secret to seven years in prison for allegedly fomenting ethnic tension and violence during a 2009 uprising in the provincial capital of Urumqi. Part of a major sweep of Uighur reporters, Bilik's prosecution occurred during a sustained campaign to censor information about the regime's crackdown in Xinjiang. In July 2010, it was reported, "Uighurbiz website manager Gheyrat Niyaz was sentenced to 15 years in prison; Nijat Azat, manager of the Shabnam website, was sentenced to 10 years; Dilixiati Paerhati, manager of Diyarim, was given a five-year term; and Nureli (who goes by one name), manager of Salkin, was sentenced to three years," according to the Committee to Protect Journalists.[30]

Beijing takes a particularly hard line against purveyors of internet news sources because authorities have difficulty controlling that medium. Make wayward action on the internet extraordinarily painful and you will get less of it, the official thinking goes.

Crucifying Believers

Like clockwork, the Chinese regime ramped up persecution of the country's Catholics during Lent 2011. Every holy season, Beijing and local cadres bulldoze churches and round up Christians to remind them that there are severe consequences to faith in the officially atheist People's Republic. Christmas, for example, is a particularly popular time to arrest priests. For millions of suffering Chinese trying to worship freely, martyrdom at the hands of the state isn't a relic of past ages; it's a fact of everyday life.[31] The 2011 Lenten crackdown was instigated by the death on Ash Wednesday of 95-year-old Bishop Andrew Hao Jinli of Xiwanzi, who had shepherded believers in the underground church in the rural northeastern province of Hebei. Ordained in 1943, Bishop Hao led an increasingly precarious life after Maoists took over China in 1949, outlawed church connections to Rome, and eventually established the communist-run Patriotic Catholic Association in 1957. Refusing to renounce his beliefs or his loyalty to the papacy, the bishop endured decades of prison, torture, and forced labor camps. Upon his death, security forces mobilized to block his flock from paying last respects or attending his funeral.

Hao's story parallels that of many Christians in the Middle Kingdom. For example, in March 2009, Julius Jia Zhiguo, a Catholic bishop who also administers to the underground faithful in Hebei, was arrested while Vatican officials met in Rome to discuss a new document defending China's persecuted Christians. The previous month, another underground bishop, Leo Yao Liang, was released after serving several years in jail for consecrating a church without government permission. In August 2004, eight priests and two seminarians were arrested in Hebei, with two being sentenced to "a period of re-education through forced labor." In the late 1990s, two bishops disappeared and several dozen clerics were imprisoned in that diocese alone. Bishop Cosmas Shi Enxiang, who was arrested in 2001 at age eighty-six, spent more than thirty years in communist prisons and labor camps, an experience all too familiar to Chinese Catholics.

The fates of these clerics reflect the rocky relationship between Beijing and the Vatican. In late 2010, the Patriotic Church consecrated a bishop without consent from the Holy See and elected an outlaw not approved by the pope to head the Chinese Catholic Bishops Association. Breaking with recent practice, these moves plunged relations to their worst point in many years between two organizations responsible, in their own ways, for over a billion souls each. "In China, Christ is living out his Passion," Pope Benedict XVI stated in May 2011. "Although there is an increasing number from this country who open themselves to Christ, there are many others who ignore and persecute them."[32]

In a strongly worded 2007 letter to Chinese Catholics about religious persecution in their country, the pope warned, "The solution to existing problems cannot be pursued via an ongoing conflict with the legitimate civil authorities; at the same time, though, compliance with those authorities is not acceptable when they interfere unduly in matters regarding the faith and discipline of the Church."[33] Critics condemned the Holy Father for openly endorsing defiance against the oppressive PRC regime, with some claiming he had endangered his own flock in China. Benedict retorted that it is more important to give public witness to the faith than to be safe, adding that although it should not be rashly sought out, the blood of martyrs nourishes the belief of the multitudes and gives them strength to face their public torments.

The Roman Catholic Church isn't the only faith community targeted by Beijing. According to ChinaAid, a Christian group that monitors religious intolerance in the PRC, persecution of Chinese Christians has increased for five years straight. An annual study released on March 31, 2011, by ChinaAid reports that the number of Chinese detained for religious reasons skyrocketed 43 percent in 2010.[34] In early March 2011, for example, police broke into a house church in central Shaanxi province, confiscated Bibles, and arrested all twelve Christians worshipping peacefully behind closed doors. On March 7, 2011, a Domestic Security Protection Squad in Henan province raided another house church, took away Bibles, and arrested the praying Christians, accusing them of belonging to an illegal cult. On March 4, 2011, paramilitary forces from Jiangsu province detained Pastor Shi Enhao, vice president of the Chinese House Church Alliance.

In late February 2011, a group of colleagues at a radio station in Hubei province were arrested and beaten for establishing an illegal place of worship by holding a discussion about Christianity during their break at work. On April 10, 2011, Beijing police raided a site and arrested 200 Protestants for attempting to hold worship services in a public space without permission.[35] The congregation was evicted from their previous meeting place because they are an unapproved Christian organization and are thus illegal. Their pastor Yuan Ling was put under house arrest. Shouwang, Beijing's largest independent Evangelical church, has a congregation of 1,000, approximately half of whom are under house arrest. And so it goes day after day, week after week, month after month, year after year in "the New China."

On March 25, 2011, Christian writer Liu Xianbin was sentenced to ten years in prison for treason by the Suining Intermediate People's Court in Sichuan province. His crime was writing about human rights abuses in China for overseas publications; the indictment charged that he slandered the CCP by referring to communist government as "autocratic rule." Imagine that. "Mr. Liu, 43, is one of the original signers of Charter 08, the document calling for democracy and constitutional reform drafted by 2011 Nobel Peace Prize laureate Liu Xiaobo," reports ChinaAid. In the late 1990s, he received a 13-year prison sentence for "inciting subversion of state power," an anti-sedition law instituted by Beijing fiat in 1997 that is so vague it can ensnare anyone for just about anything. The law is particularly dangerous to religious adherents because the legal standard for prosecution is partly subjective, taking into account things like whether an individual is sufficiently loyal to the state. In an officially atheist nation, belonging to a church or believing in God is, in and of itself, considered subversive.

These crackdowns are occurring daily in every part of China and across all socio-economic classes, demonstrating that faith is not deemed an authentic part of life in the red-lacquer prison Mao built. As longtime foreign correspondent for *TIME* magazine and Christian advocate David Aikman explains in his book *Jesus in Beijing*, "China's long record of intolerance to all religious groups is part of the original Marxist-Leninist worldview that insists on dictating not just all politics, but all of society."[36]

In an interview with us, Aikman elaborated on developments since his study was published in 2003. "China's current Christian protest is, in effect, the Chinese first civil rights campaign since the formation of the People's Republic in 1949," he explained. "It is not political—in fact China's Christians have made it plain that they are in no way endorsing the objectives of the 'Jasmine Revolution,' nor are they trying to overthrow the government and party, as Falun Gong explicitly wanted to do. The civil-rights component is whether the Chinese Communist Party is willing to live with the presence in society of any organization that it doesn't control. The answer at present seems to be a resounding no."

In an officially atheist nation, belonging to a church or believing in God is, in and of itself, considered subversive.

On December 1, 2010, the Politburo of the Chinese Communist Party officially branded the community of house churches in the entire country a cult, and thus outside the law. In effect, "China's top leaders signed off on what could become the nation's most savage campaign against Christians since the 1966–1976 Cultural Revolution," Aikman declares.[37] Comparing Beijing's current "Operation Deterrence" to the worst period of repression in the late Roman Empire, he calls the current PRC leadership "China's Diocletian," referring to the Roman emperor who unleashed the legions on Christians in 303 AD.

Interestingly, the percentage of Romans who were said to be Christian at the time—about 10 percent—is the same number that is estimated to be Christian in contemporary China. And clearly, that is too many for Beijing. "In the short run, the sheer power of the Chinese state will suppress demonstrations," Aikman told us. "But with China's Christian population broadly estimated by quite secular outside observers as at least 80 million (and by some Chinese Communist sources as 130 million), it will be a long struggle."

Communist anxiety over small religious communities is unsurprising in light of China's official paranoia about any movement or association state authorities do not directly command. Beijing can have soldiers patrol the streets, put spies in pews, have junior Marxists taking notes in the classroom, micromanage newspapers, pick and choose corporate executives, and try to censor the internet, but it's impossible to control all the people all the time—especially in a fragile, diverse nation of 1.3 billion citizens. With 75 million members in the Chinese Communist Party, there are a lot of fingers to plug leaks—but every time they do, a new one seems to break out elsewhere.

Terrified of Tibetan Monks

After arising at the crack of dawn on March 17, 2011, a young Buddhist monk named Phuntsog Jarutsang had a spoonful of rice for breakfast and meditated on the coming day. After a peaceful morning of contemplation, the 21-year-old straightened his saffron robe, walked through the monastery he called home, and ventured out into the streets of Kirti, in Sichuan province in western China. At 4:00 p.m., sitting on the pavement in the lotus position, he doused himself with fuel and set himself on fire. As a crowd gathered, police rushed to the scene and put out the flames, but then—for good measure—the officers kicked and beat the charred monk, who died ten hours later. Phuntsog's self-immolation was a desperate plea of protest against the PRC's 60-year occupation of Tibet.[38]

March is typically a heated time in China for protesting the regime's Tibet policies. At least two major confrontations have occurred over the years during that month, when anniversaries spawn annual protests to honor the memory of victims killed in crackdowns by the People's Liberation Army. Three years before Phuntsog set himself ablaze, security forces gunned down at least twenty-two protesters in what the government calls "the March 14 Riots," which have become a yearly event for expressing dissatisfaction with the regime.[39] Many of the victims were Buddhist monks making a public stand for their occupied nation. In 1959, less than a decade after PLA tanks rolled into the mountainous land, the communist military hammered protesting Tibetans, killing over 87,000. Amidst the violence, the Dalai Lama—the traditional spiritual and temporal head of all Tibetans—fled his homeland. He and his successors have lived atop a government in exile ever since.

Over the years, the communists have worked hard to keep the Tibetans down. In October 2009, the PRC executed at least two Tibetan protesters accused of having led the so-called March 14 rebellion the previous year in the Tibetan capital of Lhasa, a bout of unrest that quickly spread to other parts of the country.[40] The two protestors' deaths were really just drops in the bucket—over its six decades of military occupation, Chinese authorities have liquidated more than *one million* Tibetans. Less overtly barbarous, Beijing has also pursued a resettlement policy to move scores of ethnic Han—the ethnic majority who largely control the PRC—into Tibetan lands to water down the local culture and eventually make the regions more like the rest of China. The cultural flood offends many Tibetans as much as the presence of troops because they see their heritage being eroded one settler at a time.

Hu Jintao, the current general secretary of the Communist Party and as such the president of the People's Republic, has a lot of Tibetan blood on his hands. In March 1989, Hu declared martial law and ordered PLA troops to fire on a crowd of peaceful protesters led by shaved-headed, Saffron-robed monks. As many as 700 innocents were killed for marching in what would be considered a normal assembly that could happen any old day of the week in Washington, D.C. Hu's cold calculation to pull the trigger was partly motivated by Han racial hatred of Tibetan ethnicity. As the Communist Party secretary in Tibet at the time of the massacre, Hu related to British journalist Jonathan Mirsky that he "loathed Tibet's climate and Tibetans' 'lack of culture.' He kept his family in Beijing and visited Lhasa as infrequently as he could."[41] This is the man whom President Obama feted at a lavish state dinner at the White House during which poached Maine lobster was served alongside dry-aged ribeye steaks and $399 bottles of Cabernet Sauvignon.

Despite years of imprisonment, torture, and the killing of pro-Tibet dissidents, the Dalai Lama—winner of the 1989 Nobel Peace Price—has stuck to his guns, at least proverbial ones. Tibetans can accept nothing less than self-government. "My position is clear: autonomy. The international community supports us because we use peaceful means to call for our country's autonomy," he reiterated after the Kirti monk's suicide.

Peacefully speaking out for freedom and independence from communism does not seem to impress President Obama any more than it does Beijing bureaucrats. When the unassuming Buddhist spiritual leader visited the White House in February 2010, he didn't receive the warm welcome later extended to Hu. Instead, wary of China's feigned outrage whenever any world leader meets with the Dalai Lama, Obama's handlers forced the human rights advocate to sneak out the back door and leave via an alley where garbage bags are tossed. This disgraceful treatment was Obama's way of telling Beijing, *Look, I have to meet with the old man to appease my Hollywood donors, but don't worry—I'm on your side.* Hu Jintao is sure to remember such acquiescence the next time he has to decide whether to mow down more unarmed civilians.

Poison to the People

Beijing is responsible for the deaths of untold numbers of Chinese people not only through brutal acts of commission like the Tiananmen massacre, but through everyday acts of omission as well. The Communist Party routinely neglects the general welfare of its people, particularly in the realm of public health. This is evident in the stifling pollution that is choking China's cities, fouling its waterways, and despoiling the countryside. Air and water pollution is a fact of life for millions of Chinese who are forced to wear face masks just to breathe on public streets and who suffer myriad health problems due to contaminated drinking water. "Every 30 seconds, a baby is born with physical defects in China, all thanks to the country's degrading environment," reported *China Daily*, a government mouthpiece.[42]

The environmental crisis is rooted in the government's practice of cutting corners in its rush to develop China's economy. Smart growth isn't always fast growth, but Beijing is in a hurry to make its mark on the world. Communist leaders want to quadruple the size of their economy in twenty years, an ambitious target that threatens to degrade the environment even more in the years ahead. "The depletion, deterioration and exhaustion of resources and the deterioration of the environment have become serious bottlenecks constraining economic and social development," Environment Minister Zhou Shengxian complained in early 2011.[43] But such talk is cheap, as Chinese authorities are not doing anything serious to alleviate the country's endemic pollution.

The Communist Party routinely neglects the general welfare of its people.... Air and water pollution is a fact of life.

The regime isn't any better at ensuring safe consumer products, especially the food supply. Even China's Iron Rice Bowl has been compromised. In early 2011, it was discovered that fake rice made out of plastic resin was being sold to unsuspecting shoppers. The plastic content in three bowls of this fake rice was equal to eating a plastic shopping bag.[44] Unfortunately, even when it is real, there's no guarantee that Chinese produce is safe. Recent studies have shown that as much as 20 million tons of rice may be poisoned every year by industrial and mining sewage; that's 10 percent of China's annual rice output. In some provinces, estimates put toxic rice at 60 percent of that locally consumed.[45]

In April 2011, Chinese authorities raided warehouses and confiscated twenty-five tons of bean sprouts that had been tainted with cancer-causing chemicals to make them grow faster and look tastier.[46] That same month in Shanghai, thousands of buns were seized for containing unapproved substances and carrying sell-by dates that falsely portrayed spoiled food as fresh. In other recent toxic-food scandals, watermelons exploded because they were pumped with too many growth-boosting chemicals; leather compounds were mixed into milk to increase the protein content; dumplings were found to contain a high percentage of aluminum; pork glowed in the dark; and more than seven million Chinese takeout boxes were infected with toxins that cause damage to the kidneys, liver, and reproductive organs.[47]

Because there is no way to know what is safe, everything consumed in China could be tainted, a situation resulting in a long-simmering panic over toxic consumer goods. "Droves of Mainland tourists come to Hong Kong to buy real, untainted, non-toxic, trustworthy food and medicines, causing shortages and prices to go up," an American academic who regularly visits Hong Kong told us. "Just yesterday (May 9, 2011), I saw one man with a big bag full of pepper sauces that he was going to take back to resell in China."[48] It's a pretty chaotic scene when people have to run for the border to acquire pepper sauce.

Because there is no way to know what is safe, everything in China could be tainted.

Unwilling or unable to regulate the food supply, the Chinese government is effectively responsible for sickening and killing millions of its own citizens. Over the long run, this will further aggravate social unrest already reaching the boiling point. It's not just that Beijing doesn't care about public opinion; the communist leadership cares nothing about the public itself. Furthermore, as described in chapter six, tainted food doesn't only affect the Chinese population. According to the U.S. Department of Agriculture, $4.1 billion in Chinese food was exported to the United States in 2006. This was up from $800 million in 1995, and shipments continue to grow every year.

The Red Storm

There's an ancient Chinese legend about a poor villager who gets lost cutting through a vast forest on his way home from a faraway market. After walking for hours in the dark woods, he collapses in exhaustion at the foot of a towering *koelreuteria elegans*, a rain tree with spiked leaves and rose-colored blossoms. When he awakes, the landscape is blanketed in fog, and he stumbles from tree to rut, feeling his way along a path worn into the grass, getting hopelessly turned around with every step. Eventually he comes to a clearing with wild orchids reaching to the sky for what seems like a mile. At the end of this paradise is a large palace comprising many different ornate pagodas. Entranced by the fragrance of the flower garden, he dreamily approaches the old gatehouse, grabs hold of the massive bronze knocker, and pounds on the door.

For some time there is no response, but then there is a great clatter on the other end of the threshold and the gate flies open to reveal a sight as amazing as it is frightening. Looming over the trembling peasant is an angry red dragon, with flames steaming from its nostrils. Before the boy can turn and run, the dragon scoops him up with a swift snatch of his claws, drags him along a rough cobblestone walk, and throws him to the bottom of a deep, dry well. "You are my prisoner until I decide to feed you to my dogs," the dragon bellows, fumes sparking from his mouth. The young man rots for months in the dank dungeon, surviving by eating lotus beetles and rats, until one day the dragon appears at the mouth of the well far above.

"I will spare your miserable life if you grant me one favor," the dragon says. "Anything, master, just don't feed me to your foo dogs," the wretch replies in desperation. The red beast's evil monkey servants hoist the boy out of the well and the dragon explains his predicament: "I'm the emperor of the sky, and my lord—the rain spirit—has ordered up a storm. All my rainmakers are on the other side of the kingdom stirring up a typhoon in the South China Sea. Will you ride the shower chariot across the clouds and deliver a thunder squall for me on your little village and the surrounding farms?" The inmate—hungry for freedom and seeing his only chance for escape—readily agrees, straps himself into the duster, and uses the reins to whip the three red phoenix pulling his vehicle into the heavens.

The dragon has ordered him only to deliver a sprinkle to nourish the spring crops below, but once the humble plowman gets a taste of his awesome new power, he can't let go. Thunder and lightening shake the countryside, while gusher upon gale flood the land with more water than has been seen in 4,000 years, washing away the town and all its inhabitants. The drowning masses beg the sky to relieve them of the torment, but the tempest only grows more fierce, until at last there are no more arrows in the weather quiver.

The enemy is anyone who challenges the Communist Chinese Party.

When the phoenix pull the storm chariot back into the carriage house, the peon quakes at the sight of the dragon, knowing full well that he has abused his mandate and murdered his own people. But to his surprise, the red dragon is pleased, telling him, "The weak only understand power, and you wielded it fiercely, earning their respect. You are a mighty and capable governor." The former agricultural laborer is made overlord of the entire province, where he rules ruthlessly for seventy-five years.[49]

This old legend is a cautionary tale about the nature of the modern Chinese Communist Party. Formerly a peasants' party from the sticks, it has now ruled the Middle Kingdom for more than sixty years, enhancing its grip on power by brutalizing its own people over the decades. Respect for the CCP hasn't been diminished by the fact that it has the blood of tens of millions of victims on its hands. This means of maintaining the party's position will not change because communists only understand—

and, by and the large, the Chinese people are cowed by—pure power politics.

Americans are by nature a hopeful, optimistic people; our best days are always ahead, even when dark storm clouds hover above. This isn't the case in China. After thousands of years of despotic control by emperors and the more recent, murderous history of communism, the Chinese people have become accustomed to being governed by the fist. "The weak only understand power," as the red dragon explained. Or, as Chairman Mao put it so succinctly, "Communism is not love. Communism is a hammer which we use to crush the enemy."

The enemy is anyone who challenges the CCP. This includes 1.3 billion Chinese souls who are more persecuted now than twenty years ago. It also includes the United States of America.

CHAPTER THREE

THE CLASSLESS SOCIETY'S RULING CLASS

There is a serious tendency toward capitalism among the well-to-do peasants.

—Mao Zedong

O ne of the most widely believed myths about China today is that market reforms, a growing economy, and a purportedly more progressive government are leading to a new age of opportunity. PRC propagandists point out that the country's middle class has grown from nothing a few decades ago to 100 million or so in 2010. What is left unsaid is that the middle class makes up less than 10 percent of the nation's population (compared to 60 percent in America), and that the average person still earns a paltry income in China, where per capita GDP is just $3,744 (compared to $45,989 in the United States).[1]

Meanwhile, backed by the Communist Party, a new, privileged class is taking root and maturing into an entrenched, hereditary oligarchy. Commonly called "the Princelings," this elite cabal comprises a small number of families—led by 200 to 300 descendants of the founders of the Chinese Communist Party—and their cronies who maintain a stranglehold on business and government in China. While publicly genuflecting to the notion of a classless, communist workers' paradise, the People's Republic has been taken over by an all-powerful aristocratic clique that crushes any competition for wealth or position and is gradually becoming a billionaire's club.

Meet the New Boss

The Princelings dominate the PRC's political hierarchy. For example, on the Executive Committee of the State Council, which is the PRC's cabinet, three of the top positions—including that of Vice Premier Wang Qishan—are held by Princelings. Of the twenty-seven State Council Ministries, 74 percent have acted as *mishus*—intimate personal aides and protégés of previous national leaders.[2] Mishu status is second only to family relations in China's nepotistic system in which career advancement is based on powerful patronage and official favoritism among cronies. The chain runs up and down all rungs of the bureaucratic ladder. Of China's thirty-one provincial governors, 68 percent have served as mishus.[3] In the horse-race analysis leading up to the PRC's national leadership shuffle in 2012, many China watchers are predicting the two most powerful jobs in the nation—that of President Hu Jintao and Premier Wen Jiabao—will pass respectively to their deputies: Xi Jinping, who currently is vice president, and Wang Qishan, a former mayor of Beijing who currently is vice premier. Both are Princelings.

The National People's Congress, the PRC's highest legislative assembly, has become a perch from which the Princeling nouveau riche protect and expand their wealth and power. According to a report by the Shanghai-based Hurun group, the congress includes around forty members who are wealthier than the richest member of the U.S. Congress, which in 2009 was California Congressman Darrell Issa, whose net worth was estimated to be over $451 million. "The richest 70 of the 2,987 members have a combined wealth of 493.1 billion yuan ($75.1 billion), and include China's richest man, Hangzhou Wahaha Group Chairman Zong Qinghou [whose net worth is over $12 billion]," reported Bloomberg News. "By comparison, the wealthiest 70 people in the 535-member U.S. House and Senate, who represent a country with about 10 times China's per-capita income, had a maximum combined wealth of $4.8 billion."[4] This makes the U.S. Senate—which has a reputation as a "millionaire's club"—look like a union hall.

Backed by the Communist Party, a new, privileged class is taking root and maturing into an entrenched, hereditary oligarchy.

The Princelings now have a lock on the growing business sector in China. For example, Bo Xilai, former poster boy for China Inc. as PRC minister of commerce, is the son of Bo Yibo, one of Red China's "Eight Elders." Known sarcastically as the "Eight Immortals" (which originally were Taoist deities in the pre-atheist culture), the elders are a group of old communist cadres who fought alongside Mao before World War II, managed the country in the 1980s, generally supported economic reform, and sent in the tanks to crush dissent at Tiananmen Square in 1989. The offspring of these immortals are the center of power in modern China. Typical of the blueblood tastes and presumptions of this clan, Bo Xilai sent his son to Harrow, one of England's oldest and most prestigious boarding schools.

Other Princelings control prominent leadership positions in the huge, state-owned enterprises that dominate China's economy. Among the most powerful industrial titans are: "Tan Zuojun, general manager of China State Shipbuilding Corporation and grandson of Tan Jiashu, former vice commander of the Air Force; Kong Dong, general manager of China National Aviation Holding Company (Air China Group) and son of Kong Yuan, the first commissioner of PRC Customs; Chen Hongsheng, chairman of China Poly Group Corporation and son of Chen Zhengren, former Party secretary of Jiangxi Province; and Ren Kelei, general manager of OCT Enterprises Co. and son of Ren Zhongyi, former Party secretary of Guandong, according to the *China Leadership Monitor.*[5]

Across the economic spectrum, China's major industries are controlled by Princelings. As the *Sydney Morning Herald* reported in 2010, "The family of former President Jiang Zemin—whose adopted father was a revolutionary martyr—pulls strings in the telecommunications, railways and postal systems. The family of former Premier Li Peng—who was adopted by former Premier Zhou Enlai—has outsized influence over electricity production, transmission and hydro-electric dam building."[6] Li Peng's daughter, Li Xiaolin, is chairwoman of China Power International Development. As the head of China Power, she controls a multibillion-dollar firm that is one of only five companies that build and operate all of China's massive power plants. Winston Wen, son of Premier Wen Jiabao, founded New Horizon Capital, a private-equity firm that is building a $1 billion portfolio.[7] Levin Zhu, son of former Premier Zhu Rongji, made millions of dollars as chief executive of China International Capital Corp., a state-owned investment bank. "Liu Lefei, the son of Chinese politburo member and senior propaganda official Liu Yunshan, run the $1.3 billion Citic Private Equity Funds Management Co.," the *Wall Street Journal* reports.[8]

According to the *Times* of London, "The 12 largest property companies in China are all said to be controlled by children of high officials. So is 85% of the lucrative business of operating toll motorways." Of the 3,220 Chinese in 2010 with a net worth of over $16 million, 91 percent were the children of top Communist Party leaders.[9]

Any group aspiring to control a national economy has to control the money, so it's little surprise that the Princelings control the banks. One of the most powerful men in the burgeoning financial sector is Chen Yuan, former deputy governor of the People's Bank of China (the country's central bank) and current CEO of the China Development Bank, one of the mightiest institutions in the PRC. Chen, the son of one of the "Eight Immortals," Chen Yun, is one of the main money men for the Princeling cabal. His financial institution's portfolio topped more than

$765 billion (5 trillion yuan) in assets in 2010;[10] it did approximately $65 billion in energy development deals in five countries in 2009 and 2010 alone and made a profit of $5.4 billion in 2010.[11] It is completely state-owned, has no shareholders, and thus takes orders from no one and nowhere but Beijing. Its decision-making processes on lending and other business are considered state secrets.

It's little surprise that the Princelings control the banks.

Management secrecy aside, the China Development Bank (CDB) is one of the largest financial players on the world stage. "Since the mid-2000s, CDB has participated in some of China's most high-profile cross-border deals, including financing the acquisition of a 9% stake in the Anglo-Australian mining giant Rio Tinto by the Aluminum Corporation of China (Chinalco), bankrolling the global expansion of China's telecommunications firms Huawei Technologies and ZTE Corporation, funding the natural-gas pipeline that runs from Turkmenistan to China, and managing the China-Africa Development Fund," according to the Brookings Institution, a Washington-based think tank.[12] CDB also owns a stake in Barclay's of London, Britain's third-largest bank. At home, the development bank finances the biggest infrastructure projects in the People's Republic, including construction of the sleek, new Pudong International Airport in Shanghai and the gigantic Three Gorges Dam project.

The Chinese megabank uses its wealth to buy influence with foreign governments starved for investment. Money talks more than ever during a global economic downturn, so Chen's brokers have been busier than usual over the past few years. According to Brookings, CDB business-development officers were dispatched to 141 nations looking for new deals to cut. This outreach is part of Beijing's "Going Out" strategy to gobble up foreign companies and commodities, especially energy and natural resources. "Beijing will use its foreign exchange reserves, the largest in the world, to support and accelerate overseas expansion and acquisitions by Chinese companies," Wen Jiabao, the country's premier, explained in 2009.[13] "Everyone is saying we should go to the Western markets to scoop up [underpriced assets]," CDB Chairman Chen clarified at the time. "I think we should not go to America's Wall Street, but should look more to places with natural and energy resources."[14]

In short, the Princelings are seeking to lock down the world's resource pool. In the five-year period between 2006 and 2010, PRC direct investment in foreign firms skyrocketed to $220 billion, and that spigot continues to flow. In 2009–2010, lending by the China Development Bank and China Export-Import Bank surpassed World Bank financing to the Third World, making Beijing the major player in the internal politics of developing nations. Beijing's sweetheart deals are omnipresent, trampling on a lot of toes. "The extremely favorable loan terms that Chinese state banks can offer state companies to help them with their offshore acquisitions have become a sore point for many of the international companies trying to compete for those deals," reports the *Financial Times*.[15]

A small circle is financing Beijing's global invasion. At the close of 2010, there were approximately $14.5 trillion in assets in Chinese lending institutions. Half of this was controlled by only four banks,[16] giving their chief executives and top managers immense sway in how the PRC is run. Their access to cash allows PRC bankers to extend the regime's influence far and wide. For example, the international advisory board of the China Development Bank includes such luminaries as former U.S. Secretary of State Henry Kissinger, former U.S. Federal Reserve Chairman Paul Volcker, former International Monetary Fund Managing Director Dominique Strauss-Kahn, former Australian Prime Minister Paul Keating, and Maurice Greenberg, former CEO of insurance giant AIG.[17]

These relationships reflect the central role Princelings serve in building ties with Western institutions, especially corporations. In a way, Princelings are the gatekeepers for foreign businesses seeking entry into the Middle Kingdom. As the *Financial Times* explains, "Western companies are extremely reluctant to discuss the importance of family background in their choice of business partners, but most multinationals cultivate close connections with Princelings at one time or another."[18]

At the center of the Princeling power structure is Xi Jinping, who as vice chairman of the Communist Party, vice chairman of the Central Military Commission, and vice president of the government is the heir apparent to become the next head of state when President Hu Jintao retires in 2012. It's important to know who Xi is to understand what contemporary communist power means and to identify its likely trajectory. Fortunately, amidst all the damage done to U.S. foreign policy through the WikiLeaks data dump disclosures, some useful information came to light, including more than 1,000 pages of diplomatic cables in which U.S. officials discuss information culled about Xi from Chinese sources over many years. One January 2007 dispatch describes Xi as "very conservative like Hu [Jintao]," meaning he's a communist hardliner.

According to a childhood friend of the would-be president's, Xi was not repelled by the excesses of the Cultural Revolution—during which millions were sent to work camps to be reeducated into being better communists and countless more simply disappeared—but saw the chaos as an opportunity for career advancement, as many of his would-be competitors and rivals fearfully retreated from politics and government service. The ambitious Xi was so committed to the Maoist cause that he joined the Communist Party while his father—Xi Zhongxun, one of Mao's earliest comrades, whose career peaked as PRC deputy prime minister—was imprisoned for sixteen years in a party purge. This man has ice water running in his veins. As the U.S. State Department diplomatic cables published by WikiLeaks conclude, Xi "chose to survive by becoming redder than red."[19]

He's obviously a fitting leader for Red China, but not one who will likely deliver progressive reform.

Graft: How to Get Ahead in the New China

The concentration of so much power and wealth in so few hands has led to debilitating corruption in China, a nation of 1.3 billion that is now run like an old boys' club.

The Princelings' venality is relatively easy to hide in a closed political system that rejects even the most basic level of transparency, such as asset-disclosure requirements for government officials or members of the Communist Party. If a leader in Beijing is prudent about appearances and doesn't flaunt an ostentatious lifestyle, he can use his powerful position to cut deals and squirrel away millions of dollars without drawing attention. Inside deals are how business is done and how people get rich in the Middle Kingdom, a fact that is not lost on China's 10 million government employees.

When China Development Bank Vice President Wang Yi was tried for corruption, eight additional ministerial-level authorities came under the spotlight for similar misdeeds. This was nothing unusual—senior officials have a frequent habit of getting caught in illegal activity. In 2008, former Shanghai Communist Party chief Chen Liangyu—one of the PRC's most important officials, who led the political apparatus of the mainland's richest city—was sentenced to eighteen years in prison for taking millions in bribes.[20] Chen, a protégé of former PRC President Jiang Zemin, had been a member of the potent Political Bureau of the Central Committee of the CCP.[21]

In the summer of 2006, the top official at the Supreme People's Procurate, the nation's top prosecutor, pulled the curtain back on the enervating corruption problem found in the senior levels of the PRC bureaucracy. In the previous three years, he said, "Procuratorial organs throughout the nation have investigated or prosecuted 9,633 public servants at and above county and division level for suspected criminal offenses and investigated or prosecuted 4,024 cases of corruption, bribery and embezzlement which involve more than a million yuan."[22] In a March 11, 2011 report to the 11th National People's Congress delivered at Beijing's Great Hall of the People, Procurator-General Cao Jianming admitted that in 2010, in a single year, his office "investigated 2,723 officials at the county level and above, including 188 at the prefecture level and six at the provincial and ministerial levels" and "investigated 3,969 suspects of bribery, a year-on-year increase of 24.3 percent."

Before anyone gets too impressed with Beijing's system of checks and balances, note that the judicial system isn't trustworthy in pursuing all these corruption cases, as the authorities also "investigated 2,721 judiciary workers suspected of graft and malpractice for personal gains" and "investigated 267 prosecutors for acts of breach of discipline or the law."[23] All this high-level corruption begs the question of how many of China's senior leaders have their hands in the cookie jar but have yet to get caught. The obvious answer is: most of them.

Official malfeasance is sometimes prosecuted, but for the top strata of Chinese officials, corruption charges have a habit of melting away into nothing. In 2009, Hu Haifeng, son of President Hu Jintao, was ensnared in a graft investigation in which $13 million was diverted from NucTech, a Chinese firm that services state contracts, to a phony Namibian front company. Young Hu was the president of NucTech, and the stolen cash was part of a $55 million deal crafted on a state visit to Namibia by President Hu. In accordance with its common practice of suppressing information about serious problems, the Chinese regime implemented a total media blackout and blocked any internet search terms related to the NucTech story. When Agence France Presse asked NucTech for comment, an ostensible spokesman snapped, "We never speak to the media."[24] President Hu's son was subsequently promoted to the top party leadership position at Tsinghua Holdings, a conglomerate with $2 billion in annual revenue and consisting of dozens of firms, including NucTech.

Politicians aren't overly interested in looking closely at misdeeds by those in uniform.

Or consider the 2009 case of China Development Bank Vice President Wang Yi mentioned above. Wang was fired for taking millions of dollars in bribes, seeking preferential business treatment for family members, and using his ill-gotten gains to play the stock market.[25] Among other influence peddling schemes, he was found guilty of taking bribes to approve loans for highway construction by a Hong Kong developer and a mainland steel slag company. Before joining the development bank, he had been vice chairman of the China Securities Regulatory Commission, where his conduct and associations are now under investigation. In 2010, Wang was given a death sentence, the state confiscated all his family's property, and his membership in the Communist Party was revoked.[26] Despite getting caught red-handed and admitting his guilt, however, Wang's sentence was commuted for two years and is likely to be set aside; it never hurts to be a member of the club, especially when you're busted.

Since the PRC's founding more than sixty years ago, the People's Liberation Army has been one of the richest and most powerful political organs in China. It should be no surprise, then, that the military is run by the new privileged class, and that it is one of the most corrupt sectors of Chinese society. In 2006, the deputy commander of the PLA Navy, Admiral Wang Shouye, was sacked for taking bribes that totaled as much as $46 million.[27] This second most powerful man in the Chinese fleet was arrested after his malfeasance was exposed by a scorned mistress who bore his illegitimate child.

The episode reveals that highly publicized oversight structures supposedly intended to root out corruption are ineffective, at least at senior levels. This makes sense given the military's importance in Beijing. The influence of the brass over the Central Committee means politicians aren't overly interested in looking closely at misdeeds by those in uniform. Authoritarian states need the muscle of the armed forces to back up their repressive policies. To put it simply, it wouldn't be helpful to have the generals against you if some day the tanks have to roll in the streets again to restore order.

Likewise, there is little oversight over members of the military hierarchy because of their nepotistic relationships with civilian political leaders. As of June 2010, among the fifty-seven most senior-ranking military leaders in the PLA, two are members of the Politburo; thirty-two, or 56 percent, were full members of the Central Committee of the Communist Party, putting them at the center of the nation's political decision-making process. As Cheng Li revealed, ten of these top military leaders are Princelings, including "General Liu Yuan, the son of former PRC President Liu Shaoqi; General Zhang Haiyang, the son of former [Central Military

Commission] Vice Chairman Zhang Zhen; and Vice Admiral Liu Xiao-jiang, the son-in-law of former CCP Secretary-General Hu Yaobang."[28] Six of the fourteen (43 percent) candidates for the military's top jobs after the 2012 leadership change are Princelings. In 2009, Mao Xinyu—the grandson of Mao Zedong himself—became the youngest major general in the PLA, at thirty-eight years old.

China's class system has become so ingrained that Communist Party leaders who don't have a distinguished family pedigree are derisively referred to as "shopkeepers."

Princelings are Communist Party animals, and there's little doubt that the law of the jungle rules in a modern China run by the party. The powerful Princelings and their cronies are becoming untouchable as they grease the palms of police, prosecutors, judges, and other government officials. In February 2011, a CCP official was freed from detention without charge or investigation after his 27-year-old wife and two young children were murdered in their home.[29] The government reported the tragedy as a murder-suicide, but the dead woman's family claimed the communist cadre killed his kin after the wife complained that he was cheating on her. All three were cremated without autopsies being released to the public or even to the victims' family.

It may seem shocking that blood is spilt among this red version of bluebloods, but it shouldn't be—in fact, it's a perfectly logical phenomenon in a system in which descendants of revolutionaries believe their family history entitles them to rule their country. This attitude also imparts a feeling that they and those who serve them are above the law. Despite the official pretentions to a classless society, China's class system has become so ingrained that Communist Party leaders who don't have a distinguished family pedigree are derisively referred to as "shopkeepers." The reference is straightforward—while the millions of shopkeepers work hard and scrape by on small change taken in every day, their overlords are free to rake in the big cash as titans of industry.

Buying Off the Bourgeoisie

While the Princeling clique occupies the economy's commanding heights, the benefits of China's storied economic growth do trickle down to some individuals and families. Although upward mobility is difficult, it's certainly not impossible if one can cultivate the right connections.

The middle class, although still relatively small, has encompassed millions of new entrants in recent decades, while a growing class of businessmen have become bona fide plutocrats.[30] China apologists point to this social climbing to argue that China will become freer once the growing middle class begins demanding political liberty to match its economic freedom. But they have it precisely wrong—in fact, upwardly mobile Chinese citizens are learning to love the Communist Party that has underwritten their success.

Accepting Authoritarianism, a book by California State–Long Beach professor Teresa Wright, explains how China's prospering capitalist class has paradoxically become the strongest bulwark for the communist state. In general, reform is not appealing to Chinese business leaders because they have been co-opted by the Communist Party. No one gets rich without the tacit approval—if not the overt helping hand—of the authoritarian government. The state controls resources, property, labor, permits, and everything else needed to operate a business, so businessmen have to play ball with Beijing.[31] Contrary to propaganda about the Middle Kingdom being a new, laissez-faire Wild West where entrepreneurial gunslingers shoot it out in a competitive marketplace, the bureaucracy picks winners and losers in this centrally controlled economy.

Some of communism's biggest supporters are China's new millionaires and the white-collar professional class. The status quo in the country is working out well for them, so there's no reason to rock the boat.

Moreover, democratization is not in their interests because it would potentially create untold numbers of new rivals for their privileged positions. From the perspective of corporate titans, political reform would raise operating costs and threaten the bottom line. "Should workers gain the right to vote, they likely would support higher wages and improved working conditions, thus diminishing the profits of private capital," Professor Wright explains.[32]

The party keeps labor costs in line, which makes firms dependent on the Politburo for profitability. The extent to which entrepreneurs are in bed with party leaders—and the corruption that is part and parcel of the relationship—means big business is opposed to greater transparency in the system because it would expose this unholy alliance.

Economic development in the People's Republic is centered on intensifying class warfare and class envy among the people. There's not much to tie the 1.3 billion Chinese together in a common cause or a shared sense of nationhood. The different classes don't trust one another, and divisions exist across regional and ethnic lines. Country folk dislike urban dwellers, a feeling that's reciprocated in the cities. These divisions are countenanced by Beijing because they work to the government's advantage. The only thing that keeps these people together in such a vast land is the Communist Party, which defines what Chinese identity is. For the majority, the party *is* China. Such societal fragmentation makes it less likely that the populace will unify to protest the regime.

It's likely that China will continue to become richer without becoming freer.

Steps taken by the Politburo after the 1989 massacre of pro-democracy protesters at Tiananmen Square demonstrate how the cadres have consolidated their power. Late CCP leader Deng Xiaoping pushed dramatic economic liberalization, freer markets, and foreign partnerships while simultaneously clamping down even harder on political dissent. Although free-wheeling enterprise zones in such places as Shanghai and

Shenzhen offer material signs of modernization, people in China are less free today than twenty years ago—and party control is less challenged. Affluence and state brutality have tag-teamed the polity to quell opposition. Beijing also has increased social-welfare entitlement expenditures to deepen the population's reliance on government handouts.

Low public expectations have worked to the party's favor too. The Chinese regime's gulags, executions, and general contempt for human life are appalling, but compared to Mao's murderous rule in which tens of millions of Chinese starved to death or were brutalized in work camps, today's sundry persecutions seem like peaches and cream.

It's likely that China will continue to become richer without becoming freer, as the Communist Party has moved further away from political reform even as it promotes economic reform. Insisting they are creating a new political-economic model for one-fifth of the world's population, leaders in Beijing believe they have nothing to learn from Western economies teetering on the brink of insolvency. The communists are doubling down on that bet, with Western consumers bankrolling the wager. The wild card is whether Beijing can keep its economic expansion rolling to match public expectations while handling demographic changes. A slowdown—let alone a major crash like the rest of the world recently experienced—would undermine the myth of communist invincibility. In the meantime, wealth creation stabilizes the party's grip on power.

As described in chapter two, PRC propaganda, which is parroted all across the West, is that a new, open society—the so-called "New China"—is emerging based on widespread economic opportunity and social mobility. However, the stark reality is that a small class of 200 to 300 super-privileged scions of powerful communist families has a lock on power through its control of the bureaucracy, the military, businesses, and banks. This oligarchy will resort to any means, including mass killing if necessary, to maintain its power. Meanwhile, a growing cadre of middle-class and wealthy Chinese citizens has developed a vested interest in perpetuating the authoritarian political model under which they have thrived.

China's dark past includes long periods when the landscape was drenched in blood while dueling warlords fought for advantage and the masses suffered amidst the chaos. Wang Dan, a Chinese dissident in exile in America who spent more than seven years in prison for being a student organizer of the 1989 Tiananmen protests, warns that a similar dark age of rule by warlords awaits his country. "Heng" is the Chinese word for "brutal," he explains, in reference to power-hungry Princelings. "Once such people assume political control, their attitudes reek of heng."[33]

Nothing will get in the Princelings' way as they struggle to further empower their family members and feather their bank accounts. Contrary to the soothing assurances of "New China" advocates, China's future government will almost certainly grow more rigid and intolerant of criticism as Beijing uses its strong arm to defend the interests of this tiny, elite class at the cost of the rest of the 1.3 billion Chinese.

After the death of Mao, Deng Xiaopeng announced that "to get rich is glorious."[34] The Princelings have taken this counsel to heart. To few go the glory, a birthright that is protected at all costs.

CHAPTER FOUR

PLA = PREEMPTIVELY LAUNCHING ASSAULT

Why do winds and waves clash so fiercely everywhere?

—Emperor Hirohito

M
ost Americans think warnings of a coming war with China are crazy. Such a conflict wouldn't benefit either side, the thinking goes, especially given the hundreds of billions of dollars in trade between the two nations.

Of course, few wars start when economies are strong and everybody is making money; it's when global markets tank and things get dicey that all bets are off. That's why today's precarious global financial straits are so scary. President Obama's record deficit spending and crippling national debt have brought the U.S. economy to its knees at a time when our military is overextended across the world. If U.S. resolve were tested by a major military power such as China, it's an open question whether Washington would or even could respond. Standard & Poor's downgraded

America's debt rating in August 2011 because the credit agency determined the United States no longer was generating enough income to cover all its bills. Poor countries cannot fight expensive wars, and America is bankrupt. This invites our enemies to make mischief. U.S. weakness signals a green light to the Chinese reds.

U.S. weakness signals a green light to the Chinese reds.

The prospect of Beijing instigating war is not as far-fetched as many hope, and the communist regime has been building up its military force for a potential confrontation. Over the past five years, China's military budget has jumped an astonishing 70 percent.[1] According to the Chinese government, spending on the People's Liberation Army (PLA) increased 12.7 percent just in 2011 and 7.5 percent in 2010.[2] China officially reports a $91.5 billion annual defense bill, but the regime's opaque budget does not include large expenditures for its nuclear arsenal, foreign arms purchases, and weapons research and development.[3] What's more, with Beijing guarding its precise military spending levels as a state secret, most military analysts believe the regime spends many times more on the PLA than it admits. Despite the lack of transparency, one thing is clear: the PRC already has the largest armed force in the world, with 2.3 million troops in uniform compared to 1.4 million in the U.S. military. When reserves and paramilitary units are included in the head count, the communist fighting force strength totals 4.8 million.[4]

The threat lies not merely in the PLA's size, but its sophistication. Beijing is frantically updating its weapons systems and hardware in a determined push to surpass the U.S. military. The newest cutting-edge hazard is an electromagnetic-pulse weapon that emits a powerful signal to demobilize all the electronic equipment—including computers—within a large area. Having the potential to cripple U.S. aircraft carriers, this weapon is part of what the PLA refers to as its "assassin's mace," an arsenal of "weapons that allow a technologically inferior China to defeat U.S. military forces," according to Bill Gertz of the *Washington Times.*[5]

The stark reality of China's buildup was detailed in a 2010 U.S. Defense Department report entitled, "Military and Security Developments Involving the People's Republic of China." According to the report, the PLA is developing a repository of anti-ship missiles that could take out U.S. aircraft carriers; building up superior offensive ballistic and cruise missiles; testing systems to circumvent American missile defense shields; expanding warfare capabilities into space; running the world's most extensive cyberwarfare operations; pumping out top-of-the-line combat aircraft; creating amphibious capabilities for invasion forces; launching the region's largest and most dangerous armada of attack submarines; and ramping up a world-class surface fleet to check U.S. naval dominance in the Pacific.[6] An August 2010 briefing about the document tells of Chinese shipyards that are manufacturing Beijing's first domestically produced aircraft carriers, and in August 2011, the PRC set sail its first acquired carrier—a retrofitted 990-foot Soviet vessel that was purchased from Ukraine.[7] These ships of war will allow the PLA to project massive force across the region and beyond.

Pacific nations are uniformly concerned about Chinese militarization. Estimating that the PLA budget is twice what Beijing claims, a 2006 Australian intelligence assessment sounded the alarm about the likelihood of a military crisis caused by an ambitious, overreaching PRC. "The rapid improvements in PLA capabilities, coupled with a lack of operational experience and faith in asymmetric symmetries, could lead to China overestimating its military capability," the report cautions. "These factors, coupled with rising nationalism, heightened expectations of China's status, China's historical predilection for strategic deception, difficulties with Japan and the Taiwan issue mean that miscalculations and minor events could quickly escalate."[8]

In other words, Asia's peace and stability are hanging by a tripwire that could go off at any time. As the 2010 Pentagon report warned, Beijing's unrelenting buildup means that the military standoff between Taiwan and the PRC continues to "shift in the mainland's favor." The same dynamic is in play between China and the governments in Seoul and Tokyo: the PLA's increasing dominance is upsetting the balance of power, raising regional tensions. This has profound implications for the United States, which is obligated through mutual treaties to defend our democratic Japanese, South Korean, and Taiwanese allies if they become embroiled in a war with China.

A Japanese defense white paper released in August 2011 contained shockingly bold warnings about the PRC's aggressive military posture. For the first time in history, Tokyo—a democracy and America's most reliable ally in Asia—officially labeled China's military expansion as "assertive" and "overbearing." As the 600-page report stated, "China's future actions are worrisome given what can be interpreted as its overbearing ways to address its clashing interests with neighboring countries, including Japan." The report was part of a major rhetorical escalation from normally low-key Japan. "We are concerned about the continuous military buildup, the increasing military power and capability, which lacks transparency," a spokesman for Japan's Foreign Ministry had announced in July. "Recent Chinese maritime active exercises have caused concern in the region."[9]

Indeed, the PRC's buildup has sparked a regional arms race. To keep pace with Beijing, India increased military spending by 12 percent in 2011. According to the Stockholm International Peace Research Institute (SIPRI), "Imports of major conventional arms by Indonesia rose 84% [in the five-year period from 2005 to 2009 compared to the 2000-2004 period]. For Singapore, the increase was 146%. And Malaysia imported an astounding 722% more arms."[10] Furthermore, Vietnam is rapidly expanding its fleet of warplanes and attack submarines, and Singapore is now the first Southeast Asian nation to rank among the world's top ten weapons importers since the end of the Vietnam War. "While Southeast Asian governments still don't openly voice concerns over China, they think about it, and they are making a statement with what they are buying," explains SIPRI's Siemon Wezeman.[11]

Asians' overarching fear of Beijing is grounded in history, when another rising power rampaged through most of the continent. There are many troubling similarities between the disposition of pre-World

War II Imperial Japan and contemporary China. After Japan humiliated Russia in the Russo-Japanese War of 1904, the victorious island nation began to rapidly militarize to secure its place among the world's most powerful countries. Meanwhile, industrialization transformed the agrarian backwater into a wealthier, more modern society. Trouble started when the Great Depression upset global markets and disrupted commodity imports that were vital to keeping a resource-poor economy rolling. When Japan couldn't purchase the resources it needed to deliver goods to a population accustomed to a rising standard of living, it set to sea to take them, starting with an invasion of Manchuria in 1931 and later expanding to much of the rest of Asia.

The PRC already has the largest armed force in the world with 2.3 million troops in uniform, compared to 1.4 million in the U.S. military.

Tokyo's war pursuits served two related purposes: it stirred up nationalistic fervor to distract the public from the increasingly dire economic situation at home, and they used the military to steal resources from other countries to keep Japan's industrial machine humming. The resultant Pacific War, which America entered after Japan attacked Pearl Harbor on December 7, 1941, led to more than 25 million military and civilian deaths in eight years. The consequences of Imperial Japanese aggression continue to motivate pan-Asian defense policies today because Chinese militarization and industrialization look all too similar to what came earlier. Note that before the Manchurian invasion, the United States was Japan's largest trading partner, a lucrative relationship that didn't deter war. The same was true in 1914, when World War I wasn't avoided despite Britain and Germany trading more with one another than anyone else. Today, America is China's largest trading partner.

American leaders need to learn from history and ask some important questions: What if the current global economic malaise turns into an all-out depression and Red China can't get the resources it needs to keep its economy growing and sustain its people's rising standard of living? Could the PRC take to the seas to secure resources like Imperial Japan did in the 1930s and '40s? If not, why is Beijing in such a hurry to field and improve the world's largest military? And why does the PLA need a blue-water navy capable of projecting force across Asia?

The communists claim the Chinese military is for defensive purposes only, but its 20-year buildup has more nefarious capabilities. Singapore, a former British colony that was surrendered to Japan without much of a fight in 1942, is so worried about suffering a similar invasion that it's invested billions in port facilities large and sophisticated enough to house the whole U.S. Seventh Fleet if necessary for defensive purposes. Singapore's assumption that America would be in the thick of any war with China is based on diplomatic and strategic reality. The United States has mutual-defense treaties with Japan, South Korea, and Taiwan, all of which have volatile relations with the PRC. World War I and World War II escalated when alliances dragged numerous nations into what became global conflagrations. That could happen again.

Democrats in Washington are guaranteeing that China's competitive advantage will become even greater.

Chinese military spending is second highest in the world, behind the United States. However, Beijing has a significant advantage over America because it focuses on achieving strategic supremacy in one region: Asia. While Washington stretches U.S. forces across every corner of the planet, our competitor works on tightening its hold on the contested area in its own backyard. And while a financially strapped America cuts its commitment to defense, China has pursued a two-decade expansion marked by annual double-digit growth in defense spending. The dual trend of Chinese expansion and U.S. contraction led defense specialists

Gary Schmitt and Tom Donnelly to conclude in early 2011 that "China's military buildup could push the U.S. out of Asia."[12]

Democrats in Washington are guaranteeing that China's competitive advantage will become even greater. During the summer of 2011, President Obama and congressional liberals fought tooth-and-nail against including cuts to welfare entitlement programs as part of a deal to raise the amount of money the nation can borrow. Instead, they forced an agreement to raise the U.S. debt ceiling based on $1.2 trillion in unknown reductions to come later—but if these never materialize, half of the total cuts (that is, $600 billion) will be hacked automatically out of defense.[13] That's on top of $350 billion gutted from the military in the original deal. In total, U.S. troops could lose nearly $1 trillion in vital defense resources during wartime in order to enable Washington big spenders to borrow even more money to waste on ineffectual big-government programs.

Welcome to Obama's America, where the Land of the Free gets continuously weaker while the red dragon grows stronger. It's a weakness that could lead to war.

A Confrontation and a Cover-Up: The *McCampbell-Light* Incident

The PLA poses a major threat to the United States, both by seeking to challenge our military directly and by stoking regional instability that could pull America into war. But the military is hardly the only tool Beijing uses for these aims. Another Chinese program that threatens the United States, and indeed much of the rest of the world, is its massive but little-discussed illicit arms smuggling operation.

China's smuggling activities, and the Obama administration's shocking determination to overlook them, are evident in a recent incident involving the USS *McCampbell* (DDG 85). An Arleigh Burke class destroyer based in Yokuska, Japan, the *McCampbell* was the first U.S. Navy vessel on the scene to help with relief efforts after the spring 2011

Japanese earthquake and tsunami. When the USS *Ronald Reagan* (CVN-76) arrived on station, the *McCampbell* became part of her destroyer screen as a member of Carrier Strike Group Seven.

Relief work, however appreciated by the recipients, is only a secondary mission for the *McCampbell*. At 9,000 tons she is the size of a World War II light cruiser and every inch the warrior. Her motto, "Relentless in Battle" is not a public relations slogan. Well-armed with Tomahawk cruise missiles, torpedoes, and a five-inch gun, the ship also carries two SH-60 helos in an aft flight deck. Such a vessel is fast (over thirty knots), modern (commissioned in 2002), and an excellent representative of Maine's mighty Bath Iron Works where she was built. This is just the vessel to send on a special mission.

On May 26, 2011, the *McCampbell* was alone in the South China Sea when the crew stopped the Motor Vessel *Light*, a small (4,650 dwt) cargo ship that looks like any other tramp steamer plying the China coast. However, flying a flag-of-convenience (Belize), the *Light* is anything but ordinary. It is an arms carrier with a North Korean crew, part of a highly secret flotilla that transports the most modern weaponry, including ballistic missiles and weapons of mass destruction (WMD) from those who produce them to those who would use them. In this case, American intelligence believed the ship was carrying ballistic missile parts to Iran by way of Burma (also known as Myanmar).

The *McCampbell* stopped the *Light* on the high seas and requested to board. Unsurprisingly, the *Light*'s North Korean crew refused. After a tense standoff, the North Koreans evidently concluded that if they tried to proceed, the *McCampbell* would sink them. So they retreated back north.

End of story? Arms delivery thwarted? Not exactly.

The *McCampbell* incident occurred far at sea, and the American people knew nothing of it. However, anticipating the confrontation would get out, the Obama administration wanted to put its own spin on it. So the White House gave an exclusive to David Sanger of the *New York Times*. The *Times* report, as well as follow-up stories in the *Washington Post* and the *Wall Street Journal*, identified the *Light* as a North Korean ship. All three articles implied the Obama administration's armed diplomacy had delivered a big blow against WMD and ballistic missile proliferation, with the *Times* calling the affair "a rare victory" for Obama's team.[14]

But there is a slight problem: what Obama's news spinners didn't reveal was that the *Light* may not be a North Korean ship at all. According to a respected maritime publication, the *Maritime Executive*, the *Light* is actually a Chinese ship, owned by the Ever Ocean Shipping Agency Co. and operated by Dalian Sea Glory Shipping Co., both based at the same address in the city of Dalian, Liaoning, in China's Manchuria, adjacent to North Korea.[15] It is one thing for the *McCampbell* to have faced down a North Korean ship far from North Korean waters. It is something else if the ship is Chinese, located in the South China Sea within range of the Russian-built SU-30MKK aircraft flown by the Chinese air force. The *McCampbell* undoubtedly could have held its own against a Chinese air attack, but no one wants to test that supposition.

The Obama administration certainly didn't want Congress to know there had been another U.S.–China military confrontation, even if China was acting through North Korean surrogates. Congressional knowledge of the stand-off could have brought enormous consequences. Consider this: in the 1990s Congress passed economic sanctions legislation against foreign companies, and in some cases foreign countries, that engage in ballistic missile proliferation. This legislation is subject to oversight by the House Committee on Foreign Affairs. The chairwoman of the committee is Florida's Illeana Ros-Lehtinen, a Cuban-born Republican who has no sympathy for communists of any stripe. Additionally, the ranking Democrat on the committee is California's Howard Berman who, though liberal on most issues, takes a strong stand against ballistic missile and WMD proliferation.

Given the way shipping companies often have interlocking ties, who knows what Congress would find if it went up the ownership chain of the Dalian Sea Glory Shipping Company? The giant Chinese shipping company China Ocean Shipping Company (COSCO), which has extensive trade ties with U.S. firms, has a major subsidiary in Dalian. If Congress discovered the *Light*'s Chinese connection and adopted sanctions against Ever Ocean Shipping or Dalian Sea Glory for engaging in illegal weapons proliferation, COSCO could conceivably become ensnared in the sanctions. Thus, if the truth got out, the Obama administration risked facing the nightmare of a united congressional committee demanding action that would significantly jeopardize U.S.–China trade.

So they told reporters the *Light* was a North Korean ship, thereby covering up any U.S.–China military showdown and removing the threat to trade. It may be that the *Light* really is a North Korean ship, but until definitive proof comes in, it seems much more likely that the *Maritime Executive* is correct that the ship is Chinese. This is, after all, the *Executive*'s line of business and it has no reason to lie about the story. The Obama administration has the opposite motivation.

The confrontation between the *Light* and the *McCampell* was not the only indication from the summer of 2011 of China's widespread arms smuggling activities. Claudia Rosett, a veteran reporter for the *Wall Street Journal*, investigated smuggling operations run out of Hong Kong and found that "a Chinese state-owned firm has been helping Iranian ships get around U.S. sanctions." The company, H&T International, is a substantial player in Chinese shipping with a subsidiary in the United States. In another case, faced with embarrassing documents showing up in the chaos of war-torn Libya, the Chinese Ministry of Foreign Affairs was forced to admit that three often-sanctioned Chinese arms companies had held discussions with the Gadhafi regime as late as July to supply the dying Libyan dictatorship with a wide range of weapons to be laundered through cut-outs in Algeria. The Libyan rebels claim that new Chinese weapons did in fact reach Gadhafi die-hards, though no proof had appeared as of this writing.

In our view, the real story is this: the Chinese communist leadership and North Korea's dictator are engaged in a massive conspiracy to export ballistic missiles, probably to Iran or other rogue regimes. In the *Light* incident, they tried to disguise this trade by flying a Belize flag over a Chinese-owned ship and by laundering the shipment through the Burmese military junta. If the deal had gone through, everyone—the Chinese officials, the North Koreans, and the Burmese trans-shippers—would have made a lot of money, probably secreted abroad in off-shore bank accounts. Finally, in order to protect U.S.–China trade and forestall pressure to take a harder line against Beijing, the Obama administration is engaged in a major cover-up to keep the American people from knowing the true dimensions of China's lucrative arms smuggling operation—and that operation has been exposed in many incidents aside from the *Light* affair.

The Chinese–North Korean Arms Smuggling Axis

It's not easy being a dictator these days. Due to the vast number of enemies it has cultivated, the Pyongyang leadership travels to China and even inside North Korea almost exclusively aboard heavily armored trains. Surrounded by an elite unit of bodyguards and preceded by trusted railway workers who check the track ahead, communist voyages are impervious to anything short of a direct hit from an American smart bomb.

In April 2004, the express train carrying North Korean head honcho Kim Jung-il passed over the Yalu River back into North Korea following consultations in China on the North Korean nuclear weapons program.[16] Some four hours later, a terrific explosion rocked the rail yard at Ryongchon, a North Korean town near the Chinese border. At first, many foreign observers discerned an attack on the Dear Leader's convoy, but it quickly became clear that it was a second train that had gone up. This was the "gifts train," a train loaded with presents from Kim's Chinese hosts that typically follows a few hours behind Kim's train when he returns from a visit to China. At one of the North Korean stations near the border, the Chinese train transfers its cargo to a North Korean loco-motive and the Chinese one returns across the Yalu River.

The gifts train explosion was far too big for the North Koreans to cover up, as satellite shots of Ryongchon brought the devastation into living rooms around the world. Buildings shown in photos from 2003 simply didn't exist in 2004 images. Even the Chinese press reported that the town center had been "totally flattened" and that "the railroad sta-tion and the surrounding buildings were obliterated."[17] North Korea announced an official death toll of 161 people, but no one believes that,

especially since the Chinese reported that North Korean officials had
initially told international diplomats that hundreds had been killed and
thousands injured.[18] Even the BBC's estimate of 3,000 killed or injured
is conservative.[19]

The Chinese are supplying the North Koreans solid rocket fuel and other critical missile components for Pyongyang's lucrative arms smuggling operation with the Syrians.

The most heartbreaking victims were children. Ryongchon Elementary
School was located right across the train yard, close to the epicenter of
the explosion. The blast happened at 1:00 p.m., when the school was
filled with students and teachers. When the train station buildings
disintegrated, their steel girders turned into a cloud of flying shrapnel
heading straight for the kids. Horrific pictures of badly injured and
burned children made the international press even as the overwhelmed
North Koreans refused outside disaster aid. "Some of the victims have
lost their eyes, others have severe burns, broken or severed limbs and
internal injuries," the Australian press reported.[20] Many other children
had no chance of survival, having been playing outside in an area that
faced the train yard when the blast occurred. Foreigners found little
modern medical care available for the injured children, seeing only two
IV drips for almost 400 critical patients in one of the local hospitals.[21]
The North Koreans eventually admitted to seventy-six dead children,
although the real number was probably in the hundreds.[22]

North Korean officials attributed the horrific explosion to mishan-
dling of ammonium nitrate fertilizer. That is technically possible, though
highly unlikely. Satellite photos taken less than a week later show the
North Korean authorities occupied with filling in the blast crater with
earth-moving equipment rather than tending the wounded or trying to

find housing for those rendered homeless. The images reveal earth-moving equipment frantically going back and forth as if burying something.

The "something" the North Koreans didn't want the world to see was evidence of what was really in the ill-fated train: Chinese solid rocket fuel, missile-related equipment, and the remains of the unique containers that housed them. In addition, according to former U.S. Defense Intelligence Agency officer Dr. Bruce E. Bechtol, Jr., about a dozen Syrian missile technicians accompanying the train were casualties of the explosion.[23]

The Chinese go to great lengths to bury their true relationship with North Korea, but evidence of their mutual illicit activities emerges here and there. In this case, it's pretty clear that the Chinese are supplying the North Koreans solid rocket fuel and other critical missile components for Pyongyang's lucrative arms smuggling operation with the Syrians.

Having no oil to sell, however, means the Syrians are a cash-poor, unreliable customer—unlike Iran. In June 2006, a respected Japanese newspaper reported that ten Iranian missile engineers were in North Korea to observe a long-range missile test checking on "the performance of missile-related equipments introduced by China."[24] Former U.S. Ambassador to the UN John Bolton told Fox News, "There is no doubt that North Korea cooperates with Iran to develop long-range ballistic missile technology." Indeed, most experts believe that the Iranian Shahab-3 missile was based on a North Korean design and could be nuclear capable.[25] The Iranians don't try to hide their intentions for the Shahab-3; when the ballistic missile is displayed at official events, the Iranians cover it with banners reading "Wipe Israel off the Map."[26]

The Bush administration was so outraged by all these flagrant Chinese violations of anti-proliferation agreements that in June 2006 the Treasury Department froze the assets of eight Chinese corporations involved in the Iranian ballistic missile development program.[27] The North Koreans' defiant response was to launch seven missiles over the Sea of Japan on July 4. Later that month, a Bush administration official confirmed to then-Senator George Allen of the Senate Foreign Relations Committee that Iranian officials had indeed witnessed a long-range missile test in

North Korea.[28] And to wrap it all up in a neat package, it appears that the Iranian missile engineers flew to Pyongyang via Beijing.

The Tehran-Beijing-Pyongyang transmission belt continued operating the following year. According to a document published by WikiLeaks, in November 2007 Secretary of State Condoleezza Rice was asking the U.S. ambassador to press the Chinese "urgently" to stop a shipment of North Korean missile parts to Iran via Beijing. Rice's cable notes that "the U.S. has raised its concerns with Chinese officials on numerous occasions and lists at least 10 instances in which it claims North Korean shipments of ballistic missiles parts to Iran passed unimpeded through Beijing."[29]

The axis continues today. In May 2011, the Chinese blocked the release of a UN report on an unnamed third party allowing Iranian advanced weapons specialists to travel to North Korea. The UN leaked the name of the third party—China—first to Reuters[30] and then to almost any reporter who asked. Eventually the report showed up in the *Weekly Standard*.[31]

Few UN reports are as candid as this one. Apparently exasperated by Chinese and North Korean lies, the report's authors charged:

- "The Democratic People's Republic of Korea (North Korea) remains actively engaged in illicit activities relating to its nuclear and ballistic missile-related programmes."[32]
- "Prohibited ballistic missile-related items are suspected to have been transferred between the Democratic People's Republic of Korea and the Islamic Republic of Iran on regular scheduled flights of North Korean Air Koryo and Iran Air, with trans-shipment through a neighboring third country."[33]
- "The country (North Korea) has been engaged in the export of complete systems, components and technology to numerous customers in the Middle East and South Asia."[34]

Some of the items being smuggled are heavy, such as the "complete systems" noted above. Before the fall of the Shah, the U.S. sold

C-130 cargo planes to Iran. Since the C-130s of the 1970s era have a range of about 2,000 miles and the flying distance from Tehran to Pyongyang is 4,000 miles, a fully loaded military cargo plane can't fly between the two cities without refueling at a military airport in western China. Likewise, the commercial airliners Air Koryo and Iran Air don't have the range for a direct flight. So the North Korean and Iranian WMD engineers get a chance to see a bit of western China while they gas up.

The transmission belt evidently goes both ways. At the same time the Chinese were spiking the UN report, the Japanese press was reporting that 200 North Korean missile and nuclear weapons engineers with false passports were in Iran. They were scattered over at least twelve WMD production facilities, including a uranium enrichment site.[35]

Perhaps the North Koreans were preparing the Iranians for their first overseas assignment—installing medium-range ballistic missiles in Venezuela. In May 2011, the German press reported that the Iranians had signed a "secret agreement on strategic cooperation" with Venezuelan dictator Hugo Chavez to build missile silos on the Peninsula de Parguana, which marks about the closest distance between Venezuela and Miami and is at the very outer range of the Iranian Shahab-3 ballistic missile. The planned Iranian missile base is extensive, including underground bunkers for warheads, rocket fuel storage, and a command and control center.[36] The North Koreans and Chinese are the world's leaders in constructing underground military facilities, something they developed during the Korean War. The Iranians, enriched by the high price of oil, are reportedly paying for the facilities.

As of this writing, the German report on the Iran-Venezuela pact remains unconfirmed, but it is certainly feasible in light of the close relations Chavez has cultivated with Iran. Such an agreement would offer Chavez the prospect of using Iranian missiles to establish Venezuelan regional dominance. This would certainly cause alarm in neighboring Brazil, which once had its own nuclear weapons program and a long-range missile program, both of which it scrapped in the 1980s but could easily restart.

Needless to say, a nuclear arms race in our South American backyard is hardly in U.S. security interests. Furthermore, a missile facility in Venezuela would dangerously complicate U.S. ballistic missile defense for the simple reason that our land-based sensors don't look south. The United States would have to rely almost completely on U.S. Navy (Aegis) ships and space satellites for warning.

However, placing such a facility on a peninsula jutting into the Caribbean Sea, relatively exposed to a late-night visit from SEAL Team Six, doesn't seem wise. Of course, it might be a risk Chavez and his Iranian allies are willing to take in exchange for bringing the U.S. mainland into effective range. The point is, America's enemies, from the socialists in Caracas to the mullahs in Tehran, are collaborating to make the U.S. homeland vulnerable to nuclear weapons stationed within our own hemisphere—and Beijing is providing the capability.

Through these kinds of activities, Pyongyang is raking in unchecked amounts of Iranian oil money while giving China a piece of the action. Characteristically, the North Koreans use most of the money to develop their own next generation WMD. This is unconscionable when you consider how far this gusher of cash could go in alleviating the suffocating poverty of the North Korean people.

America's enemies … are collaborating to make the U.S. homeland vulnerable to nuclear weapons stationed within our own hemisphere—and Beijing is providing the capability.

As an illustration of the depths of North Korean poverty, consider this: many foreign visitors to Seoul take the bus trip north and east of town to the "Peace Village" of Panmunjom, which is situated in the middle of the Demilitarized Zone (DMZ) in the place where the Korean

War Armistice was signed in 1953. Tourists can inspect the negotiating table while North Korean soldiers glare. Technically, it's located in North Korea but it's difficult to get a feel for the place since everything within sight is for show. Even the North Korean buildings within view are only false fronts, like a movie set—a textbook Potemkin village.

The best way to get a glimpse of the real North Korea is to go by car north and west of Seoul toward the Yellow Sea to an overlook of the Imjin River valley. From this spot, the contrast of North Korea with its southern neighbor is overwhelming. In early September, the South will still be green in those places where urbanization hasn't laid down the asphalt. On the North side there is nothing. There are no towns, roads, fields, or people in view—just brown hills and an oversized statue of the late North Korean dictator Kim Il-sung looming in the distance. It appears that the North Korean peasants have carried away every stick for fuel and every blade of grass for the cooking pot. In a sense, the land itself has a lot to say, confirming the reports of those refugees lucky enough to escape the desolate hellhole North Korea is today.

But not everyone suffers there—the top leadership lives in luxury. The Dear Leader has so many palaces and villas scattered around the country that he doesn't visit some of them from one year to the next. Stories abound of rich food and the high life—fancy cars and motorboats—of the North Korean elite. Illicit arms profits, which they share with Beijing, help to make this extravagance possible. The North Korean people bear the burden with their poverty and sometimes their lives.[37]

There's no sign of change in the North Korean–Chinese relationship, and there likely won't be even with a change in the North Korean leadership—the Chinese are already running gift trains for Pyongyang's heir apparent, Kim Jung-un, as seen in news reports of a minor derailment of such a convoy in December 2010.[38] Beijing's arms smuggling deals with North Korea have already resulted in the deaths of hundreds of children at Ryongchon—and that was an accident. If these weapons begin to explode on enemy targets around the world as they are designed to do, the casualty list will grow exponentially.

Remembering the *Hanit*

It doesn't take a lot to exacerbate the broiling political crisis in the Middle East, and Beijing's international arm sales pour fuel on the Muslim-Jewish fire. In mid-July 2006, during the Second Lebanon War, a Chinese C-802 anti-ship missile struck Israel's INS *Hanit* off the Lebanon coast. Four Israeli sailors were killed in the incident—Yoni Hershkovitz from Haifa, Shai Atias from Rishon Letzion, Tal Amgar from Ashdod, and Dov Shtienshos from Carmiel. The oldest was thirty-seven, the youngest just nineteen. All of them had families.[39]

The casualties could have been much worse. The majority of the *Hanit*'s eighty crew members were sitting down to a "Sabbath eve dinner, an error of complacency that ironically in retrospect ended up saving lives."[40] Most of the crew was in the ship's mess, a central location away from the spot where the missile struck.

There could have been a more direct hit on the vessel. The *Hanit* is a corvette (called a Saar 5 class ship by the Israeli navy), which is substantially smaller than an American frigate or destroyer. It's about 1,200 tons loaded, built at the Ingalls shipyard in Mississippi. The Chinese C-802 anti-shipping missile is a sea-skimmer, an advanced conventional weapon—not a ballistic missile—and carried a 400-pound time-delayed semi-armor-piercing high-explosive warhead that blew up near the fan tail of the ship. As it was, the explosion caused substantial damage, engulfing the aft section in flames and caving in the ship's helicopter pad.[41] But the *Hanit* didn't sink. If the Chinese missile had struck amidships where most of the ship's company was eating, or had impacted at the water line, many more crew members would have been killed or permanently injured, and it's unlikely the ship would have survived.

Fortuitously for the *Hanit*, a second C-802 fired at the same time flew over the ship, zeroed in on a small freighter forty miles away, and sank it. A ship the size of the *Hanit* could never have taken two missile hits.

There was never any doubt about who fired the missiles. The chief of the terrorist organization Hezbollah announced the attack first, declaring, "You wanted all-out war—and that is what you will get! You have no idea who you are dealing with!"[42] Israeli officials believe Hezbollah may have had its hand on the lanyard, but Iranian specialists manned the firing batteries, and Lebanon's military radars provided the guidance for the missile.[43]

The Israeli Board of Inquiry determined that the *Hanit* suffered no technical malfunctions prior to the attack. Rather, it attributed the ship's vulnerability to negligence by the commander and other crew members. Apparently, the sailors had such little apprehension of danger that a junior officer turned off the ship's defensive systems, rendering the *Hanit* effectively blind to the threat. The ship's captain lost his command and other officers were disciplined.[44]

The Chinese missile attack on the *Hanit* came about primarily due to intelligence failures, but it highlighted a tragic blindness in the Israeli military: it simply refused to believe that Chinese authorities would put a dangerous missile system of this magnitude in the hands of a non-state actor. At the Board of Inquiry, the Israeli navy commander explained that the prospect of Chinese advanced conventional missiles in the hands of Hezbollah seemed "unrealistic and imaginary."[45]

No one doubts that the Chinese have been and still are deeply engaged in illicit nuclear weapons assistance to numerous countries. The bomb designs for the nuclear weapon programs of Saddam Hussein's Iraq,[46] Muammar Gadhafi's Libya,[47] and Pakistan[48] were all Chinese. The PRC is trading nuclear weapons designs to Iran for oil and, through front companies, has funneled dual use nuclear goods bought by North Korea to Syria.[49] Specialists in the field widely agree that China also secretly trades in other types of WMDs, ballistic missiles, and advanced conventional weapons.[50]

Israeli military officials knew it as well. But they didn't understand *what*—advanced conventional weapons—China would sell to *whom*—non-state actors. They knew the Chinese sell WMD to rogue states like Iran or North Korea, but the Israelis, like national security policy makers in most of the free world, assumed the PRC was just nasty, not crazy. Top Israeli security officials evidently thought, "Even the Chinese would not go so far as to arm terrorist groups with advanced conventional weapons."

They were wrong. But to be fair to the Israelis, surprise attacks against America, like Pearl Harbor or 9/11, are reminders that the Jewish state is not the first to tragically underestimate its bloodthirsty opponents.

The C-802s fired by Hezbollah at the Israeli navy originated in China either as fully manufactured missiles or as kits assembled by the Iranian Revolutionary Guard. At any time, the PRC could have told the Iranians not to deliver them to any terrorist organization, but Beijing obviously issued no such instructions. The Chinese Communist Party simply thought the West and certainly the UN would never call out China—a permanent member of the UN Security Council—on its skullduggery.

The arming of Hezbollah, like most of the PRC's illicit weapons trade, all boils down to money. Arms smuggling is highly profitable, and the Chinese Communist families that control Beijing's end of the various arms smuggling operations with the North Koreans, Iranians, or the Syrians would have gotten their cut of whatever went down. As one expert recently noted, "Most remaining proliferation disputes don't pertain to the actions of the government in Beijing, but to the practices of China's state-owned defense industries. The country's large State-Owned Enterprises (SOEs) are some of the world's most prolific exporters of weapons and dual-use technologies."[51] And recall, as discussed in chapter three, that the SOEs are dominated by the so-called Princelings, sons and daughters of high-ranking officials.

In a private briefing in Hong Kong in 1988, a Chinese arms dealer described the relationship between the Chinese Communist elite and Beijing's arms smuggling trade. According to him, this lucrative business was carefully divided so that each family received a share of the profits depending on where they are in the Communist Party pecking order.[52] His account immediately brought to mind the mafia families in *The Godfather* dividing up the New York crime scene. In discussing the most important arms exporting firm in Beijing, "Polytechnologies Inc.," he noted that the company's officers were in the same hierarchical relationship with one another as their sponsors (fathers, fathers-in-law, and the like) were within the Communist Party. He explained that this implied a deliberate division of the arms smuggling pie based on Party rank order.[53]

At the time of the briefing, Polytechnologies was headed up by none other than the son-in-law of Deng Xiaoping, the former leader of China.

Painting Taiwan Red

From the air, Taiwan looks like any other lush, green island in the Pacific Ocean, replete with a mountain range, sandy beaches, and high rocky cliffs overlooking the crashing surf of the Philippine Sea. Arriving passengers peering down on the Hualien airport in the largest town in east Taiwan would have to look carefully to see the structures unique to an island constantly prepared for hostility from China. Running along the western side of the airport's single runway is a line of concrete bunkers housing Taiwan's American-made F-16 Fighting Falcons. They're gassed up and ready to roll at a moment's notice.

What can't be seen from above is a taxiway crossing the airport's runway that disappears into a nearby mountain. Inside the mountain is enough space to hold 200 aircraft and everything the Taiwanese air force would need to fight—fuel, spare missiles, bullets, and bombs. Carved out of solid granite, nothing short of a direct hit from a nuclear weapon would impact the people and warplanes inside. There are several entrances to the complex, many of them hidden. An attacker would have to take them all out at once to shut down the base's operations, while also contending with aircraft that can be launched from at least three directions.

"Shan" means "mountain" in Chinese. The JiaShan complex is Taiwan's most important military facility after the command and control center in the north of the island. In an armed conflict with China, if Taiwan loses Hualien and JaiShan before the Americans can arrive in force, they've probably lost the war.

The stakes are immense in the Taiwan Strait, where tensions always run high. The governments in Beijing and Taipei have been enemies since before most people in both countries were born. In 1949, Mao's Communists won a hard-fought victory in a long civil war against Nationalists led by Chiang Kai-Shek. When his anti-communist, pro-Western forces could no longer fight, Chiang fled the mainland and established a government on the island of Formosa, now known as the Republic of China (ROC) but popularly called Taiwan. Neither Taipei nor Beijing accepts the legitimacy of the other, and both claim to be the "real China." Since Chiang's escape, one of the PRC's existential objectives has been to subdue its democratic "rebel province" and "reunify" it with the mainland.

China's relations with the ROC are of crucial interest to the United States, mainly because under the terms of the Taiwan Relations Act passed in 1979, America is committed to coming to Taiwan's defense if the island is attacked. Meanwhile, we have armed Taiwan to the teeth to prevent that from happening. The United States regards Taiwan as the lynchpin of our interests in the Pacific Ocean; if Taiwan were taken over by communist China, the U.S. would suddenly be confronted with a major shift in the region's strategic balance. A communist Taiwan could host Chinese nuclear missile subs at Su-ao, the modest base that currently homeports three of Taiwan's modern frigates. In that scenario, China's sphere of influence would dramatically expand, especially if it began operating out of the deep water directly off the Taiwanese coastal shelf. Only a mile offshore, the subs could dive deep enough to render them impossible to find.

America is committed to coming to Taiwan's defense if the island is attacked.

Yet Taiwan is not as vigilant as might be expected of a nation living in the shadow of a sleeping dragon. Communist Chinese fishing junks regularly anchor off the island's coastline. As Dr. "Peter" Chen Pi-chao, former Deputy Defense Minister of Taiwan, pointed out,

> Chinese commandos could easily hike up the coastal highway
> and attack Hualien Air Base. [Taiwan's defense ministry] has
> no idea if they are coming ashore on dark nights and running

simulations against the base's defenses. It's been going on for years. I've tried to get someone to put guards out here or better yet, run them off but nobody listens. I only get the usual bureaucratic response. Who would pay for the guards? Should we stir up the dragon over a few fishermen? I have no doubt that if we took a count we would find Chinese fishing junks off nearly every Taiwan beach on most nights.[54]

The Chinese are building at least one new class of SSBN, nuclear powered ballistic missile subs, and having them operate out of Su-ao would be no trick at all. They could just slip into the deep blue and be gone, potentially altering the strategic balance in the Pacific against the United States and its allies.

If China were to establish its domination over Taiwan, it would be disastrous for any Taiwanese citizens who couldn't immediately leave the island for the United States, Canada, Japan, or any other free country that would take them. In Taiwan, as in the United States, every government official above the civil service was either elected by the people or appointed by someone who was elected. In China none of the equivalent officials are popularly elected; they are all selected by the Communist Party. The Taiwanese would have to get used to life without basic freedoms and human rights. With ninety years to fine-tune its torture, brainwashing, and extortion techniques, the Chinese Communist Party would have all of it available to extract information and grudging cooperation from a beaten-down population.

Because Beijing has successfully lobbied Washington against U.S.–Taiwan military-to-military exchanges, the Taiwanese military is not as well-versed in U.S. and other NATO systems as we would like. However, they do know quite a bit; the ROC army is American-equipped, the ROC air force flies U.S. and French fighters, and the ROC navy mans American, French, and Dutch-built ships. Tens of thousands of Taiwanese men have passed through the ROC armed forces in recent years, where they were exposed to NATO equipment. They have test-fired American-made Harpoons so they know how well our missiles work and areas where they don't.

The danger here is that if China were to subsume Taiwan, all these men could expect to be rounded up and drafted into the PLA. All of the ROC armed forces' surviving equipment, including the latest American Patriot III missile batteries, would go into the PLA's stockpiles. Every Taiwanese military base including JiaShan would be taken over by the PLA. Furthermore, Taiwan has a respectable military R&D establishment that makes some of its own gear including missiles and radars—this too would go to China. In addition, Taiwan has a world class industrial base, especially electronics, which would be absorbed into the PLA's military industrial base. We can think of "Painting Taiwan Red" as an elevator ride—straight up—in communist Chinese war fighting capability.

And then there is the geographic problem. Taiwan lies exactly in the middle of a chain of nations and islands stretching from Japan in the north, heading south through the Philippines, and ending with Australia. All these countries are either in formal alliance with the United States—Japan, South Korea, Australia—or are otherwise counted as friendly. A loss of Taiwan to the communists would blow a huge hole in the middle of this pro-American chain. A Red Taiwan would allow the PLA air force's Russian fighters and ground attack aircraft to operate over a huge area reaching almost to the Japanese main islands to the north and, to the south, covering most of the northern Philippines. It would more than double the Chinese air force's current range in the middle Pacific, allowing it to threaten American citizens in Guam as well as our navy and air force bases there.

A free and democratic Taiwan, on the other hand, ensures that the islands around it remain free as well. If Taiwan were to fall to China, the Quemoy and Matzu islands right off the Chinese coast would be lost —and with them, the capability to look deep inside the Chinese mainland via radar.

We can expect China to escalate its aggression against Taiwan as the PLA becomes ever stronger. But the ROC is hardly the only nearby nation feeling the heat from Beijing. China is throwing its growing military strength around all of eastern and southeastern Asia, bullying its neighbors and threatening to draw the United States into war.

There Goes the Neighborhood

South and west of Taiwan is the Pratas Reef, roughly 200 miles southeast of Hong Kong. Right now it only has a runway and a military garrison, but there is talk in Taipei of developing recreational facilities there. Located in the northern part of the South China Sea, Pratas's takeover by China would hold out some military value to the PLA, but the real value would be a substantial territorial claim to offshore oil prospecting in the region. China already produces oil in fields to the west of Pratas. Gaining Pratas would enlarge Chinese territorial claims by hundreds of square miles.

China has been moving south at least since January 1974, when it kicked the South Vietnamese off the Paracel Islands. These islands are much closer to Vietnam than they are to China or its Hainan Island. But in 1974 South Vietnam was preoccupied with a communist insurgency and President Nixon was preoccupied with Watergate, so Beijing saw an opportune moment to make a land grab.

The PRC's territorial claims are now ridiculously large. On a map, they look like a giant tongue sticking down from the south of China all the way to Borneo. It's 2,700 miles from Beijing to Borneo, the world's third largest island which is home to parts of three different nations: Indonesia, Malaysia, and Brunei. That's the distance between Washington, D.C., and Los Angeles. In other words, the PRC's maritime claims into Southeast Asia stretch as far as the entire continental United States. Such expansive territorial ambitions combined with the PLA's massive armaments buildup belie China's claim that its huge standing military is for defensive purposes only. Sure it is—if one concedes Beijing's claims across the entire western Pacific region.

A key source of tension throughout Asia is China's claim to the Spratly Islands, parts of which are also claimed by numerous other Asian nations. In 1988, the PLA attacked the Vietnamese in the Spratly Islands, and the result was the same as in 1974—dead Vietnamese soldiers and sunken Vietnamese navy ships. Beijing is clearly frustrated because some of the areas it continues to hold on to in the Spratly Islands are not even above water at high tide. They've taken to building standing structures above the coral, armed lighthouses in effect. Anything else of development value already has someone else's flag flying over it.

China's most valuable target in the Spratly Islands is the Taiwanese-controlled island of Itu Aba. It's about a thousand miles south of Taiwan, right in the middle of the South China Sea with only one source of fresh water and a landing strip big enough for serious aircraft. The ROC lands a C-130 here from time to time, and it is guarded by Taiwanese marines. Although the PRC has not employed force against the island, it would almost certainly succeed if it did; Itu Aba is far beyond the range of Taiwan's air force. Taipei could send its fleet, but that would be a suicide mission. Furthermore, the United States would not go to war with China to protect Taiwan's offshore claims, while other Asian nations, distracted by their own competing claims, lack the muscle to challenge Beijing.

China's territorial claims are ridiculously large.

For now, China seems content to wait, knowing that if it takes Taiwan, Itu Aba will come as part of the dowry. But patience has its limits, and some PRC officials are undoubtedly arguing for a stronger policy. "China's big goal in the 21st century is to become world number one, the top power," wrote PLA Senior Colonel Lin Ming Fu, a professor at China's National Defense University, in his 2010 book *The China Dream*. According to Liu, confrontation with the United States is inevitable in the "competition to be the leading country, a conflict over who rises and falls to dominate the world." Once Red China has the planet's most powerful military, America "would not dare and would not be able to intervene in military conflict in the Taiwan Strait," he writes.[55]

The prominence of this view within the PLA leadership exposes the lie that today's PLA brass is more moderate than in the past when, for example, General Zhur Chenghu declared in 2005 that "we will have to respond with nuclear weapons" if the U.S. interfered in a war with Taiwan.[56] This attitude is consistent with the shocking 1995 warning from General Xiong Guangkai, the PLA's deputy chief of staff, that Americans won't come to

Taiwan's defense if we "care more about Los Angeles than Taipei."[57] This isn't mere saber-rattling; China's first aircraft carrier, the *Shi Lang*, is named after a Chinese admiral who invaded and conquered Taiwan 300 years ago.[58]

In the summer of 2011, a respected Australian think tank, the Lowery Institute, made news when two of its researchers claimed that escalating disputes between China and everyone else could lead to war.[59] But their conclusion was really just common sense in light of Beijing's bullying in the area. Just in 2011, China fired warning shots at Vietnamese fishermen, cut the cables of a Vietnamese ship doing oil surveys, sent a warship into areas claimed by the Philippines, launched its first aircraft carrier, and defiantly told the United States to stay out of its way.

While China watchers continue to debate the reasons for Beijing's aggressive posture in the South China Sea, the PRC may have let the cat out of the bag. An article in *People's Daily*, the PRC daily rag, reported that Li Yongwu, president of the China Petroleum and Chemical Industry Association, revealed China depends on imported oil for 55 percent of its consumption needs—a higher rate even than the United States—and by 2030 it may have to import a staggering 70 percent.[60]

Oil indeed seems to be at the center of many of China's territorial disputes. Vietnam is already pumping about 300,000 barrels a day from offshore fields to the west. On the eastern side, the Philippines' oil production jumped 33 percent from 2009 to 2010 mostly based on new production offshore. To the south, Malaysia and Brunei are major oil producers on the shore of Borneo. In the middle sit the Spratly Islands. No one can say the islands sit in a giant basin of oil, but with oil prices hovering around $100 per barrel, the mere prospect of exploring for oil is enough to capture the attention of national governments as well as international oil companies. For example, since the Obama administration shut down Gulf of Mexico drilling operations, the Diamond Offshore Company has been forced to move one of its giant deep-water rigs to Vietnamese waters to drill two wells and possibly two more for BP.[61] It will be the third Diamond rig to leave U.S. waters since the drilling moratorium.

At the outset of 2011, China began stepping up the role of the bully in the South China Sea, firing at Vietnamese and Filipino fishermen and harassing oil exploration teams from both those nations. Chinese air force planes began acting aggressively with the forces of the countries of the region. With air-to-air refueling, Chinese SU-27s have some limited linger time over the Spratly Islands, but not a lot. Moreover, Beijing has begun a campaign to build on the various bits of territory it has managed to secure. By early June 2011, the Chinese ambassador to the Philippines baldly announced that China had not started to drill for oil and that neighboring countries should not drill for oil in disputed waters either.[62] What he neglected to mention was that two weeks before, in Shanghai, China had launched a billion-dollar oil platform designed to drill in deep waters, and that rig would be on station to begin drilling in July 2011—in the South China Sea, right on the doorstep of the Philippines.[63]

How much oil and gas are we talking about in the South China Sea? No one really knows because the area has not been completely surveyed. Estimates vary wildly, from a Chinese estimate as high as 213 billion barrels to a twenty-year-old U.S. estimate of just 28 billion barrels.[64] Either way, China is putting forward an ever-expanding list of territorial claims and is fielding an ever more powerful military that could soon begin enforcing them.

A Feckless Response

In 2008, Richard Fisher, senior fellow of the International Assessment and Strategy Center and one of America's foremost authorities on the PLA, gave a lecture at the United States Naval Academy at Annapolis.[65] The event was held in Mahan Hall, named for the famous naval theorist Admiral Alfred Thayer Mahan, and about 1,000 midshipmen attended. At the end of the lecture, there was a question and answer period.

A midshipman stood up and introduced himself as one of the academy's international students from the Republic of China (Taiwan). He said, "In case anyone has any doubts, the Republic of China's armed forces will defend Taiwan ... to the last man!" With that, a thousand U.S. Navy Midshipmen jumped to their feet and roared their approval.

Compare that attitude to the one that prevails in the Obama White House, which informed Capitol Hill on June 28, 2011 that it would not permit the United States to sell new model F-16s to Taiwan. And that was just one of many indications of the Obama administration's disinterest in protecting U.S. interests vis-à-vis Beijing. With their constant focus on protecting trade ties with China, Obama administration officials largely respond to PRC aggression by obfuscating the facts, minimizing the threat, and changing the topic.

The administration's blasé position toward Chinese arms smuggling is particularly outrageous. Until the United States acts effectively to shut down Beijing's family business of weapons smuggling, the world runs the risk that a terrible weapon of Chinese origin will eventually end up in the hands of a terrorist organization inspired by a twisted sense of religious duty.

The administration's blasé position toward Chinese arms smuggling is particularly outrageous.

Here's exhibit A in the Obama administration's apathetic approach to Chinese arms smuggling: in July 2009, Secretary of State Clinton sent a cable to the U.S. Embassy in Beijing asking then-U.S. Ambassador Jon Huntsman Jr. to deliver a "talking points/non-paper" to the Chinese regarding nine WMD (ballistic missile technology and nuclear weapons) smuggling cases that the United States had raised with the Chinese Foreign Ministry over the past year. Among others, Clinton accused Polytechnologies by name as having exported under "false documentation" a critical piece of machinery for ballistic missile production as well as "integrated optical chips" that have military uses.[66] (See Appendix I.)

Polytechnologies is far from the only Chinese family firm collecting money from WMD sales. After Muammar Gadhafi decided to halt his WMD programs and cozy up to NATO in 2004, he turned over a treasure trove of documents related to Chinese and North Korean arms smuggling. According to one press report, one of the Chinese documents "contained detailed, step-by-step instructions for assembling an implosion-type nuclear bomb that could fit atop a ballistic missile."[67] Remarkably, a U.S. official who saw the Chinese blueprints reported that there were handwritten notes in the margins that "made reference to Chinese ministers, presumably involved in the deal."[68] A signed confession couldn't have been more explicit.

Clinton prefaced her cable to the U.S. Embassy in Beijing by complaining that the United States has "received little or no response from China" on these cases. It concluded with soothing diplomatic language: "We appreciate your interest in advancing our mutual nonproliferation goals." Clinton's long list of Chinese WMD smuggling cases, which Beijing has totally ignored, makes it clear the U.S. and China really have no "mutual non-proliferation goals." Of course, nothing came of her entreaties to Beijing.

Further examples abound of the Obama administration's listless response to continued Chinese WMD and ballistic-missile arms smuggling. For example, one of the companies on Hillary Clinton's list, China Precision Machinery Import and Export Corporation (CPMIEC), was banned by President George W. Bush from doing business with U.S. firms in 2006. However, in late December 2009, on Clinton's watch, The Wisconsin Project on Nuclear Arms Control, a highly respected Washington think tank, found that "lax enforcement of U.S. sanctions is allowing Chinese companies to continue to ship goods to the United States even after being hit with an import ban for proliferation to Iran," among them over 300 illicit CPMIEC deals with U.S. firms.[69]

The cable also notes a number of other Chinese companies, such as China Precision Machinery, that have been sanctioned by the United States for past smuggling operations. All the Chinese companies listed by Clinton are State Owned Enterprises (SOEs) ultimately controlled by the Chinese Communist Party.

The list of companies in the cable proves Beijing's arms smuggling scheme has continued for decades hidden under layers of cut-outs and proxies within the SOE system. According to the Chinese arms dealer's

1988 description, the profits from this dirty business are used by Chinese Communist aristocratic family members for foreign travel, tuition at Ivy League universities, and maintaining a luxurious lifestyle far beyond the comprehension of the vast majority of poor Chinese people. Over time, more and more Princelings stake claims to this pot of money, making it difficult for Beijing to eliminate the smuggling cash cow even if it wanted to do so. As the number of claimants on the smuggling proceeds grows, so too does the danger posed to the West as Beijing grows increasingly reckless. The C-802 anti-ship missile that struck the *Hanit* is an advanced weapon but still a conventional one—imagine if it had been a ballistic missile or a weapon of mass destruction such as a nuclear bomb.

The nine arms smuggling cases identified by Clinton—spanning WMDs, nuclear weapons expertise, and ballistic missile technology— were serious blows to global non-proliferation efforts, but at least the customers were all national governments. In its continuing quest for cash, however, the likelihood rises of Beijing transferring ballistic missiles, WMD, or the means to build them to new villains—terrorist groups that are *already* their customers for advanced conventional weapons. Unsurprisingly, the Obama administration has made no concerted effort to tell Beijing that the United States will hold it accountable if it continues to sell dangerous weapons to terrorists.

Trying to determine a person's motivation is always tricky. Certainly the reluctance of some Obama officials to confront Beijing's arms smuggling and regional bullying stems from concern over their post-government employment prospects. Since trade ties with China are based on the Chinese Communist Party's system of dictatorship, changing the status quo in Beijing could hurt American companies that profit from the current conditions. Those companies won't want to hire people who hurt their business, and China won't want to do business with uncooperative former officials. In short, they're trying to follow in the footsteps of disbarred lawyer Sandy Berger, who established a lucrative China business after he served as Bill Clinton's national security advisor, and Clinton Secretary of State Madeleine Albright, who did the same.[70] As China reporter and author Jim Mann argued, "The proclivity of American elites to refrain from public criticism of China's repressive system is reinforced all the more by the influence of money. There are huge and growing financial incentives for prominent Americans to support the status quo in China."[71]

The People's Republic of China is the most significant long-term threat to U.S. national security, and Barack Obama is not defending America against it. He is derelict in his duty as commander in chief of this great nation and as the leader of the free world, which is once again in danger of being dominated by a communist power.

CHAPTER FIVE

THIEVING AND SPYING: THE CHINESE REGIME IN ACTION

Secret operations are essential in war;
upon them the army relies to make its every move.

—Sun Tzu

More than five dozen Americans were prosecuted for spying for Beijing between 2008 and 2011.[1] A U.S. intelligence official told us, "The scary thing is not the relatively few of our citizens we catch that are spies, but the realization that for every one we nail, there are hundreds or even thousands that we don't know about—and they're still out there selling vital national secrets to our enemies." When asked what country currently poses the biggest threat to U.S. interests, this official—who works for the director of national intelligence—stated, "China, no question about it. We can't forget about the Russians, because they still think of themselves as a major check to U.S. power, but it would be a costly mistake not to view Beijing as an enemy—because they are out to get us. All you have to do is look at their elaborate espionage network in America if you want to get an idea of their bad intentions towards us."

Intelligence operations are an essential component for any national security apparatus. We must know and understand the enemy in order to create adequate defenses against them. In this cloak-and-dagger world, covert operations often deliver a lot of bang for few bucks. For mere tens of thousands of dollars, foreign agents can bribe bureaucrats or scientists to acquire blueprints for weapons systems that cost tens of billions to research and develop.

In Beijing's efforts to leapfrog ahead of America, communist officials have launched a major espionage program to achieve technological sophistication that otherwise would take China decades to achieve. To get this valuable information, communist agents pay off government officials, engineers, security guards at top-secret facilities, university professors, and business executives. Many of Beijing's spies among us are ethnically Chinese, but there is a growing number of U.S.-born, non-Chinese citizens who are selling out our nation.

This spy war between states is a zero-sum game. When the People's Republic of China wins, the United States loses.

"The Chinese espionage threat has been relentless recently," according to former U.S. National Counterintelligence Executive Joel Brenner. "We've never seen anything like it. Some of it's public. Some of it's private. And some of it lies in that ambiguous area in between."[2] Chinese business and government officials act in unison for the purpose of increasing the power of their homeland. It's a lesson U.S. officials need to learn. This spy war between states is a zero-sum game. When the People's Republic of China wins, the United States loses. And today, America is losing badly.

Far and Wide: The Extent of China's Espionage

An entire book could be written on the number of Chinese technology espionage cases alone. According to an extensive search of Department of Justice files, at least fifty-seven people have been charged with trying, and in some cases succeeding, to illegally export critical U.S. military hardware and software to China—and that is just since 2008.[3] The following are accounts of just a few of the most recent and egregious cases.

- In the summer of 2011, two Chinese aerospace executives pleaded guilty to attempting to export radiation-hardened military microchips to China.[4] "Radiation-hardened" are the magic words that raise this far above the average Chinese technology smuggling case—the process allows these microchips to be used in outer space or even in a nuclear war.

- While President Obama decided to end manned space flight by the United States, the Chinese have huge space ambitions, mostly with military applications.[5] So, it should come as no surprise that they are trying to steal every space secret we have. One of their instruments was 73-year-old Dongfan "Greg" Chung, an American citizen born in China who worked as an aerospace engineer, with that position's high security clearance. Chung stole the secrets to the American space shuttle and shipped them to China, earning him a 15-year prison sentence in early 2010.[6]

- American stealth technology is another major target of Chinese espionage. Noshir S. Gowadia, a former engineer with the U.S. defense contractor Northrop-Grumman, gave China the keys to that kingdom. According to the FBI, during his career with Northrop-Grumman, Gowadia "contributed to the unique propulsion system and low observable capabilities of the B-2 Spirit bomber, sometimes

known as the 'Stealth bomber.'" So he knew how to make
aircraft almost disappear from radar. With this knowledge,
he did two things for the Chinese. First, he taught the Chinese the vulnerabilities of the B-2 and how its stealth capabilities could be defeated. Second, he helped design China's
own stealth cruise missile that could be used against us. He
went to China and gave a remarkable Power Point presen-
tation: he displayed a picture of their existing missile and
told them what it looks like on American radar; then he
displayed a blank screen and declared that this is what their
missile would look like on American radar after they
installed a certain modification he had designed for them,
if the price was right.

Gowadia betrayed his adopted country for money,
enabling him to enjoy a nice retirement lifestyle with a
luxurious house in Hawaii. To keep from having to pay
taxes on his ill-gotten gains, he laundered the Chinese
money through a phony children's charity he set up in
Liechtenstein. In January 2011, Gowadia was sentenced
to thirty-two years in federal prison. Since he is sixty-six
years old, he will be ninety-eight when he gets out, minus
any time off for good behavior. With taxpayer-funded
healthcare, he might yet see the Hawaiian sunset once
again. In the meantime, his actions have jeopardized the
lives of American sailors and marines and our allies in the
Pacific.[7]

America is a major priority for Chinese spies, but their activities stretch
far beyond America's shores. Four South Korean officials were caught
in a Chinese "honey trap" in 2011.[8] French intelligence documents
leaked in the same year accused the Chinese of "widespread industrial
spying."[9] In Britain, Chinese espionage is so prevalent that the UK's
MI-5 security service has begun circulating a document entitled "The
Threat from Chinese Espionage" among British business executives.[10]

Tokyo was deeply embarrassed in 2007 when a computer disk containing sensitive information about the American Aegis combat system showed up in a police raid of the home of a Japanese naval petty officer married to a Chinese woman.[11]

According to a former high-ranking American defense official, the Chinese also stole secrets from the Russian Mikoyan and Sukoi Design Bureaus, where high-tech Russian weapons systems such as the famous MiG aircraft are developed.[12] That may explain how the Chinese were able to roll out a fifth generation fighter jet just a year after the Russians announced theirs.

In order to improve their agents' already impressive tradecraft, Beijing has announced the opening of a string of spy schools attached to Chinese universities. As might be expected, the students at Shanghai's Fudan University, the site of one of the new spy schools, "have been largely kept in the dark about its existence."[13] This announcement may be designed to divert attention from a parallel set of long-standing, little-known spy schools.

Chinese spymasters employ all the tricks of the cloak-and-dagger trade. Of late, they have used a kind of "false flag operation" in which an American becomes involved in an international transaction with what appears to be an allied country but in reality is Beijing. Department of Defense official James Fondren went to prison under just those circumstances when he sold classified information on U.S. arms sales policy to Taiwan to someone he thought was representing the island country but in fact was working for Red China.[14] The specifics are damning. Fondren, a retired lieutenant colonel in the Air Force, sold classified military reports to Tai Shen Kuo, a naturalized U.S. citizen originally from China.[15] Before being sentenced to three years in prison, Fondren served as deputy director for the Washington liaison office of the U.S. Pacific Command.[16] He had the goods on U.S. operations in Asia, and that information is worth a lot of money. If Beijing can get inside Pacific Command, it can get in anywhere.

Arguably the most interesting recent case is that of American Glenn Duffie Shriver. A somewhat aimless wanderer and sometime student, Shriver found himself in China, where he was approached by Chinese agents and offered $70,000 to go home and apply to join the CIA or the

State Department. He took the money, made the application, was caught lying during his polygraph examination, and will be in prison for the next four years.[17]

American counterintelligence experts are debating the meaning of the Shriver case. Does it mark a shift away from the Chinese intelligence tradition of targeting ethnic Chinese by extorting or bribing them into spying for Beijing? Or does it signal an expansion of espionage tactics, adding new groups to the stable of ethnic Chinese agents they already have?

America needs an army of whiz kids to take on China's massive intelligence apparatus.

Or perhaps it's a more subtle game—recruit a gullible American kid, make certain he gets caught, and thereby force America to spread its counterintelligence resources even thinner. Additionally, these episodes could complicate U.S. intelligence efforts by casting a veil of suspicion over any young Americans who ever studied in China and want to serve their country in the CIA, FBI, State Department, or military intelligence. That last point is an important one—if Chinese intelligence can taint anyone who spent a year abroad studying in Beijing, it can seriously inhibit the United States from recruiting the national security team our nation needs to keep tabs on the PRC for the next ten to twenty years. America needs an army of whiz kids to take on China's massive intelligence apparatus, but Beijing's clever spy game is taking a lot of our talent off the table.

Soft Targets and Glaring Vulnerabilities

China doesn't really need to physically infiltrate our organizations when it can target us by exploiting its stranglehold on American trade and cheap technology.

Take SCADA systems, short for "Supervisory Control and Data Acquisition." Tied to computer systems, they monitor and control overall projects such as manufacturing processes, electrical grids, oil refineries, power generation, oil and gas pipelines, and telecommunications, among others. For example, a SCADA monitors ("Data Acquisition") the temperature at certain points of a nuclear power plant and sends an electronic signal ("Supervisory Control") to a valve telling it to open when needed to let in a certain amount of cooling water to keep a nuclear meltdown from occurring. SCADAs are vitally important to keeping society orderly and functioning. Consequently, they are a major national security vulnerability.

The weakness of SCADAs lies in the two parts of the system—the data acquisition and the supervisory control. Suppose there is some flaw in the data acquired. For example, could the thermometer inside a critical component of a nuclear power plant be defective, telling the supervisory control that the temperature is lower than it really is and therefore cooling water is not needed? Or suppose the thermometer is fine but there is a failure of the supervisory control system—that is, the supervisory control system knows something is running hot, so it sends an incomplete message to the valve and it opens, but not far enough or long enough. In any variation of these possibilities, it's easy to see how a malfunctioning SCADA—whether by accident or design—could cause a disaster. Consider the following:

- SCADAs are most often connected to the internet, making them vulnerable to hackers.
- Vital components or even the entire SCADA system itself may be purchased from the lowest cost producer abroad— making a hostile power's efforts to design weaknesses in the components or software relatively easy.
- Commands are sent from a central point to the valves by wireless (radio) communications whose encryption costs would be an attractive target for naive project managers looking to save money.

Scientists at our National Laboratories have already run realistic simulations against a refinery showing how someone could enter the plant's computers system and disable a re-circulator pump, causing an explosion. When they used the internet to attack a 27-ton U.S. power generator, it shook, emitted smoke, and destroyed itself.[18]

If a hostile force can get in, it can make a SCADA system malfunction and suppress alarms until it is too late. As the *Chinese Army Daily* threatened, "Perhaps one day people [foreigners] will wake up in the morning to find out all the phone systems are down, computers hacked by viruses, the state treasury being emptied."[19]

As far back as 2000, Steve Kroft of *60 Minutes* painted a horrific picture of what could happen if a malevolent actor exploited our systemic vulnerabilities: "Radar images can be changed, planes can be erased from the screens and false data inserted in the National Weather Service could confuse and misdirect pilots, causing chaos in the air."[20] Depending on how widespread it is, tens of thousands of Americans and foreign visitors flying in our skies would lose their lives. No one would be immune—neither the VIP in a private jet nor the family on its way to Orlando.

The idea that a nation could damage its enemy through these kinds of attacks is far from theoretical. In 2010, we got a glimpse of how vulnerable sophisticated, expensive operating systems can be to problems with their cheapest parts. That summer, computer experts discovered a new kind of virus circulating in computers around the world. Specifically targeting SCADAs made by the German industrial giant Siemens, the virus attacked control components in nuclear centrifuges, causing machines to malfunction and eventually break down. It was essentially harmless to anything else, but was capable of great destruction of the specific, targeted equipment. The experts called this high-tech attack "Stuxnet" after a word found in its computer code.[21]

The Iranians just happen to use Siemens SCADAs to control their illicit uranium enrichment program, and the target of this attack wasn't a U.S. facility but one run by the Islamic fanatics in Tehran. Stuxnet caused the Iranian nuclear weapons machinery to damage itself, dealing a significant setback to the regime's nuke program. When asked about the source of the virus, national security officials from the apparent creators of Stuxnet—the United States and Israel—act like cats that swallowed the canaries. Nobody knows anything, but it was a job well done.

Here's how Stuxnet worked: The Iranian nuke program depends on Pakistan-supplied centrifuges—machinery with high-speed rotors that cause uranium to separate ("enrich") into various forms ("isotopes"), one of which is the critical ingredient for atomic bombs. The United States and Israel duplicated the Siemens SCADA system and tied it to the same kind of centrifuges Iran possesses. The package was set up secretly in the Israeli desert and tested on various computer viruses until one was found that would work. Apparently there wasn't a way to implant the virus directly into the Iranian system, so it was released worldwide in the hopes that someone in Iran would insert an infected thumb drive into a console. Once it was unleashed, Stuxnet disabled the alarm systems and sent the Iranian centrifuges running wildly out of control until the whole thing crashed, at least for a while.

Using an infected thumb drive against the Iranians was ironic since, as Deputy Defense Secretary William Lynn announced, "[I]n 2008 ... a foreign intelligence agency used a thumb drive to penetrate our classified computer systems—something we thought was impossible."[22] Now, American government computers are designed so that it is impossible to insert a thumb drive or similar device into a console.

Organizing the Stuxnet operation must have been an incredibly complex endeavor. Programming the virus to attack only those Siemens SCADAs that control Iranian nuclear equipment, and not identical Siemens SCADAs working on harmless projects elsewhere in the world, is quite a trick. It would have taken a lot of expert computer specialists at least months of effort and millions of U.S. dollars (and Israeli shekels) out of various black budgets to pull it off.

In light of Iran's secrecy surrounding its nuke program, the precise extent of the damage inflicted by Stuxnet is unclear. But the virus clearly took a toll, an outcome that invited replication. In the spring of 2011, an ad hoc group of twenty-one American academics, senior military officers, and code breakers united to work on a program they called "Project Cyber Dawn"—an effort to infect Muammar Gadhafi's Ras Lanouf refinery that runs on the same Siemens SCADAs that the Iranians were using. Unfortunately, the group's plans appeared on the internet after something calling itself "Luz Security" hacked the group's internal emails.[23] It's unclear whether their cover was blown before they put any of their plans into operation, but presumably somewhere in NATO such a scheme or something similar is under consideration. The tech war is real, as is America's need to ensure our geek patrols are better than the enemy's.

An Electronic Pearl Harbor

In November 1997, Deputy Defense Secretary John Hamre testified before the Senate Subcommittee on Terrorism that "we're facing the possibility of an electronic Pearl Harbor.... There is going to be an electronic attack on this country some time in the future."[24] Two years later, he told a secret session of the House Armed Services Committee, "We are at war—right now. We are in cyberwar."[25]

"There is going to be an electronic attack on this country some time in the future."

Fast-forward more than a decade, to 2011. President Obama's choice for secretary of defense, Leon Panetta, tells the Senate Armed Services Committee at his confirmation hearing that the United States faces a possible "electronic Pearl Harbor." Panetta had been the CIA director for the previous two years—so he should have known.

Two extreme, nearly identical warnings twelve years apart should have brought home the magnitude of the electronic threat facing the country. Yet nothing was done. When former Director of National Intelligence Admiral Mike McConnell was asked directly by Congress about our ability to withstand such an onslaught, he replied, "The United States is not prepared for such an attack."[26]

The Obama administration has shown a shocking disinterest in this threat, earning it a blunt rebuke from former White House national security official Richard Clarke. While "our government is engaged in defending only its own networks ... it is failing in its responsibility to protect the rest of America from Chinese cyberattack," Clarke wrote in the *Wall Street Journal*. In other words, the federal government has taken action to protect itself, but not the rest of us. Clarke further declared that "senior U.S. officials know well that the government of China is systematically attacking the computer networks of the U.S. government and American corporations," and yet, "In private, U.S. officials admit that the government has no strategy to stop the Chinese cyberassault."[27]

This searing denunciation of the Obama administration's passivity toward China is made all the more powerful by the fact that Clarke is no Republican partisan. To the contrary, he had a bitter falling out with the Bush administration during his service with it, after which he became a generous contributor to liberal groups such as Moveon.org and to Democratic candidates including Barack Obama himself.[28]

The Obama administration at least claims to recognize the problem. Deputy Defense Secretary William Lynn told a European audience in June 2011, "The third and most dangerous cyber threat is destruction, where cyber tools are used to cause physical damage.... It is possible to imagine attacks on military networks or on critical infrastructure—like the transportation system and energy sector—that cause economic damage, physical destruction, or even loss of life." However, the administration's grand solution is, as Lynn took great pride in announcing, merely to institute "a pilot program with a handful of defense companies to provide more robust protection for their networks."[29] The commanders of the Chinese Army must be quaking in their desk chairs.

Game Over

Most Americans don't realize the Chinese have already successfully attacked many U.S. government and civilian computer systems. The *Wall Street Journal* noted that in one major Chinese intrusion, the attackers were "able to copy and siphon off several terabytes of data related to design and electronics systems, officials say, potentially making it easier to defend against [American F-35 fighter-jets]."[30] Consequently, "Chinese spies enjoyed months of access to the personal Google emails of U.S. officials and human rights activists," reported London's *Telegraph* in 2011.[31]

In 2006, network intrusions caused authorities to shut down the entire computer system at the U.S. Naval War College. Air Force General Richard Goetze, a professor at the military school who previously was the commander in charge of developing America's strategic nuclear war plan, told his students the Chinese "took down" the war college's network. Even the school's website and email systems went down. For weeks afterward, military officers—both students and professors—at the school were forced to use private email accounts such as yahoo and gmail instead of their official addresses, exposing government business to untold security risks. This embarrassing attack exposed a serious Pentagon vulnerability—the Naval War College was where the Defense Department created a cyber-warfare center specifically to counter the threat from hackers. Two days after the incident, U.S. Strategic Command raised the security alert level of America's entire military computer network. Alan Paller, a security expert at the SAND Institute, observed, "The depth of the penetration is more than anybody is admitting."[32]

America isn't the only target; financial institutions and international organizations are also vulnerable to Beijing's cyber offensive. Chinese hackers blew through the defenses of the Indian company Satyam that held the computer services contract for the World Bank in 2008. Internal World Bank emails called this an "unprecedented crisis," as World Bank officials held angry closed door meetings with China's executive director with the bank.[33] Similarly, the IMF won't say who penetrated its information systems in the spring of 2011, but most experts point to China.[34] In 2009, a Canadian think tank identified China as the source of a cyber network that "tapped into classified documents from government and private organizations of 103 countries."[35]

CNN's computer expert Dr. Adam Segal notes that Chinese hackers stole proprietary information from "DuPont, Johnson & Johnson, General Electric, RSA, Epsilon, NASDAQ and at least a dozen other firms."[36]

Moreover, a 2011 Chinese cyber assault on major Western oil companies, nicknamed "Night Dragon," was discovered by cybersecurity firm McAffee, Inc,[37] which also found that a "one state actor" had successfully penetrated scores of industrial companies in what McAffee dubbed "Operation Shady Rat." The firm didn't specify which nation was behind Shady Rat, but a major clue is found in the operation's targeting of the International Olympic Committee, the World Anti-Doping Agency, and various national Olympic committees, all this occurring just before and just after the 2008 Beijing Olympics.[38] Finally, Oak Ridge National Laboratory, where the first atomic bomb was produced, was victimized by Chinese hackers in the fall of 2007 as a follow-on to a larger penetration of U.S. national security just months before.[39]

The Chinese hackers appear to be a vast army of chair-borne warriors associated with or downright part of the People's Liberation Army. According to a secret U.S. State Department cable revealed by WikiLeaks, American specialists have tracked some of the most serious attacks back to sites known to belong to electronic espionage units of the Chinese military.[40] In 2007, angry U.S. defense officers leaked an internal review reporting that the Chinese military had attacked Pentagon computer networks, including the one serving Defense Secretary Robert Gates.[41]

The Chinese hackers appear to be a vast army of chair-borne warriors associated with or downright part of the People's Liberation Army.

We now know that the attack on the Pentagon network was more serious than initially reported, to the point that one expert, Dr. James Lewis, director of the technology and public policy program at the Washington think-tank Center for Strategic and International Studies, called it an "espionage Pearl Harbor." In 2010, Mr. Lewis told *60 Minutes* that "terabytes of information" had been downloaded from "all of the high tech agencies, all of the military agencies"—the State Department, the Department of Energy (which runs our nuclear weapons labs), and the

Department of Defense. Asked how big a "terabyte" is, Mr. Lewis replied, "The Library of Congress, which has millions of volumes, is about 12 terabytes. So, we probably lost the equivalent of a Library of Congress worth of government information in 2007."[42] If the American intelligence community conducted a damage assessment afterward, it has not publicized the details.

The Huawei Wars

Huawei is China's poster child for every conceivable kind of bad corporate behavior. An undeclared arm of the Chinese army, the company is a center of Chinese spies, proud partner of Iranian military industries, thief of American technology, recipient of Chinese government favoritism, dispenser of bribes, and sponsor of a mysterious after-hours raid on its competitors.[43]

Huawei was formed by Ren Zhengfei, a PLA officer who remains in nominal control as CEO, while the actual owner of the company has never been revealed. The company's second ranking officer, chairwoman Sun Yafang, is a veteran of China's Ministry of State Security, Beijing's overseas spy division. Perhaps through her ministry contacts, she helped obtain critical loans to keep Huawei afloat in its early years, and grateful ever after, no doubt.[44]

As the RAND Corporation, an American think-tank reporting to the U.S. Air Force, reports, "Huawei maintains deep ties with the Chinese military, which serves a multi-faceted role as an important customer as well as its political patron and research and development partner. Both the government and the military tout Huawei as a national champion, and the company is currently China's largest, fastest-growing, and most impressive telecommunications-equipment manufacturer."[45]

Huawei has spread its tentacles widely. The Chinese embassy in Tehran bragged that the firm "has gained the trust and alliance of major [Iranian] governmental and private entities within a short period.... [M]ilitary industries ... are among the clients of this telecom giant."[46] Closer to home, U.S. Export-Import Bank president Fred Hochberg cited

Huawei's $30 billion line of credit from the Chinese Development Bank as an example of Chinese "state-directed capital" giving a Chinese company a vital competitive edge over a vast array of U.S. businesses.[47] In its competition with American rivals, Huawei doesn't fight fair. When Cisco Systems sued Huawei in 2003, the U.S. firm claimed Huawei infringed at least five of its patents and stole its source code.[48] Likewise, Motorola sued Huawei in 2010, accusing the Chinese firm of conspiring with Chinese-born Motorola engineers to steal Motorola technology through an outside dummy corporation they had established.[49] Both cases were settled out of court.

The most brazen case of Huawei malfeasance took place in 2004, when a Huawei employee armed with a phony identity badge and carrying all sorts of industrial espionage tools got caught in Chicago making an after-hours raid on a Japanese competitor at a trade show. As the general counsel of Japanese computer firm Fujitsu's American subsidiary, Fujitsu Network Communications (FNC), wrote in an angry letter to Huawei, "Specifically Mr. Zhu reportedly went to FNC's booth after the exhibition hall had closed to the conference attendees and removed the casing from a proprietary optical networking device owned by FNC. He was caught by a contractor of FNC while he was examining certain circuit boards within the device (after removing the casing of the device)."[50]

That FNC circuit board is a million-dollar piece of equipment. When the trade show's security officers shook down Zhu, the Huawei employee, they found a digital camera; memory sticks with all sorts of goodies including at least "two pages of proprietary diagrams of an AT&T Corp central office"; and a notebook "packed full of hand-drawn diagrams and other data" as well as a list of other competitors Zhu was targeting.[51] FNC's general counsel copied her Huawei letter to executives of Cisco, Lucent, Nortel, and Tellabs, suggesting that Huawei's spy also broke into those firms or at least intended to do so.[52] It looks like Zhu had already cleaned out AT&T at the Chicago show and had intended to approach other targets there before he was caught rifling through the FNC booth.

The tradeshow's security team stripped Huawei's emissary of his phony ID, digital camera, memory sticks, and magic notebook, and tossed him out of the exhibition hall. FNC turned all this paraphernalia over to the FBI. Later, Huawei released a short statement saying it had fired Zhu, though there is no way to verify that claim in a 100,000-strong corporation like Huawei. Zhu could certainly be in a position somewhere deep inside China, lecturing Huawei's next class of foreign representatives on espionage and theft techniques.

Among other things, Huawei makes telecom gear such as switches for large IT systems. It would be very useful to get its equipment inside U.S. national security computer systems—and it has made multiple attempts to do so. The pattern seems to be the following: Huawei and its American partners cook up some mergers and acquisitions scheme hoping nobody will notice. The U.S. intelligence community finds out about it and tips off people on Capitol Hill. Letters fly down from the Hill to the Treasury Department's Committee on Foreign Investment in the United States (CFIUS). Huawei's Democratic Party lobbyists try to protect the deal, but it gets nixed. Then, everyone waits for Huawei to think up a new angle of attack on the American national security system.

The game began in 2008 when Huawei tried to take a junior position in the American firm 3Com, a maker of internet router and networking equipment. Huawei probably thought the $2.2 billion deal was a cinch since it was put together by Bain Capital of Boston. However, the Pentagon noticed that 3Com also made anti-hacking software for the U.S. military. CFIUS killed the move and with it Beijing's opportunity to undermine our anti-hacking program.[53]

In the next case, in 2010, instead of attempting to merge with a U.S. firm, Huawei tried to become an important equipment supplier to American firms that in turn supply "important equipment to the U.S. military and law enforcement agencies," as the alert letter from Capitol Hill read.[54] That is, the plan was to hide behind the American supplier, counting on the U.S. government not to realize that the U.S. firm would install Huawei switches and other gear. The government did catch on, however, and the scheme collapsed.

In a 2011 case, Virginia Senator Jim Webb noted that Huawei's takeover of an American firm "was specifically designed to ensure the transaction avoided review by U.S. regulators."[55] Huawei had bought the assets of an insolvent U.S. computer firm that produced off-the-shelf systems linked to more powerful computer systems, but once again it was blocked from proceeding.[56]

It would be nice to declare "strike three, you're out," but it's unlikely Huawei will simply give up. After being thwarted in that last deal, the corporation published an open letter complaining about its treatment in the U.S. and asking the government to make a formal investigation to clear up any "concerns it may have about Huawei." Where subtlety has failed, apparently, a play for American sympathy might succeed.

Theft vs. Manipulation

On the theft side of Chinese hacking, there is, of course, traditional espionage—military secrets, such as the stolen data from the F-35 stealth fighter. As Northrop-Grumman told the U.S.–China Economic and Security Review Commission, "China's defense industry is producing new generations of weapon platforms with impressive speed and quality.... Chinese industrial espionage is providing a source of new technology without the necessity of investing time or money to perform research."[57]

Likewise, Chinese companies' commercial theft speeds up their innovation. Commercial theft via computer intrusion has been part of Beijing's overall program of supporting key Chinese firms, a program that also includes patent and copyright theft as well as employee stealing. Just as it is easier to steal defense secrets by computer hacking than to develop a new weapons systems yourself, it is certainly easier to steal a competitor's technology and trade secrets than it is to innovate a commercial product in-house.

Worse than computer espionage is the threat of manipulation. Steve Kroft of CBS imagined this scenario a decade ago when he spoke of the possibility of hostile powers making jetliners disappear from the FAA's radar screens. The Stuxnet virus in Iran was another case of manipulation—the affected Iranian SCADAs made uranium enrichment machinery run wild. Stuxnet was a national security victory for the United States, but unless our firms are vigilant, similar capabilities could victimize our whole society. For example, prepared food, such as baby food, is made in factories where the assembly line is sometimes controlled by SCADAs. The same is true for pharmaceuticals. It might be possible to change the mixtures to cause great harm or even death.

Commercial theft via computer intrusion has been part of Beijing's overall program of supporting key Chinese firms.

Even the Defense Department is alarmed at the possibility of hostile manipulation. For example, suppose a hostile power simply changed the GPS coordinates of a B-2 bomber meeting with its refueling tanker—both could show up in different parts of an empty sky, and the bomber would crash into the ocean when it ran out of fuel.

As of this writing, the Obama administration is shooting at hostile targets in Iraq, Afghanistan, Pakistan, Libya, and Yemen. Predator drones, smart bombs, and guided missiles all rely on accurate information, right down to the square foot. If a hostile power intervenes in the process, it could engineer a terrible case of "friendly fire," resulting in the death of our own troops or of friendly civilians. In June 2011, NATO had a single bomb go astray in Libya that killed nine civilians including a baby. There is no indication this was anything more than the fog of war, but a hostile hand directing the targeting could turn a limited tragedy into a catastrophe.

Money Buys Friends

While China is concentrating immense resources in its massive campaign of technological espionage against the United States, it also continues engaging in old-fashioned, Cold War-style spying operations against the U.S. military. For example, in 2006, former Defense Intelligence Agency (DIA) analyst Ronald Montaperto was sent to prison after being convicted of illegally holding classified documents. As part of his plea bargain, he signed a document that divulged quite a bit about his relationships with Chinese embassy attachés and the intelligence he gave them. Though blandly titled "Statement of Facts," it's essentially Montaperto's confession, which he signed in order to avoid facing more serious charges than possessing classified documents in his home. (See Appendix IV.) In the document, Montaperto agreed that if his case had gone to trial, the government would have been able to prove "beyond a reasonable doubt" that he maintained decades-long inappropriate relationships with Chinese intelligence agents. Or, as one U.S. intelligence official stated bluntly, "He was a spy for China."[58]

Practically from the time Montaperto joined the DIA in 1981 to the time he pled guilty in 2006, he was a divisive figure inside the China-watching community.[59] By his own choice, he became the prime example of all that was wrong with the U.S. government's approach to the growing China threat. It took a sting operation by the Naval Criminal Investigative Service (NCIS) and the FBI to show that Montaperto was not just a moderate in the China debate, as he portrayed himself to be, but had gone over to the other side, decades ago.

Montaperto told his Chinese contacts about two major Chinese ballistic missile smuggling operations the U.S. had discovered. He confessed that his "knowledge on this topic was derived from information on those cases that came from highly classified sources and sensitive compartmentalized information," in other words, from top secret information.[60] A law enforcement official assigned to the case told *Washington Times* national security editor Bill Gertz that one of the smuggling operations involved ballistic missile sales to Iran.[61] Moreover, a U.S. official told Gertz that shortly after Montaperto told the Chinese spies we were on to their Iranian operation, our intelligence source dried up.[62]

In the end, the Montaperto case reveals two activities that make the Chinese regime a major threat: WMD proliferation and effective espionage, a dangerous combination indeed.

Checking the Luggage

On an official trip to China in the 1990s,[63] one of this book's authors stopped over in a hotel in Guangzhou, formerly known as Canton. Before going down to dinner on the first night, he scrambled the combination lock tumblers on his luggage and remembered the setting. When he returned to his room, all the tumblers had been changed. The message from Chinese intelligence was aggressively clear: "Not only did we go through your luggage, we made certain you know we did."

In a meeting with Chinese officials the next morning, he casually mentioned the episode with the comment, "We're all adults here and obviously I'm not carrying anything sensitive, but rubbing my nose in it was unnecessary." The communists seemed embarrassed, though in fairness they probably didn't know anything about it, since he was meeting Chinese economic officials, not security officers.

On a subsequent stop in China, he left his hotel room and again scrambled his luggage lock tumblers, remembering the setting. This time, when he returned to his room, all the tumblers were exactly as he had left them except the last one, which was changed by a single number. This was Chinese intelligence communicating, "Message received."

This little story illustrates two things: first, Chinese spying is pervasive, and second, if you stand your ground, they will back off—or at least be a little more polite about their espionage.

Examining the record to date, there are hardly any public quotes by Obama administration officials warning the American people or the Congress of the PRC as a major intelligence, economic, or military threat. One exception is Treasury Secretary Timothy Geithner, who apparently got a sniff of reality in September 2011, when he accused China of enabling "systematic stealing of intellectual property of American companies."[64] By and large, however, Obama's team seems oblivious to the looming threat across the Pacific. To the extent China is mentioned at all in the annual public hearings held by the Congressional Armed Services and Intelligence Committees on worldwide threats facing the United States, the prepared texts of administration officials bury it in the back with the also-rans.

Ridiculously, Obama officials sometimes begin their China discussion with false platitudes such as "China shares many interests with the United States," as they did in the administration's "National Intelligence Strategy" of August 2009.[65] As for Obama himself, about the only time he invokes China is when he cites it as a model for his own policies. "Building a world-class transportation system is part of what made us an economic superpower. And now we're going to sit back and watch China build newer airports and faster railroads?" Obama intoned as he urged more infrastructure spending in his jobs speech of September 2011.[66]

About the only time Obama invokes China is when he cites it as a model for his own policies.

Retired government officials with business ties to China often assume the role of China apologists, as described in chapter seven. But those without such links often speak bluntly about the China threat. Michelle Van Cleave, America's first chief counterintelligence officer, told the Associated Press that Chinese spying is like a "cancer … that can really, really hurt you." Her successor Joel Brenner told the same reporter, "The Chinese espionage threat has been relentless."[67]

So if former officials are outspoken about the China threat, why don't current intelligence professionals warn the American people about it? Their hands are tied by the Obama White House which, after Obama's election, quietly downgraded our intelligence priorities directed against the PRC and consequently our counterintelligence effort against Chinese spying—just as we are trying to fight off waves of Chinese spies who are successfully targeting our most important military secrets. Professional intelligence officers were so appalled by this reorientation that they took their complaint to Bill Gertz at the *Washington Times*. According to him, the Obama administration directed that China be moved from "Priority One," a category it shared with the likes of Iran and North Korea, down to "Priority Two," which places it alongside humanitarian problems such as the earthquake in Haiti. Both Director of National Intelligence Dennis

Blair and CIA Director Leon Panetta reportedly challenged the move, but both lost to the Obama White House hacks.

John Tkacik, an experienced China watcher and former U.S. intelligence official, told Gertz that changing China from "Priority One" to "Priority Two" means "the Obama Administration doesn't understand the profound challenge that China has become." Counterintelligence expert Michelle Van Cleave was dumbfounded: "Chinese intelligence is going after the U.S. with a vengeance," she noted. "So why are they doing this?" It's an important question.[68]

When publicly addressing the issue of Chinese espionage, most experts begin by noting the unprecedented size of the problem. Former FBI Special Agent I. C. Smith was posted to the State Department as chief of investigations, counterintelligence programs, where he looked into a number of high-profile Chinese spying cases. He told the U.S.–China Economic and Security Commission, "Never has this country faced such massive attacks, on virtually all fronts, from a single country, as China does right now."[69]

Agent Smith worries about the huge numbers of Chinese students in the United States, many of whom are studying in the hard sciences that have potential military applications. He told the commission that the FBI doesn't have the resources to track all these students.[70] There are an estimated 128,000 Chinese students studying at U.S. colleges and universities, and perhaps most worryingly, that number is increasing at a phenomenal rate of 30 percent per year.[71]

This is yet another vulnerability added to an already perilous situation. The technological savvy of U.S. industry and the U.S. military is one of the few remaining advantages we have as China leverages its vast resources in an all-out effort to eclipse American power. If we develop valuable technology just to allow Beijing to steal it from our grasp, our woeful lack of vigilance will come back to haunt us—sooner rather than later.

CHAPTER SIX

WHEN CHINA RULES THE U.S. ECONOMY

If the U.S. monopoly capitalist groups persist in pushing their policies of aggression and war, the day is bound to come when the people of the whole world will hang them.

—Mao Zedong

In his farewell speech upon leaving office, George Washington warned against entangling foreign alliances. America's first president was worried about the new nation squandering its hard-fought independence by establishing relationships with foreign powers that could inhibit our government's freedom to act in its best interests. Treaties, by nature, limit policy options. In strident terms, Washington cautioned that developing special attachments risks "facilitating the illusion of an imaginary common interest" that can ultimately transform a free country into a slave of another power.

Today, the United States is in such a relationship with the People's Republic of China. American lawmakers cannot do what's best for America because it could upset our relations with Beijing, which exports more to us than anyone else and owns the dragon's share of U.S. public debt. While policymakers delude themselves about common interests and cooperation, year by year the U.S. economy is becoming more enslaved to China.

The United States is more than $14.8 trillion in debt, and the PRC owns more of those bills than any other nation. In 2010, the U.S. trade imbalance with the PRC was $273 billion in Beijing's favor.[1] Americans bought $365 billion in Chinese products that year. Every day, we borrow money from the Middle Kingdom so we can buy their merchandise and keep Chinese people working while U.S. unemployment hovers around 9 percent. U.S. GDP grew by a paltry 1.8 percent in the first quarter of 2011 as the PRC's economy expanded 9.7 percent.[2] While the United States battled recession and insolvency in 2010, the PRC grew at a brisk rate of 10.3 percent.[3] As America has become the largest debtor nation in world history over the past two decades, China's economy has grown on average more than 10 percent per year.

Year by year the U.S. economy is becoming more enslaved to China.

In April 2011, the International Monetary Fund dropped an atomic bomb on the financial world by predicting that Red China's economy will overtake America's by 2016.[4] The comparison was made using purchasing power parity, which measures what given products cost in comparative markets in relation to income, with exchange rates being a neutral factor. In other words, it's how much a can of Coke costs in China and America given what Chinese and American workers earn respectively.

A mere decade ago, the PRC economy was only one-third the size of the U.S. economy. Now the much-vaunted U.S. standard of living is facing a big slide. No matter when the changing of the guard occurs, it's on the way unless this nation drastically changes course. The American Age, which commenced when the U.S. economy surpassed the British Empire in the last decade of the nineteenth century, is giving way to a new Age of China. The numbers don't lie; the PRC is getting stronger and America is getting weaker. The writing is on the wall.

As the United States struggles with a sputtering economy and an existential debt crisis, Beijing is canvassing the world to establish ties and ink development contracts to fortify its growing global influence. America's position as the primary distributor of largesse around the world is being contested as the loyalties of billions around the world are being bought from under our noses. This is a dangerous posture for a nation with trillions in debt. As Pulitzer Prize-winning columnist George Will asked an audience of senior military leaders at a speech at the U.S. Naval War College on February 28, 2011, "How can the world's largest borrower be the world's greatest power?"[5] Obviously, there is a direct correlation between a nation's power and its fiscal state. Without a dramatic turnaround, future generations of Americans will be poorer, more isolated, and increasingly dependent on China for loans, business, and perhaps even aid as our Asian competitor displaces America as the world's preeminent economic power.

Energy: A Chinese Hand on America's Throat

Energy is the mother's milk of an industrial economy, but even in this most fundamental sector, Beijing is becoming America's nursemaid.

Filling up a pickup truck with gas can cost over $100 these days. Not only do high fuel prices make it more expensive for the average family to get to work and drive the kids to school, but pricey gas raises the costs of all the food we eat and products we use because it raises the cost of transporting all those things.

After trending upward for many years, gasoline costs have skyrocketed in the United States recently, stoking national anxiety about our economic vulnerability to unpredictable global oil markets. For some reason, God put a lot of crude in unstable hellholes run by dictators. When some desert sheikh invades his neighbor, a Venezuelan thug nationalizes Western refineries, or tribal warfare breaks out in the jungles of Indonesia, prices in Peoria jump as world supplies contract. The uncertainty—along with the pain of filling up SUVs—has led to a popular demand that America lessen our dependence on foreign oil by tapping into our own neglected sources of energy. As former Alaska Governor Sarah Palin put it so well during the 2008 presidential campaign, "Drill, baby, drill!"

If only the solution were so simple.

The first part of the problem is that Obama's "green" agenda is making Americans more dependent—not less—on foreign energy by restricting the development of U.S. domestic resources. While blaming high gas prices on oil companies that ostensibly refuse to increase production, President Obama himself has kept new oil sources off the table, making it nearly impossible for domestic firms to ramp up output. After BP's Deepwater Horizon oil spill in the Gulf of Mexico in 2010, the White House established a year-long ban on almost all drilling in the Gulf and along both coasts.[6] Even when the ban was technically lifted in 2011, the government was so stingy with permits that for all practical purposes the ban remained in effect.

Even more devastating is the liberal refusal to allow oil exploration and extraction in Alaska's Arctic National Wildlife Refuge (ANWR). Out of a huge total region of 19 million acres, the proposed site for oil exploration is only 2,000 acres, an area that could yield as much as a million barrels of crude per day for thirty years.[7] ANWR holds about half of America's known recoverable oil, or roughly 10.4 billion barrels, according to the U.S. Energy Information Administration. Oil drilling in ANWR is an obvious step toward America's energy independence, but Barack Obama refuses to allow action even in the middle of a recession or during times when gasoline prices exceed $4 a gallon.

The scary reality is that the United States has surrendered much of our chance at energy independence by allowing Chinese companies to gobble up land that holds valuable sources of power. This is a particular problem in America's wild west, which Beijing is rapidly subduing. Chinese corporations, which all answer and report to Communist Party leaders back home, have been buying up ranches that sit on known or suspected oil fields. In other words, even if politicians in Washington had the foresight to lessen our foreign energy dependence, we are losing our ability to "drill, baby, drill" because Americans no longer own or control many of the resources in our own country—Chinese kingpins do.

Beijing's control of American energy stretches beyond crude; America's natural gas is also being gobbled up by communist concerns. In January 2011, Cnooc Ltd., a Chinese state-owned energy giant, paid $1.3 billion to the U.S. firm Chesapeake Energy Corp. to purchase one-third of the rights to its shale-oil-rich land in Colorado and Wyoming and to take over 67 percent of Chesapeake's drilling and production responsibilities until 2014.[8] A month later, PetroChina Co., another state-owned firm, invested $5.4 billion to acquire a huge stake in Canada's natural-gas reserves. These contracts followed an October 2010 deal in which Cnooc paid $1.1 billion for control of approximately 200,000 acres worth of Chesapeake's oil and natural-gas fields in Texas.[9] These transactions have made North America dependent on China by giving Beijing a voice in how our own commodities are used—whether that entails Chinese state-owned companies having the final say over U.S. business decisions or American customers having to pay China for gas obtained from U.S. fields.

The PRC's grip on U.S. shale-gas has severe long-term consequences because these fields hold several times more shale-gas than all known sources of conventional gas. "U.S. shale-gas resources total 650 trillion cubic feet," according to BP. "By comparison, proved U.S. gas reserves at the end of 2009 totaled 244.7 trillion cubic feet."[10] Some analysts believe this mother lode of natural gas is enough to guarantee U.S. self-sufficiency for half a century and that America could even be poised to become one of the world's largest gas exporters.

For some reason, God put a lot of crude in unstable hellholes run by dictators.

Shortsightedly, U.S. companies—some in a pinch during a recession—gave away the store to cut deals with PRC firms. The hope was that if communist conglomerates were given a share in U.S. assets, they would reciprocate by welcoming U.S. companies into China's huge energy market. Not so fast, *gweilo*,[11] that's not how it works over there. In 2009 and 2010 alone, Chinese state-run entities paid out a total of more than $42.3 billion to buy up oil and gas resources around the world.[12] Meanwhile, Chinese resources remain out of bounds for many foreign firms.

The natural gas industry is hampered by technology-transfer agreements that benefit PRC firms to the long-term detriment of U.S. companies. In 2011, New York-based Hess Corp. signed long-term cooperative arrangements with the Sinochem Group and China Petroleum and Chemical Corp., while Cheniere Energy Partners of Houston has a contract with ENN Energy Trading Company of China. In many collaborative arrangements between Chinese and U.S. firms, the PRC provides the working capital while Americans contribute the expertise, that is, until the Asian counterparts learn how to do the skilled work themselves.

The U.S. posture toward the People's Republic results from too much short-term thinking going into policy decisions that have long-term consequences. Selling away our energy independence is a case in point. Many problems in the Middle East have been exacerbated by spending trillions to pump oil out of the sand, but the Arabs don't have the intent or the capability to build a navy to challenge America at sea, a space program to attack us from the stars, or a national economic policy to cut us off at the knees. Beijing is pursuing all those goals. China's growing power over U.S. energy resources is just one case study showing the dynamics at play across the board in America's relationship with Red China—a relationship in which the communists increasingly have the upper hand. That hand, it is clear, is on our throat, strangling our ability to breathe freely on our own.

Tech Bandits

There is rarely equal reciprocity between partners in Chinese business dealings with foreign entities—because communist leaders know there doesn't have to be. Western businesses are so anxious to get into the

Chinese market that they will sign unequal deals with PRC outfits for even a hint of a chance at the Chinese pie.

It's been going on for years: struggling American businessmen go to China with dreams of a cheap production center and 1.3 billion consumers dancing in their heads. The proffered quid pro quo is too much for many business leaders to pass up: transfer some technology to the Chinese and get access to the Middle Kingdom's massive market. Amidst a lot of wining and dining by their Chinese counterparts and grandiose promises by PRC politicians about future partnerships, U.S. experts set up shop in the mainland and show the Chinese how to build and operate complicated systems. As the Chinese learn the systems, however, they have less and less need for an American partner, who predictably will be cut off.

In 2009, China was home to between 750 and 1,500 R&D labs sponsored by international firms, which use the sites to train local Chinese in industrial tradecraft. And that number is increasing. As James Mulvenon, vice president of Defense Group Inc's Intelligence Division, testified to the U.S.–China Economic and Security Review Commission in 2009, "There is some frustration among multinational executives who have to deal with this situation because they know they're training people for their competition, but they also know that the establishment of that lab was a quid pro quo to get into the market."[13] The consequence of this trend is that it will be increasingly difficult for the next generation of Americans to find high tech jobs as the R&D labs move from Palo Alto to Shanghai.

Business contracts may contain ostensible guarantees, but good luck enforcing any of those in a PRC courtroom. In 2001, for example, the Educational Testing Service (ETS)—a Princeton, New Jersey company that conducts 50 million standardized tests annually—sued New Oriental Education & Technology Group, a Chinese firm, for illegally obtaining and infringing the copyright on questions for the Graduate Record Exam (GRE) and the Test of English as a Foreign Language (TOEFL). Chinese students were using the absconded information to game the U.S. testing system to gain admission and win scholarships to prestigious U.S. universities because they had access to test questions and methodology before taking the exams. New Oriental CEO Michael Minhong Yu warned ETS

General Counsel Stanford von Mayrhauser against suing in China, predicting, "You're going to lose, no Western company can win in Beijing."[14] A lower court initially awarded the U.S. company $1.2 million in damages, but higher courts knocked that down to a paltry $450,000— far less than what it cost to fight an international trademark case in a foreign court.[15] Helping students cheat to get into U.S. schools is par for the course in China; as New Oriental founder Yu made clear, he "was only following standard Chinese business practices."[16]

In Beijing's sprint to lead the pack in technology, communist leaders have pursued the quickest path to innovation: steal everything. In August 2010, under the cover of darkness, armed guards encircled a U.S.-owned factory in China while trucks loaded up the multimillion-dollar manufacturing machinery inside. Fellowes Inc.—a family-owned Illinois company founded in 1917 that makes a patented line of "the World's toughest shredders"—was the victim of a Chinese joint-venture partner that decided to literally take away the whole business. Since the confiscation of its Chinese operation, Fellowes has lost $100 million of its $168 million business and can't fill global orders, knocking the firm onto the ropes.[17]

"No Western company can win in Beijing."

Not all instances of corporate theft are as brazen as looting a competitor's facilities in the dead of night; PRC bureaucrats also exploit the regulatory process to steal foreign technology. When outside products are waiting for government approval to be allowed into the Chinese market, communist inspectors routinely pass along design information to Chinese companies that copy it. This practice, euphemistically called "re-innovation" and "co-innovation," is outright theft. "It's a huge long-term strategic issue," an executive for an American technology firm told the *Wall Street Journal*. "It isn't just the crisis of the day for U.S. business. It's THE crisis."[18]

Across the board, PRC practices are making it more difficult—not easier—for U.S. companies to protect their intellectual property rights.

The fact that so many firms view China as a strategic imperative for future business growth means executives are often hesitant to press their case. They're damned either way: complain and be denied market access; say nothing and have your company's products stolen, copied, and sold out from under you. It's a deliberate, systematic policy by Beijing to leapfrog from being a low-cost producer of simple manufactured goods to a high-end innovator of sophisticated, high-tech merchandise. According to the *Wall Street Journal,* this policy, which comprises a thorough effort at thwarting the rights of foreign entities, includes the following key components: "new patent laws that could make it easier to seize foreign innovation; the setting of standards that require products to be reengineered to meet Chinese specifications; national-security initiatives that give preferential treatment to Chinese companies in several industries; limitations on market access for U.S. services companies; continued weak enforcements of intellectual property rights."[19]

Even when a company is burned in China, it usually goes back for more because American corporations have become dependent on China for profits. Despite all the past litigation over copyright and trademark infringement of standardized examination material, ETS and New Oriental entered into a business partnership in 2007 to jointly market test-prep products in China.[20] In a similar case in 2003, America's Cisco Systems Inc. sued China's Huawei Technologies for illegally copying and selling its internet software.[21] The expensive case was eventually settled, with the Chinese company admitting guilt and making significant concessions, but Cisco is again partnering with Huawei.

A lot of theft of U.S. intellectual property happens here at home, with Chinese employees and interns of U.S. companies sending sensitive corporate data back to the fatherland. In February 2011, Wen Chyu Liu, a Chinese immigrant who had worked for Dow Chemical Company as a research scientist since 1965, was convicted of stealing his employer's trade secrets and selling them to PRC outfits.[22] Admitting to causing as much as $100 million in damage to his employer, a Chinese worker at Ford Motor Co. was convicted of stealing 4,000 Ford documents and providing forty-one trade secrets in 2006 to Beijing Automotive Company, for whom he was secretly employed.[23] In 2010, two Chinese engineers for Wyko Tire Technology, a Chinese outfit, were convicted for taking cell-phone pictures to steal trade secrets of Goodyear tire-manufacturing equipment while on a consulting visit. That same year, a Chinese national working at Dow Chemical was convicted of economic espionage for providing Dow trade secrets about organic science to Hunan Normal University, a PRC government institution that was conducting competitive research on the same subject.

There are thousands of similar examples of Chinese intellectual property theft amounting to billions of dollars in damage every year. The bottom line is this: while Chinese companies benefit from stolen technology and make new hires as their businesses grow, America's sons and daughters can't find jobs in a depressed economy with dwindling domestic production facilities.

U.S. Debt in Yuan

There is no more painful example of America's waning lack of will to survive than our refusal to get our national financial house in order and live within our means. A country needs discipline to survive, especially if it wishes to remain a thriving superpower. But a decade into the twenty-first century, the United States has not proven it has the resolve or the discipline to maintain its preeminent place in the world.

By the summer of 2011, the U.S. national debt hit $14.6 trillion, enough to erase a whole year's economic output in the planet's richest and most productive nation. Too many people view this debt as an illusory figure, an abstract amount of money that we don't actually have to pay back. Every government owes every other nation a prince's ransom, the thinking goes, and in today's world everybody gives a wink and understands that nobody has to repay any of it. But that is not true; severe consequences arise when a country can no longer pay off even the interest on its debt. America is rapidly approaching that point of no return, and the growing power poised to exploit our bankruptcy is Beijing, which owns more U.S. debt than any other nation.

Overall, China owns more than $1.2 trillion in U.S. debt. That's the amount of a whole year's economic output in Australia, a first-world nation with one of the highest standards of living on the planet. This gives the communists frightening leverage over the American economy and even our political decisions. For example, Beijing protested the "Buy Made in the USA" provisions found in President Obama's exorbitant, near-trillion-dollar "stimulus" spending package.[24] The Chinese, you see, were worried our government spending spree wouldn't give its usual jolt to Chinese employment. Unsurprisingly, the Obama team didn't make a peep when the PRC's own massive economic stimulus package had even stronger provisions guaranteeing its government spending went for products and services almost exclusively made in China. But that's the point: the same rules don't apply to both sides. Beijing is holding more cards, so to a troubling extent, Washington has to manage with the hand it is dealt by its communist lenders. This subservience to Beijing will only get worse as the PRC expands its control of the American economy in pace with U.S. debt growth.

According to financier Robert Agostinelli, the United States simply cannot afford to support the current level of deficit spending. As he explained to an audience of senior officers during a February 2011 lecture at the Naval War College, "Unless policymakers face this head on, the U.S. will continue to give China greater sway over our affairs. China controls hundreds of billions of U.S. dollars, most from buying U.S. debt, and while there is currently a mutual interdependence between China and the U.S., this could change over time. U.S. policymakers must therefore be prepared for possible national security repercussions."[25]

Competing bureaucratic spending bills aside, it is embarrassing how U.S. officials have had to go hat in hand to Red China to keep the loan spigot turned on. In her first mission early in the Obama administration in 2009, Secretary of State Hillary Clinton journeyed to the Middle Kingdom to meet with America's most important lender. "The Chinese know that in order to start exporting again to its biggest market, the United States, the U.S. has to take some drastic measures with the stimulus package. We have to incur more debt,"she said.[26] The message was loud and clear, and it sounded an awful lot like blackmail from a desperate party in dire straits. In effect, Mrs. Clinton was saying, "You need to sell to us, but we're too broke to buy your stuff, so you have to give us a loan to keep trade going."

It's a humbling reflection of how far America—long the world's richest and most powerful industrial country—has fallen. As if that groveling weren't pathetic enough, Clinton went even further to clarify that she was asking Beijing to fund Obama's stimulus package. "We are truly going to rise or fall together," she said of America and the PRC. "By continuing to support America's treasury instruments, the Chinese are recognizing our interconnections." No doubt, the Chinese are also recognizing that the United States can no longer stand up on its own without a financial crutch "made in China."

In a rough and tumble world in which dangerous controversies and conflicts erupt constantly, Washington's decision-making is constrained by our inability to do anything that risks upsetting the PRC to the point that it might consider divesting its U.S. holdings. Granted, that might not be a smart move for Beijing because it is so heavily invested in our debt that it has an interest in keeping America solvent. But China is definitely in the driver's seat. In the case of a diplomatic disagreement, it could dump some of our debt and take the hit, knowing America would be worse off because nobody else wants our Treasury securities in bulk like the Chinese, and if we can't continue to borrow, our deficit-driven economy will grind to a halt.

The United States can no longer stand up on its own without a financial crutch "made in China."

Not everyone on the other side of the world thinks investing in America is a safe gamble. Yu Yongding, a former adviser to China's central bank, bemoaned Washington's "reckless policies" and expressed fear that the value of the PRC's U.S. assets will significantly erode.[27] What makes economists like Yu nervous is the U.S. government's heavy deficit spending during a recession in which there is no new economic growth on the horizon to underwrite new debt. When spending continues to increase but revenue is stagnant, eventually the system will hit the wall. "Personally, I don't think we should increase [U.S.] holdings because the medium- and long-term risks are quite high," Zhang Ming, secretary general of the international finance research center at the Chinese Academy of Social Sciences in Beijing, told Bloomberg News.[28]

The tables of prosperity have surely turned when a rising PRC legitimately fears its economy could be dragged down by U.S. government spending. At the dawn of the twenty-first century, the teetering U.S. economy is vulnerable to a developing nation's lack of confidence in America.

In a darkly ironic twist, however, there is proof that government spending in the People's Republic actually boosts the U.S. economy. While the Obama administration's spending policies delay recovery by depriving the private sector and investors of funds to instead focus on government programs, centrally planned spending across the Pacific offers major benefits to some U.S. industries active in the Middle Kingdom, at least in the immediate term. This is particularly the case for heavy manufacturing and commodity firms that are integral to the PRC's massive infrastructure development projects. Of the more than $586 billion in the PRC's 2008 stimulus program, at least 69 percent was earmarked for infrastructure projects.[29] Government-sponsored projects already mean the PRC consumes more than 30 percent of the world's steel annually; all the construction in Beijing's stimulus created demand for tens of millions of additional tons of steel, helping stabilize world steel prices and giving a sales boost to struggling U.S. producers.

In the summer of 2009, American firms Caterpillar—maker of large industrial machinery—and United Technologies Corp.—maker of jet engines, helicopters, military aircraft, electronic fuel cells, and life-support systems for NASA—reported that profits in China related to Beijing's stimulus helped make up for a soft market at home in America.[30] As U.S. automotive sales plummeted to their lowest level in decades, Ford Motor Company's sales were up 14 percent in China. Reflecting the world's desperation for productive output during the global financial meltdown, stock markets across the world perked up when Beijing announced its stimulus plans in November 2008. For instance, "Oil prices increased about 6%, gold rose 2.5% and London copper jumped 8.5%" on the news.[31]

U.S. firms that are attached at the hip to China face manifold risks. For example, new profits related to Beijing's stimulus give many U.S. businesses an excuse to put off the inevitable downsizing that is necessary to "right-size" operations when the stimulus silver pieces stop coming. Eventually industries must rationalize to absorb the blows of a soft economy, but the artificial bump provided by government funding temporarily blinds many managers to the inevitable. "The risk is that producers will expand capacity [to meet stimulus demand]," warns Arthur Kroeber, managing director of the Beijing business consultancy Dragonomics.[32] That means the fall will be much harder when reality sets in and growing companies will suddenly have to suffice with sales that couldn't sustain smaller operations in the past.

In a startling wake-up call showing just how dependent U.S. companies are on Chinese business, stock in U.S. aluminum giant Alcoa Inc. fell 18.6 percent on news that Beijing wasn't announcing an expected second stimulus package in 2009 that would have accelerated importation of U.S. raw materials.[33] So much for U.S. self-sufficiency.

"We Hate You Guys"

Mutual dependency can guarantee a certain amount of pragmatic behavior by both sides, but there should be no romantic illusions about how the Chinese communists feel about America. "We hate you guys," China Banking Regulatory Commission Director General Luo Ping fumed about the PRC being forced into buying U.S. Treasuries to protect Beijing's massive U.S. debt holdings. "Once you start issuing $1 trillion–$2 trillion … we know the dollar is going to depreciate, so we hate you guys, but there is nothing much we can do."[34] He says there is nothing they can do because Beijing needs Americans to keep buying their consumer goods.

Approximately 20 percent of imports into America come from the PRC,[35] and that percentage is on the rise. China's huge pool of cheap labor means the country can produce more stuff at lower cost than anyone else. As if the peasant advantage weren't enough for its production facilities, Beijing has pursued monetary policies to keep the yuan artificially low to guarantee that its products can undercut any competitors' prices even more.

This is a mixed blessing, or mixed curse, depending on one's point of view. With a flood of inexpensive products coming from China, American homemakers can spend less on most household goods, which leaves more income to save, invest, spend on luxury goods, or dedicate to children's education. On the downside, artificially low prices for Chinese goods create an unlevel playing field on which U.S. companies can't compete, a situation that unquestionably led to untold numbers of U.S. jobs being sent overseas and the resultant collapse of America's domestic manufacturing base.

"Eighty percent of the computer software in China is counterfeit."

There is an uneasy alliance of some political factions on the left and right on this issue. Even devout free-traders agree that a working system of free trade depends on a regime of rules that prohibits uncompetitive national practices that prop up or unduly support domestic industries. A May 2011 editorial in the *New York Times* offers a critique of Beijing practices with which almost anyone on the ideological spectrum can agree. "The list of complaints is long: 80% of the computer software in China is counterfeit. Beijing just published a new investment catalog that keeps a long list of industries off limits for American firms," the old Gray Lady protested. "It changed the investment vetting process to allow Chinese companies to recommend barring acquisitions by foreign rivals. It has done nothing to reduce the enormous subsidies in the form of cheap credit to favored state-owned firms."[36]

The catalog of Beijing's sins goes on and on, but the point is that the People's Republic can essentially do what it wants and it gets away with it. As Thea M. Lee, policy director for the AFL-CIO, testified before the Commission on U.S.–China Economic and Security Review, "Enforcement of wages, hours and health and safety rules is lax or nonexistent in many areas of the country, and forced and child labor are prevalent in some sectors."[37] It's no surprise many U.S. labor unions have staked out a tough stance on the PRC, and some of it for good reason. Along with child labor, Beijing has a penchant for openly pursuing unfair trade practices and violating international trade rules. One of the most common practices is direct government financial subsidies for PRC industries so they can sell goods below the price of production, thereby stealing market share.

The other major way Beijing cheats to get its companies ahead is by forcing state-owned banks to provide low-interest loans to businesses and making these financial institutions absorb losses by exporters. Chinese businesses have a significant and unfair competitive advantage by not having to pay market-priced interest rates on borrowed money and not having to cover losses on their books. As Republican congressman Duncan Hunter put it succinctly, "China is cheating on trade."[38]

At the center of the PRC's trade strategy are machinations to keep their currency under-valued, which makes the price of their exports cheaper in relation to products from nations with stronger currencies. Washington's sale of so much U.S. debt to Beijing unwittingly strengthens this communist ploy. "Because of their under-valued currency (and large trade surplus), abundant U.S. dollars are officially overpriced in China," Jonathan Rothwell, a research analyst at the Brookings Institution, explains. "Chinese banks take deposits from exporters in dollars, convert them to yuan, lend them out, and get artificially high returns by virtue of the enhanced buying power of yuan."[39]

In effect, the Chinese get more bang for the buck than Americans do by using the relative high value of the dollar in their own markets, where prices are low because of the artificially depressed value of their own currency. To keep the value of the yuan low, China has bought more than $3 trillion in foreign currency reserves. "Its reserves are the world's largest, accounting for 31%," according to *Business Week*.[40] "China still closely manages the level of its exchange rate and restricts the ability of capital to move in and out of the country," U.S. Treasury Secretary Timothy Geithner complained in January 2011. "These policies have the effect of keeping the Chinese currency substantially undervalued."[41]

The Obama administration is crying wolf about Beijing manipulating its currency, but so what? Secretary Geithner has insisted that Beijing strengthen the yuan to help improve U.S. price competitiveness, but this clearly isn't in China's interest, and the U.S. Treasury has little leverage with its biggest creditor. It's hardly China's fault that we're so dependent on their largesse that fluctuations in the yuan are dangerous at home in the place formerly recognized as the Land of the Free. In no uncertain terms, America is not free if we're shackled to the economic policies and monetary decisions of a communist state.

Geithner has warned that President Obama believes the PRC is "manipulating" its currency,[42] but there is nothing the United States can do about it because we depend on the PRC continuing to prop up our markets. As the *Augusta Chronicle* of Georgia put it so aptly, "If you took out a sizable loan from your neighborhood bank, you're not likely to strut into the bank president's office and tell him how to run the place."[43] But that's what Obama and Geithner are doing, or at least doing for the cameras. They don't have a leg to stand on.

America is not free if we're shackled to the economic policies and monetary decisions of a communist state.

America's addiction to cheap Chinese consumer products, as well as our reliance on a constant flow of Chinese loans to buy the junk, stem from economic indiscipline and weak political leadership in Washington. At the root of the problem is an obstinate refusal to live within our means. While both political parties have had a poor recent track record on spending, it appears that Republicans now understand the imperative to mend

our ways while Democrats are bitterly resisting change in a more responsible direction.

This standoff was painfully obvious during budget battles in 2011
over raising the debt ceiling so government can continue to borrow from
future generations to pay today's bills. President Obama and Democratic
leaders in Congress resisted any Republican attempts to tie an increase
in the debt ceiling to corresponding cuts in federal spending or entitlement
reform. On April 11, 2011, just a few days before tax payments were due
to the IRS, White House spokesman Jay Carney said, "We believe that
we should move quickly to raise the debt limit and we support a clean
piece of legislation to do that." Translation: give Capitol Hill big spenders a credit card with no limits.

House Speaker John A. Boehner, a Republican, insisted that any
increase in the debt ceiling must be equaled or surpassed by corresponding cuts in government spending, but he was ignored in the other chamber by Democratic Senate Majority Leader Harry Reid. So the cycle
continues: a U.S. government on the verge of insolvency spends more
than it has on big government programs it cannot afford. The sugar
daddy underwriting the spending spree lives in Beijing. Eventually those
bills will come due.

Shipping American Jobs to Guandong

The June 18, 2008 cover of *Business Week* asked a compelling question: "Can the U.S. Bring Jobs Back from China?" It's a subject of increasing importance as America's unemployment rate hovers around 9 percent
with no relief in sight. According to the magazine, there are some factors
that could help create a welcome climate for moving jobs back home.
For example, high oil prices have dramatically increased the price of
shipping products across the globe; the sinking value of the dollar lowers
the price of U.S. goods compared to products from countries with stronger currencies; and the cost of Chinese products is gradually rising as
Chinese wages increase 10–15 percent annually.

Add on top of all this a growing nationalist sentiment among Americans who want to buy products made in America. The problem is that consumers often cannot find American-made products even if they try. One of the authors of this book was committed to purchasing a domestic-made shower curtain, or at least one not produced in the People's Republic. After visiting two dozen stores, he gave up on the search and made do with a shower curtain made in Guatemala. Every other option in the entire metropolitan D.C. area was made in China. Friends and colleagues have tried similar hunts for housewares ranging from dishes to lamps to framed art to hand and power tools. It's almost all made in China by Chinese workers instead of underemployed Americans.

There is a long list of industries that have mostly or completely ceased to exist in America: shoes, clothes, toys, sporting equipment, glassware, underwear, computers, appliances, and even statues of Jesus. The list continues. In November 2010, a condom manufacturer in Alabama laid off 300 employees after its main customer—the U.S. Agency for International Development (USAID)—dropped "Buy American" language in its acquisitions policy. USAID, which has distributed more than 10 billion jimmies around the world, now uses its taxpayer funds to source these products from China.[44] Similarly, a 2011 ABC News report found that catalogues sent to incoming students by schools and colleges across the United States offer dorm-room furnishings largely made in China and other foreign countries. Although ABC investigators found American-made alternatives that actually cost less, the colleges are locked into contracts with the catalogue companies, whose reliance on foreign suppliers costs the United States thousands of jobs.[45]

When U.S. factories began closing, some people argued that American workers cost too much to make a profit on cheap goods. How can a company make money paying U.S. middle-class wages to a factory full of employees producing pencils, flip-flops, or bicycles? That argument becomes less plausible as China gets into and gradually takes over more expensive products such as high-end furniture, medical equipment, and even automobiles.

One sophisticated product that's moved overseas recently is electronic circuit boards for complex medical and defense operations systems. "A decade ago, the U.S. accounted for one-third of global circuit-board output," according to *Business Week*. "Today, that's down to 10%, with China making 80%."[46] Other complex goods ranging from pricey plasma TV sets to multi-ton industrial presses are also increasingly produced in China. This wholesale transfer of high-paying jobs to China hurts individual Americans as well as our national finances—workers who lose well-paying jobs to China or lose access to the dwindling supply of them don't pay as much in taxes, reducing our ability to maintain important infrastructure, support first responders, or pay down the national debt.

A nation has to produce something to have the income to consume anything. Unfortunately, trends are still going in the wrong direction as whole sectors pack up and move to lower-cost facilities in the Middle Kingdom because of a Chinese cost advantage of 50 percent or higher. As Roy Nersesian, an instructor at Columbia University, explains the simple economic dynamic, "You can hire a hardworking Chinese laborer for a week for the hourly wage in the United States."[47]

The Chinese have established particular dominance over the growing green economy. As environmentalism has gone mainstream and many consumers look for ostensibly "earth-friendly" options for everyday necessities such as appliances and energy production, what was once a cottage industry has exploded into a major market for supposedly green goods. Rugs are made of recycled clothes; furniture is made from timber felled by natural causes; recycled plastic is seemingly in everything (even in some rice found in China); and windmills are promised to replace coal-burning electricity generators. There are potentially millions of jobs in this alternative economy, and President Obama has staked his reputation, for what it's worth, on the proposition that America's future is in so-called green technology. "I do not accept a future where the jobs and industries of tomorrow take root beyond our borders," he said of the green economy. "It is time for America to lead again."[48]

When Mr. Obama uttered these words in 2009, the United States was hemorrhaging green jobs to the Middle Kingdom. More than $100 billion of his $787 billion stimulus spending spree was devoted to solar power, wind energy, and other inefficient enviro pet projects, but it couldn't stop the bleeding. One problem is Chinese "green-collar" workers only earn $141 per month, 89 percent less than their American counterparts.[49] Another glitch is that 70 percent of renewable-energy equipment is made overseas.[50] Of the top ten employers in "clean tech" industries, three were Chinese in 2008, and that number doubled to six just two years later. [51] Only two of the world's top providers of green jobs are American, demonstrating how government spending does *not* lead to private-sector initiative. Obama's green rhetoric hasn't done anything for green jobs in America, which are moving to China faster than ever.

The anecdotal evidence of missed opportunities in this field is overwhelming. Do a Google search for "green jobs," and most of the articles that pop up are about factories closing in America and reopening in China. In January 2011, Evergreen Solar announced it was closing its Massachusetts facility and moving 800 jobs to China.[52] Evergreen had received at least $58.6 million in incentives from the commonwealth to support production there.

The previous year, 2010, was particularly bad. In July, BP Solar closed a plant in Frederick, Maryland, and moved 430 jobs to China.[53] In September, General Electric closed its last American factory—this one in Virginia—producing light bulbs the company had produced almost since Thomas Edison invented the marvel a century and half earlier. That was 200 jobs gone. Overall, GE Lighting has cut its U.S. workforce by 68 percent since 1980 and closed fifteen factories in Ohio alone in the last decade.[54]

> ## Obama's green rhetoric hasn't done anything for green jobs in America, which are moving to China faster than ever.

The death knell for the light bulb—and all the domestic jobs to produce them—was a self-defeating law passed by Congress in 2007. Supposedly meant to boost energy efficiency, the law effectively outlawed typical incandescent light bulbs. "Rather than setting off a boom in the U.S. manufacture of replacement lights, the leading replacement lights are compact fluorescents, or CFLs, which are made almost entirely overseas, mostly in China," the *Washington Post* informs.[55]

In many instances, the U.S. government subsidizes American companies that have more employees abroad than here at home. In 2010, the Obama administration gave $2.1 million to Suntech Holdings Co., which has seventy workers in Arizona but 11,000 in China.[56] The Obama administration gave $16.3 million to First Solar Inc., which planned to add 200 jobs in Ohio but has 4,500 employees overseas. A mega-wind farm backed by Senate Majority Leader Harry Reid, Nevada Democrat, sought $450 million in stimulus funds for an operation in Texas; the turbines would be made in China and run by a Chinese company.[57] The United Steelworkers Union accuses the PRC of illegally subsidizing its "clean energy" exports.[58] That's ironic given that the only exports the Obama White House seems to be subsidizing are jobs.

When U.S. companies invest heavily in cutting-edge new facilities in America, they find they just can't compete with their subsidized Chinese counterparts, even when the U.S. firms themselves are subsidized. In mid-2011, California solar-panel maker Solyndra announced it was closing down, laying off its entire workforce of around 1,000 employees, and filing for bankruptcy. Undermined by cheap Chinese competition and a dubious business model, Solyndra failed spectacularly despite having received federal loan guarantees of half a billion dollars. In late 2011, Congress opened an investigation to determine whether Solyndra received this taxpayer cash as a reward for large contributions company executives made to Obama's 2008 presidential campaign.

Some analysts have characterized the U.S.–China relationship as a domestic anti-jobs policy. Whether or not one agrees with that assessment, the numbers are startling. In the decade since 2000, the United States lost more than 5 million manufacturing jobs. Total job losses top 10.5 million. U.S. manufacturing jobs are down more than 40 percent since 1979, from 20 million then to 11.6 million in 2010. This collapse in blue-collar work occurred as the U.S. population grew steadily from 225 million in 1979 to 312 million today.[59]

Official government reports undercount the real crisis by not including those who have stopped looking for work, but even skewed statistical methodology can't obscure the fact that more Americans are underemployed today than at any time in almost a century. In the summer of 2011, there were 14 million jobless Americans, and if you include the numbers of people who settled for part-time work to make ends meet but haven't been able to find a real, full-time gig, the real unemployment rate is 16 percent. As billionaire publisher Mortimer Zuckerman summarized our national predicament, "We now have more idle men and women than at any time since the Great Depression. Nearly seven people in the labor pool compete for every job opening."[60] Perhaps the six out of seven who have no chance for a job in the Land of the Free ought to seek employment where the jobs are: China.

Cheap Junk Poisoning Our Kids (and Pets)

The jobs angle isn't the only concern with having all of our consumer goods made in Red China. There's also a real safety danger in depending on products from a nation that has loose and unenforced safety regulations. A few years ago, one of the authors of this book was in Hong Kong on business. Having a couple of hours to spare and needing a wedding present for family friends, he went to the large Chinese Communist Department Store on Nathan Road. Housewares were on the second floor, and there was a sale on hand-painted Chinese tea sets. It was a good deal for nice-looking merchandise. He was walking down the aisles looking at the various patterns when he realized he was being watched by a woman who turned out to be an ex-patriot British housewife. She was in a different department but was close enough to see the tea sets. Ignoring her, our would-be buyer walked down more aisles and examined different teacups while the observer grew increasingly agitated. Finally, unable to stand it anymore, she broke the famous British reserve and came over to warn, "Don't even think about it!" What followed was a thorough lesson in the dangers of Chinese cookware and tableware, which are commonly made with lead, cadmium, and other dangerous toxins.

The Chinese have peddled numerous toxic products to American consumers, including everything from children's toys to adult vitamins to pet food. In fact, the U.S. government regularly stops more poisonous or faulty products at the border that were imported from the PRC than from any other nation. In April 2011, for example, the Food and Drug Administration issued 197 import refusals for Chinese goods, compared to 107 for India and 105 for Mexico, the two next most prolific purveyors of bad merchandise.[61] Some of the 197 goods refused for entry into America included hazardous cardiograph machines, cosmetics, pet medicine, diet drugs, orthodontic parts, surgical bandages, frozen spinach, asparagus, and candy.

The Chinese have peddled numerous toxic products to American consumers.

These examples were compiled by simply taking the first ten products from the list, not by searching for the most egregious cases. The inspector's note on a batch of refused fish gave this reason for his thumb's down: "The article appears to consist in whole or in part of a filthy, putrid or decomposed substance or be otherwise unfit for food." This incriminating judgment speaks to the huge risks associated with a vast range of products exported from China. Unfortunately, merely stopping a poisonous product at a port of entry doesn't necessarily prevent it from ending up in an American home because corrupt Chinese exporters often re-ship refused products, hoping they will eventually slip past U.S. officials. In no uncertain terms, nothing from China can be assumed to be safe.

In February 2011, a research team from Thomas Jefferson University Hospital tested lead levels in ceramic plates, bowls, teacups, spoons, and other items that were made in the PRC and offered for sale in shops in Philadelphia's Chinatown neighborhood as well as Chinese-made wares sold at stores elsewhere. Among all this kitchenware, 25.3 percent of the products from Chinatown were lead-positive and 10 percent of the

Chinese goods from outside Chinatown had lead in them. "We were astounded—*astounded*—to find so many of them positive for lead," said Dr. Gerald O'Malley, a toxicologist who spearheaded the study, who warned that lead in Chinese products presents a serious public health threat.[62] Lead in eating utensils can seep into food and beverages, poisoning unsuspecting innocents.

Perhaps the most outrageous aspect of China's toxic trade is the thousands of contaminated toys that are shipped abroad to unsuspecting toddlers. In 2008, Healthytoys.org found that 21 percent of toys made in China contained detectable levels of lead. In 2009, Mr. Squiggles—a stuffed hamster toy made for kids three years old and up by Zhu Zhu Pets that was one of the most popular gifts that Christmas—was found to contain a cancer-causing metallic chemical called antimony.[63] In 2011, Tween Brands Inc. recalled 137,000 pieces of jewelry marketed for kids twelve years old and under for containing dangerously high levels of cadmium, a metallic chemical that can cause cancer and damage to the liver and bones, resulting in death or brain retardation in the young. The state of California limits cadmium content in jewelry to a tiny 0.03 percent; some of the recalled Tween Brands products had cadmium levels of 69 percent.

Chinese-made jewelry pulled off the shelves by the Consumer Products Safety Commission in 2010 included items that had cadmium levels of over 90 percent.[64] "On the CDC's [Centers for Disease Control] priority list of 275 most hazardous substances in the environment, cadmium ranks No. 7," according to the Associated Press.[65] In the past few years, toxic Chinese products sold to American kids have included dolls, toy trucks, Elmo, Big Bird, Dora the Explorer, Rudolph the Red-nosed Reindeer, the Princess and the Frog, and Best Friends bracelets, to name just a few. Many of these were distributed by Mattel, Fisher-Price, and other famous toy brands. More than 80 percent of all toys are made in China.[66] Many are potential killers.

Chinese toys are dangerous because they often contain lead, cadmium, and other toxins that are harmful for little kids who put things in their mouths they're not supposed to. But people of all ages are equally at risk when putting Chinese goods in their mouths that are intended to be there: food. A 2011 lawsuit against the Whole Foods grocery chain alleges that frozen vegetables sold at its stores are made by prisoners in China and irrigated by a polluted river.[67]

That kind of allegation against exported Chinese food is nothing new; there are thousands of cases of rotten and contaminated Chinese produce being sold in America. The U.S. Food and Drug Administration only inspects 1 percent of imports, which means a lot of bad stuff ends up on our plates. In 2011, there were cases in America of Chinese berries laced with salmonella and rotted fish coated with pesticides. In one four-month period, "The FDA rejected 298 shipments from China that included 'filthy' fruits, cancer-causing shrimp and 'poisonous' swordfish," according to *Consumer Reports*.[68] In many cases, to hide dodgy items such as rotten meat, Chinese exporters label the containers as something entirely different, such as dried flowers. Other common but dangerous food items exported here from the PRC include frozen catfish pumped with illegal antibiotics, pesticide-packed mushrooms, apples with carcinogenic preservatives, and bacteria-plagued sardines and scallops.

Next time you set the table for dinner, you could be endangering the health of your family with contaminated food from China.[69] In fact, it might not even be safe to sit at the table at all. Glass-topped patio sets sold by Martha Stewart Living have exploded into thousands of shards for no apparent reason; Stewart refused to give refunds or exchanges, instead conveniently blaming a Chinese supplier that had since gone out of business.[70]

There are thousands of cases of rotten and contaminated Chinese produce being sold in America.

In June 2011, Food & Water Watch, a consumer advocacy group, released a shocking exposé of imported Chinese food products. "China's food exports to the U.S. have tripled over the past decade to nearly 4 billion pounds of food in 2010, worth nearly $5 billion. The U.S. Food & Drug Administration prevented over 9,000 unsafe products from entering the country between 2006 and 2010," according to the report.[71] This is important because many staples of the American diet now come mostly from the PRC, including two-thirds of our apple juice (400 million gallons a year), over 75 percent of our tilapia (288 million pounds in 2010), 50 percent of cod, 20 percent of spinach, 90 percent of vitamin C supplements, and more than 88 million pounds of candy.

It's not just our human loved ones that are at risk from toxic Chinese products; our little furry friends aren't safe either. In 2007, 154 brands of pet food with Chinese ingredients were recalled after thousands of cat and dog deaths and illnesses were reported in connection with poisoning from melamine, a chemical used in fertilizer, pools, and fire retardants.[72] The same year, the U.S. government held back 20 million American chickens from going to market because PRC-sourced feed contained melamine.[73]

Americans are putting our nation in hock to a communist power for loans so we can buy more stuff at a lower price. In return, we are getting tainted produce, exploding patio tables, and killer stuffed animals. Lead toys threaten our kids and poisonous pet food kills our animals. Moreover, there has been no discernible improvement in the safety of Chinese imports in the past decade, showing that Beijing has no interest in cleaning up its toxic trade. In fact, the opposite is the case; more contaminated products are making it into our stores as we buy more Chinese merchandise every year.

Health and safety standards should not be so hard to guarantee, especially in China. Supposedly, the authoritarian government has iron-fisted control of the country, which means it should be able to put a lid on the regulatory violations behind the toxic trade. Of course, in reality the communists don't want to clean up many of their exports because doing so could hurt the bottom line. They will cut any corner—or any throat—to get ahead, and American consumers continue to feed the beast.

Manifest Destiny, Mao-Style

A book came out in 2009 with the chilling title *When China Rules the World*.[74] It's a grim future that American leaders need to contemplate without illusions. Across much of the globe, the past two centuries have been marked by democratization, a rising standard of living, and the expanding recognition of universal human rights. This progress is the result of Anglo-American influence in world affairs that has prioritized the dignity of the individual, especially in opposition to an all-powerful government, and a belief that all people rightfully yearn for freedom. America has fought numerous wars and sacrificed hundreds of thousands of our best and brightest to help spread the dream of freedom to other lands.

This era of benevolent stewardship will be turned on its head when China rules the world because the regime in Beijing believes in power over principle, the prerogatives of the state over the individual, and in the destiny of the Chinese people to dominate the planet. The communists will stop at nothing to further this vision of domination. Already, the People's Republic has a stranglehold on the world economy, especially America's.

If current trends continue, Red China is poised to surpass the U.S. economy by 2016. That's a mere two presidential election cycles away.

The data chronicling our decline and heralding the PRC's rise are thorough and unmistakable. If current trends continue, Red China is poised to surpass the U.S. economy by 2016. That's a mere two presidential election cycles away. Whether or not Barack Obama wins a second term, if we don't radically change our governing policies, the commander in chief who takes the oath of office in January 2017 will be the first in history to take over a nation less prosperous and less powerful than the Middle Kingdom.

President Obama likes to refer to Beijing as a "strategic partner." In November 2009, for example, he said, "On critical issues, whether climate change, economic recovery, nuclear non-proliferation, it is hard to see how we succeed or China succeeds in our respective goals, without working together."[75] Mr. Obama is kidding no one but himself. As financier Robert Agostinelli more realistically summarized the showdown to us, "China is committed to asserting its role as a global power in the fullest sense of the word. From their perspective it is their manifest destiny. They are patient in a very impatient manner."[76] America's status as the world's lone superpower is in the way of Beijing's perceived destiny to become the world's preeminent power. Make no mistake about it, China's rise is at the expense of the U.S. position in the world. As communists from Lenin to Mao predicted, the day has come when our own policies have given our enemies the rope they need to hang us. The communists in Beijing are obliging hangmen.

CHAPTER SEVEN

BEIJING'S AMERICAN AGENTS OF INFLUENCE

PERCEIVED POWER =
[POPULATION + TERRITORY + ECONOMY + MILI-
TARY] x [STRATEGY + WILL]

—Ray Cline, former CIA official[1]

The tables are being turned on America's traditional position of power in the world. Once the richest, freest nation on earth, the United States is increasingly hobbled by challenges at home and abroad. The equation at the top of this page was used by the U.S. government during the Cold War to assess U.S. strength compared to our enemies. In the 1970s, especially in America's weakest period during the lackluster presidency of Jimmy Carter, the international consensus was that Moscow was stronger than Washington. Dusting off this equation and considering the same factors today leave the impression that communist China is gradually inching its way ahead of Barack Obama's America. Other chapters have detailed Beijing's booming economy and military build-up in the face of the U.S. recession and defense cuts; this chapter is about an even more fundamental problem undermining America's destiny: a lack of national will to do what it takes to remain great. President Obama has officially described his foreign policy as "leading from behind." This losing strategy is allowing Beijing to overtake America.

In the 1980s, the great fear was that the U.S. economy was going to be buried by the rising sun emanating from Japan. The first page of economist Pat Choate's blockbuster book, *Agents of Influence*, warned that "America has the most advanced influence-peddling industry in the world. Washington's culture of influence-for-hire is uniquely open to all buyers, foreign and domestic.... Its lawful ways of corrupting public policy remain unrivaled."[2] The more things change, the more they stay the same. The Tokyo threat subsided, mostly because of an inefficient government bureaucracy that suffocated Japan's private-sector economy, but the pay-to-play lobbying apparatus is more open to foreign influence than ever, and the People's Republic of China is funneling millions into the U.S. political system to purchase support for Beijing's policies.

This is part of a concerted strategy to use all the instruments of statecraft to force China's will on us. In the 1990s and the first decade of the twenty-first century, Beijing focused on narrowing the gap with America in terms of hard power, which is constituted by quantifiable elements such as economic growth and military forces. Now the communists are advancing to stage two of their offensive, which is a battle waged using soft power.

Joseph Nye, former dean of the Kennedy School at Harvard and assistant secretary of defense under President Clinton, describes soft power as "the ability to get what you want through attraction rather than coercion or payments. It arises from the attractiveness of a country's culture, political ideals and policies. When our policies are seen as legitimate in the eyes of others, our soft power is enhanced."[3]

The Chinese Communist Party would be a poster child for Dr. Nye's ideas. In the spring of 2010, a press account revealed that China would be initiating "a $6.6 billion global strategy to create media giants that will challenge agenda-setting Western behemoths such as Rupert Murdoch's News Corp, the BBC and CNN."[4] This program was not initiated by ambitious businessmen seeking to exploit profit-making opportunities. Dictates for the creation of Chinese media behemoths came straight from the top—Chinese Communist Party leader Hu Jintao and CCP propaganda chief Li Changchun. They have unleashed a flood of money into media of all kinds. China Radio International has even taken over the programming of American radio stations WILD in Boston and KGBC in Galveston, Texas.[5] Using what the U.S. Census calls "combined statistical area" and depending on the station's signal strength, as of the summer of 2011 the Chinese could broadcast their propaganda to as many as 13 million Americans.

What follows is an ugly story of lies, subversion, intimidation, and extortion. America's most important political, military, and academic institutions—the ones charged with maintaining and protecting our liberties—are under political attack by Beijing. Some very bad guys have sold out their country, preferring the glitter of mammon to the colors that don't run.

The Foreign Agents

The Foreign Agents Registration Act was enacted shortly before World War II so that the FBI could keep tabs on Hitler's American henchmen. It remains American law and is administered by the Department of Justice (DoJ). In a nutshell, anyone getting paid by a foreign government or foreign company to influence the U.S. government has to register with the DoJ and disclose how much is being disbursed and what will be done with the money.

Being a hired gun for Beijing used to be a largely Republican Party operation. As John Judis explained in *The New Republic*, "A Republican administration first re-established ties with China in 1972, and ... Republicans controlled the White House for most of the next twenty years."[6] These days, however, it's predominantly Democrats who are in bed with Beijing. The Justice Department's files of foreign agent registrations reveal that for a long time, China has had the highest level of representation in Washington through senior Democratic Party political figures and associated firms. This strong association with the Democratic Party begins with Chinese money being funneled to Democratic politicians and to their firms which, in turn, have long-standing ties to elected Democrats in the White House, House of Representatives, and U.S. Senate. For example, during the first six months of 2008, the PRC embassy's American lawyers told the DoJ of their meetings with the United States Congress on behalf of Beijing. There were sixteen meetings—all with Democrats, including then-Speaker of the House Nancy Pelosi and Senate Majority Leader Harry Reid. There were no Republicans.[7]

We will look at a few of the most prominent cases, the first of which is the law firm of Akin Gump Strauss Hauer and Feld, lawyers and advisers to the PRC embassy until the summer of 2005. The "Strauss" is the firm's founding partner, Ambassador Robert S. Strauss, formerly the chairman of the Democratic Party. Campaign contribution filings at the Federal Election Commission run for pages and pages on Akin Gump employees and on the company's political action committee, which have contributed to well-known Democrats including Hillary Clinton, Congressman Barney Frank, and others. Ambassador Strauss himself gave the maximum political contribution allowed by law to the campaign of Barack Obama in 2008. In fact, in the FEC records it's difficult to find any Democrat running for national office in the past decade who has not received Akin Gump support, amounting to a multi-million dollar campaign, depending on how far you go back.

According to Akin Gump's agreement with the PRC embassy, the firm was to produce for the embassy "strategies pertaining to critical policy matters" and "the dissemination of materials representing the views of the People's Republic of China." Both the Congress and the executive branch were targets of this enterprise, about which there were no details.[8]

Although the Chinese embassy began in part to work with another Democratic Party politician in 2002, looking at the Akin Gump website today reveals that the firm remains deeply engaged in China. It has an office in Beijing and is the lawyer for several major Chinese firms including the China National Overseas Oil Company (Cnooc), the same firm buying American oil and gas production assets. The firm brags that "Mr. Strauss welcomed Deng Xiaoping to the United States in 1979 and accompanied the Chinese leader on his tour of America."[9]

An Afternoon Meeting

Former Democratic Senator Bennett Johnston registered with the DoJ for the PRC embassy in the fall of 2002. He fit in well with Beijing's plans because as a senator in 1995, he had been the only member of Congress to vote for barring Taiwan's president from visiting the United States. By 2002, Johnston was out of the Senate, and the House had passed legislation drafted by Republican House Majority Whip Tom DeLay allowing the U.S. military to have closer relations with Taiwan's military. It was pending in the Senate on July 17, 2002, when Johnston arranged for his "friend," the Chinese ambassador, to state Beijing's case to Democratic Senator Carl Levin, chairman of the Senate Armed Services Committee.[10] After the three of them met, the pro-Taiwan legislation was watered down in the Senate to become a mere study of whether the U.S. should have closer military relations with Taiwan. After that, it effectively disappeared altogether.[11]

Just like that, in one fell swoop, months of work were demolished. DeLay had the support of numerous congressmen from both parties in addition to congressional staff members, mostly on-duty and retired military officers and other national security officials who wanted to strengthen Taiwan's defense by increasing that nation's contact with the world's finest military. If isolated from the armed forces of the United States and other democratic countries, Taiwan's military risks atrophy— which only benefits China.

DeLay accomplished his job of rounding up House votes for the pro-Taiwan measure. All this effort was undone by one short meeting between a retired Democrat senator, the Chinese ambassador, and the Democrat chairman of the Senate Armed Services Committee. Chairman Levin had control over the legislation in the Senate—and that's why that meeting occurred. Seeing how easy it was for Beijing to defeat a significant national security initiative, Taiwan's American supporters lost heart. This story went around Washington national security circles in 2002, energizing the Chinese Communist Party's American friends and discouraging its enemies. It is still discussed today as a case study of Beijing's influence in Washington.

As an active Washington-based lobbyist, Johnston remained a strong supporter of Democratic causes. According to FEC records, he gave $1,000 to the "Friends of Carl Levin"—Chairman Levin's campaign arm—and an additional $500 on June 16, 2002, just a month before the three-way meeting with the Chinese ambassador. Coincidence? While no one would like to believe that the chairman of the Senate Armed Services Committee could be bought for $500, it certainly doesn't look good for the senior senator from Michigan.

Tommy Boggs

Passing the Chi-Com baton yet again in 2005, the current recipient is Thomas ("Tommy") Hale Boggs Jr., a true Democratic Party Princeling. Both his parents were Democratic members of the House of Representatives from Louisiana, his late father rising to the post of House majority leader. His sister, Cokie Roberts, and her husband are prominent TV and radio journalists of the liberal persuasion. Running the Federal Election Commission campaign numbers just for Tommy's own contributions and not even those of his law firm, Patton Boggs, is a repeat of the Akin Gump experience—we find another gusher of cash for Democratic candidates and liberal causes. Tens of thousands of dollars in soft money has been funneled to Democratic organizations and candidates including Congresswoman Debbie Wasserman-Schultz—the new head of the Democratic National Committee—and the late, embarrassingly corrupt Congressman John Murtha.

Tommy Boggs and his law firm are reputed to have the best political contacts in Washington and therefore the highest influence, certainly among Democrats. According to the Foreign Agents records at the

Department of Justice, beginning in 2005, the Chinese embassy was willing to pay $22,000 per month, plus expenses (payable quarterly, in advance) for this political access to the American government. After Senator Obama became President Obama, the price went up to $35,000 per month, almost a 60 percent increase, reflecting the value Beijing placed on having Washington's number one Democrat law firm on the payroll at a time when the Democratic Party held the White House and both houses of Congress. The Hale Boggs' contract with the Chinese embassy (marked "confidential" in a file with the DoJ) promises that the "Patton Boggs team will continue to be led by Thomas Hale Boggs, Jr." Only the best for Beijing.[12]

Only the best for Beijing.

It is worth noting that like Akin Gump, Patton Boggs has a number of commercial clients in China. For example, in the fall of 2010, Hale Boggs gained the Chinese Ministry of Commerce as a client operating through two trade associations. First it signed a $175,000 contract, payable in full and in advance, with the Chinese trade association responsible for minerals export. A second contract with the Chinese machinery and electronics exporters group filed the same day with the DoJ calls for another $175,000 payment. Mr. Boggs is listed on both DoJ filings as servicing this account.[13]

Patton Boggs' online "China practice areas" section proudly announces the following:

> As for our representation of Chinese companies, Sinopec, one of China's largest oil companies, retained the firm to assist with labor and political aspects of its initial public offering in the United States after other Chinese firms experienced great difficulty with such offerings. Working collaboratively with the client, Patton Boggs worked to lessen potential public opposition. As a result of these efforts, Sinopec's offering was

successful. The firm also assisted Sinopec with its interests in post-war Iraq's oil industry.

It's unknown outside Patton Boggs what assistance the firm provided for Sinopec's efforts to gain Chinese control of Iraqi oil, but it's instructive to note that the PRC has a long history of hindering allied efforts in Iraq. In this case, Patton Boggs is not required to post the Sinopec contract with the DoJ, but it was doubtless a highly lucrative arrangement.

The firm also claims to represent an unidentified Chinese bank operating in the United States in some sort of lawsuit it didn't want to describe. It further says it is advising the Chinese embassy and unnamed Chinese companies on matters relating to the U.S. federal government's Committee on Foreign Investment in the United States (CFIUS), the organization that can use national security grounds to block foreigners' investments in America. There is no indication which particular Chinese CFIUS cases are involved, but a number of them, particularly the cases involving Chinese telecom giant Huawei, have been controversial. All in all, Hale Boggs claims to have about twenty Chinese government and other entities as clients.

The Hong Kong Connection

Our next foreign agents case is the China-U.S. Exchange Foundation and its public relations and consulting agency, Brown Lloyd James. There are no heavy-hitting Democrat politicians here, though a Brown Lloyd James principal in Washington is a former mid-level Clinton administration official, Peter Brown, who signed the Foundation contract and contributed $4,200 to Hillary Clinton in 2006, according to FEC records. The client is certainly interesting, but it is what Brown Lloyd James, perhaps inadvertently, claimed to have done for the China-U.S. Exchange Foundation and its future plans that is truly extraordinary.

The Foundation is a Hong Kong non-profit established by shipping magnate C. H. Tung. In 1985 Beijing rescued Tung's company with a $100 million loan, and he has been the CCP's man ever since, getting appointed as Beijing's first chief executive for Hong Kong after the former British Crown Colony became part of the PRC in 1997. After Tung resigned his post amidst public displeasure in 2005, Beijing gave him a face-saving position on one of the governing committees that the Chinese Communist Party uses in place of democracy.

Tung formed the Foundation in 2008 and remains its chief. The Foundation's board of directors is a sort of Who's Who of pro-Beijing business and academic leaders in Hong Kong. Stanley Ho, the Macau gambling czar, is listed on the Foundation's website as a "funding ... Patron."[14] Crucially, its "Honorary Advisors" include two high-profile American Beijing apologists: former Nixon-era Secretary of State Henry Kissinger and former Clinton-era Secretary of the Treasury Robert Rubin. That gives Tung and his group political access at the highest levels, Republican and Democrat, of the American political system. The Foundation further claims links with two prestigious Washington think tanks, the Center for Strategic and International Studies and the Carnegie Endowment for International Peace.

In the seventy-plus years since the Foreign Agents Registration Act became law, the foreign agents who have been forced to register have habitually tried to provide as little information to the DoJ as they can get away with, particularly those who represent controversial clients. Blandness and blather are typical. For example, in the summer of 2008, Patton Boggs gave the DoJ the following description of its previous six months of work for the PRC embassy: "Met with legislative and Executive Branch officials to discuss bilateral issues of importance." That was it—no more details. This is a pretty common non-disclosure/disclosure found in DoJ records. For this, whatever it is, the PRC embassy pays the firm over $400,000 per year.[15]

Unusually for a communications company, Brown Lloyd James went the other direction with C. H. Tung's Foundation. In a January 1, 2010 contract labeled "CONFIDENTIAL" filed with the DoJ, Brown raised the curtain on what some of these companies are really expected to do for the hundreds of thousands of dollars they receive. Even before it got to what it was going to do for the Foundation, Brown said its first named service would be "defending and promoting China ... in the media."

Only after that did it mention it would promote the Foundation. This indicates that the real client here is the Chinese Communist Party and that propaganda for the Party is the name of the game. To most Americans, the word "Exchange" in the Foundation's title would imply an exchange of views, but clearly, the only thing being exchanged is cold, hard cash for influence in the U.S. press.

Brown didn't stop there. It added an astounding appendix to its DoJ FARA filing that details its work—and it's all about China. It goes on and on for seven single-spaced pages outlining what it has already done for this program (prior to January 1, 2010) and its future plans. We have reviewed many FARA filings over several decades, but we have never seen a document like this. Here are some highlights of the accomplishments Brown Lloyd James claims on behalf of its Chinese client:

- Brown "arranged for two journalist visits consisting of four high-level journalists to visit China," resulting in "28 media placements." The journalists were not named, but Brown claimed they were from *Newsweek*, the *Nation*, and other well-known publications.
- Brown "directly influenced the publication of 26 opinion articles and quotes within 103 separate articles." Brown's scorecard is three articles per week, which they have "contributed to or influenced" to the ultimate benefit of the Chinese Communist Party.
- Tung apparently made three trips in 2009 to the United States, where Brown arranged for him to be received by "nineteen individuals at the top-tier of media."
- Brown claims to have "secured placement for Mr. Tung's op-ed in the *Washington Post*." The *Post* did run Tung's op-ed, "In China, There's a lot to Celebrate," on October 31, 2009. It claimed, among other things, that "in China's long history, prosperous times were always associated with a strong and enlightened central government, which has led the Chinese people generally to believe in strong government. Today we have such a government, with

clear vision and enlightened policies. While ideological and principled, the government in Beijing has also proved pragmatic and flexible when necessary."[16]

- Brown claims to have arranged for a meeting between Tung and "Bill Daley," who is not further identified but is most likely to be William M. Daley, chief of staff to President Obama.
- Brown arranged for Tung to sit for an on-air interview with PBS' Charlie Rose.
- Brown arranged for Tung to give speeches at Georgetown University and New York University.

Turning to the future, Brown's DoJ filing envisions a pro-PRC propaganda program of truly epic proportions. Again, some highlights:

- For an additional $3,000 to $5,000 per event, Brown will arrange private dinner "salons" with "top-tier media figures [DC and NY]."
- Media interview targets include Fareed Zakaria of CNN, Al Hunt of Bloomberg, and Christiane Amanpour, moderator of *This Week* on ABC News and wife of former senior Clinton administration official James Rubin, who later was an informal advisor to Secretary of State Hillary Clinton and President Barack Obama.
- Brown suggests arranging free trips to China for journalists and placing thirty op-eds in major American newspapers "to secure statements of support for China."
- Making clear the long-term aim of this program, Brown's FARA filing says, "In order to educate the next generation of U.S. journalists on China" it will organize "familiarization trips" for a group of journalism students.
- Brown says its objective is to "develop and foster a community of like-minded experts."
- Brown's "Tibet Factual Review" deserved its own separate heading on par with the journalist junkets to China.

Brown sees China's position in Tibet as "deeply misunder-
stood," and the American understanding of Tibet can,
they predict, be "reversed in public perception" i.e.,
through its propaganda campaign.

- Brown proposes an obscene "Religious Freedom Program"—more China junkets, this time for pliable American
"cultural and religious leaders" who might not notice that
Christians and other believers are in jail and being tortured.

Thanks to Brown's explicit filing, Beijing's strategy has been exposed:
spend hundreds of thousands of dollars (some of it derived from
Macau gambling dens) to hire American toadies who can influence the
U.S. government and the American people in ways the Chinese Communist Party wishes. By focusing on journalism students, they have
tipped their hand to the long-term effort to brainwash generations of
young Americans. And as we are about to see, this is only part of the
CCP's American propaganda program.

A Real Teaching Experience

James R. Lilley was ambassador to China in the George H. W. Bush
administration from 1989 to 1991. During lunch with one of the authors
of this book in the spring of 1989,[17] Lilley outlined a disturbing trend:
former high-level U.S. foreign policy officials were exploiting a loophole
in the Foreign Agents Registration Act, keeping their relationships with
Beijing a secret and making enormous sums of money in the process.

At a small lunch table, Jim explained that the scam works in phases
with three actors: a respected former U.S. government official with good
relationships in Washington, a Chinese Communist official, and a U.S.
businessman. In phase one, the former U.S. official takes the businessman
to see the Chinese official. In phase two, the Chinese official grants some
sort of lucrative monopolistic deal to the businessman, per China's typical practice of crony capitalism.

At this point Jim stopped to ask rhetorically, "Now why is the Chinese official doing this? He's not a public charity, yet he is putting money into the pockets of both the U.S. businessman and the former U.S. official because the businessman will pay off the former U.S. official, either with a big fee or by putting him on his board of directors." Jim answered his own question by pointing to the third phase: the former U.S. official "will pay off the Chinese politically" with an op-ed in a prestigious newspaper defending Beijing's position during some crisis, a telephone call to a legislator about to take a tough position on an issue of importance to Beijing (trade or Tibet, for example), or a letter to the administration signed by a group of "like-minded experts" such as the kind Brown Lloyd James is trying to organize.

In the end, everybody gets something: the U.S. businessman gets a lucrative deal, the Chinese Communist Party gets its position supported by a respected former U.S. official, and the U.S. official makes a pile of loot.

In the end, everybody gets something: the U.S. businessman gets a lucrative deal, the Chinese Communist Party gets its position supported by a respected former U.S. official, and the U.S. official makes a pile of loot he doesn't have to reveal to the DoJ since no Chinese money comes directly to him. The big loser in all this, of course, is the American people, who have no clue that it's all one big money charade.[18]

Dr. Henry Kissinger

On June 4, 1989 the Chinese People's Liberation Army turned its guns and tanks on the Chinese people. The killings occurred both in and around Beijing's central Tiananmen Square and, we now know, later that summer in hundreds of other cities across China. By happenstance, Beijing was filled with foreign reporters gathered to cover a meeting between Chinese and Soviet leaders. Consequently, the carnage was broadcast across the world and repeated night after night throughout the summer of 1989. Gruesome photos of slaughtered Chinese citizens filled the front pages of foreign newspapers, while "the man in front of the tank" video quickly emerged as an iconic image that remains an internet favorite today.

Horrified officials in democratic countries struggled to find an appropriate response. Sanctions against the CCP seemed to be a no-brainer considering the scale of the massacre, but even this minimal action drew vociferous objections from a prominent American statesman who has distinguished himself as one of the country's leading China apologists: former Secretary of State Henry Kissinger. In a famous op-ed running in the *Los Angeles Times* of July 30, 1989 and reprinted in the *Washington Post*, Kissinger wrote, "No government in the world would have tolerated having the main square of its capital occupied for eight weeks by tens of thousands of demonstrators who blocked the area in front of the main government building."[19] China watchers around the globe were stunned. Everyone knew Kissinger was favorably disposed toward the Beijing leadership, but no one expected he would blame unarmed demonstrators for their own murder.

Kissinger's self-interested missive drew international attention to his top-level business connections in China. In fact, he had become wealthy in large measure through his door-opening in Beijing for major multinational firms. For example, Maurice ("Hank") R. Greenberg, then chairman of insurance giant AIG, appointed Kissinger as chairman of AIG's international advisory board in 1987. AIG was founded in Shanghai and thrown out of China by Mao, but returned after Kissinger took Greenberg to Beijing.

Following his cold-blooded op-ed, it was only a matter of time before someone pointed out Kissinger's conflict of interest. The task was taken up by veteran *Wall Street Journal* reporter John Fialka, who wrote an article, "Mr. Kissinger has Opinions on China—and Business Ties," that ran on the *Journal*'s front page on September 15, 1989. Fialka related that Kissinger then headed a firm called China Ventures that had a joint venture relationship with the People's Bank of China, China's state bank. Revealingly, Kissinger's firm was distributing a brochure announcing that the company only invested in projects that "enjoy the unquestioned support of the People's Republic of China." Outraged by the exposé, Kissinger threatened both Fialka and his editors at the *Journal*, to no avail.

Sadly, Fialka's report did not lead free-world statesmen to take an unwavering stand against the PRC's murderous outrages. Although the United States and other nations did eventually impose sanctions, they were considerably weaker than those originally proposed, and by now nearly all of them, except direct arms sales, have been lifted.

It would be fitting if Kissinger's defense of the indefensible caused Western businessmen to shy away from hiring him for their China deals, but that didn't happen. Kissinger still seems highly active in China, though he's so secretive about his China business that he turned down the chairmanship of the 9-11 Commission when he found out government regulations would require him to reveal his client list.[20] According to a 1986 *New York Times Magazine* profile, "Kissinger Associates requires a clause in its contracts stating that neither the firm nor its clients will divulge a business connection."[21] In his recent book *On China*, Kissinger spends 608 pages avoiding details of his business deals in China—but he does say he has been there fifty times.[22] Unless he's the PRC's best tourist, he'd only visit that many times to conduct business. Regrettably, so far as anyone can tell, Kissinger's China business only expanded after his 1989 intervention on Beijing's behalf.

Kissinger's secretive China activities are a pressing matter of public concern. Consider this: it is not widely known that President Obama's Treasury Secretary, Timothy Geithner, is an Asia specialist. He majored in Asian studies at Dartmouth College and studied at Chinese universities in Beijing in the early 1980s. After obtaining his U.S. graduate degree, he got his first real job with Kissinger Associates just as Kissinger was making his big money move in Beijing. From there he segued into the Treasury Department and helicoptered his way to the top.

Geithner is the administration's point man on the issue of China's under-valuing of its currency. The next time he testifies on Capitol Hill, Congress should ask if he has received any intervening communications from Kissinger or his firm.

The Sanya Initiative

Vincent Mai is a trained accountant who grew up in South Africa. He is the head of AEA Investors, a New York-based private equity firm with over $4 billion in assets and offices in Hong Kong and Shanghai.

In addition to his duties as the head of AEA Investors, Mai was a leading member of the board of directors of the Federal National Mortgage Corporation, widely known as Fannie Mae, from 1991 to 2002, effectively overlapping the tenure of then-Fannie Mae Vice Chairwoman Jamie Gorelick (Bill Clinton's former deputy attorney general) and then-Fannie Mae CEO Franklin Raines (Clinton's former director of the Office of Management and Budget). After Fannie Mae unraveled in the mid-2000s, an outside investigation produced a scathing report about the company's board of directors.[23] Compensation was the piggy bank that broke Fannie Mae, and during the relevant period, Mai was chairman of Fannie Mae's Compensation Committee. The report concluded, "Despite the sophistication of the Compensation Committee members and its chair, Mr. Mai, who was a former chairman of the Audit Committee, the Compensation Committee failed in its duty to align compensation with appropriate objectives for internal auditors."[24]

Vincent Mai had the requisite accounting training, financial experience, and the power to stop the lending practices that resulted in immeasurable pain in the lives of millions of Americans—men, women, and children—and that remain a dark cloud over the entire United States economy. But he did fail in his duties. His legacy as the chairman of Fannie Mae's Compensation Committee is hundreds of millions of dollars in unwarranted compensation raining down on Clinton cronies, millions of Americans losing their homes, and the American taxpayer having been exposed to tens of billions of dollars in losses. And since Fannie Mae is still losing billions of dollars, the hemorrhaging will likely continue.[25] At this point there is no light at the end of the Fannie Mae tunnel for the American taxpayer. As David Brooks of the *New York Times* wrote, "The Fannie Mae scandal is the most important scandal since Watergate. It helped sink the American economy."[26]

Unsurprisingly, top-level Fannie Mae executives who presided over the company's self-destruction—people like Mai, Jamie Gorelick (who received more than $26 million in compensation during her six-year tenure at Fannie Mae) and Franklin Raines (who reeled in more than $90 million in Fannie Mae largess)[27]—have cried all the way to the bank. Taxpayers even paid for Raines' lawyers who defended him against civil suits.

Looking at Mai's and his wife's campaign contributions in the FEC records, we find another flood of cash for Democratic Party candidates and committees, as was the case with Akin Gump and Patton Boggs. All the usual Democrat suspects—Congresswoman Barbara Boxer, Congressman Barney Frank, Senator Al Franken—appear in page after page of lists of contributions to the Democratic Party totaling millions of dollars. The Mai's were particularly generous to Hillary Clinton, giving the maximum to her presidential ambitions as early as March 2007, this coming after supporting her Senate races.

After Hillary Clinton's primary challenge to Obama ended in July 2008, Mai donated $2,000 to the Obama campaign. That was a meager sum compared to Mai's donations to other Democrats, but his engagement with Obama may be rising. In May 2011, Jason Horowitz of the *Washington Post* wrote a feature piece on the Obama campaign approaching donors whom it "shunned" during the 2008 campaign. Horowitz stated that this time around, Obama's money men "are apparently more than willing to hold their noses" to solicit money from prospective donors who previously had a "political odor emanating from the crystal chandeliers and European masterpieces" of the high rollers' drawing rooms. Horowitz specifically named Vincent Mai as a participant in one of these new gatherings with the Obama moneymen who are "holding their noses."[28]

So what do the Fannie Mae scandal and Mr. and Mrs. Mai's generosity to the Democrats have to do with China? Here's the answer: Mai, his employee (retired Admiral William A. Owens), Henry Kissinger's financial benefactor Hank Greenberg, and C. H. Tung's China-U.S. Exchange Foundation are the tip of the spear in Beijing's top strategic policy goal: to disarm Taiwan so the PRC can take over the island. This is the aim of the little-known Sanya Initiative, which is fronted by Owens and funded by Mai, Greenberg, and C. H. Tung.

Beijing's top strategic policy goal: to disarm Taiwan so the PRC can take over the island.

The Sanya Initiative, named after a vacation destination in south China that is reputed to be near a secret underground Chinese submarine base, brings retired American generals and admirals together with ostensibly retired Chinese PLA officers to chat about U.S.–China relations and make recommendations for improvement. The Chinese side is led by the notorious PLA general Xiong Guangkai, whom we last encountered in chapter four making veiled threats of nuclear war against Los Angeles. Xiong stepped down officially as the head of Chinese military intelligence a few years ago, but in China, senior PLA generals do not really retire. In that tradition, Xiong still runs the PLA Intel's China Institute for International Strategic Studies and, more consequentially, acts as the Chinese facilitator for all the North Korean weapons of mass destruction programs.[29]

The U.S. side is led by retired Admiral William A. Owens, Bill Clinton's vice commander of the joint chiefs, and includes at least four other American retired generals.[30] Since leaving the U.S. Navy, Owens has had a controversial career in private business. He was CEO of Canadian telecoms equipment firm Nortel for only a year and a half, but demanded a huge severance package as he went out the door. Once a $28 billion-dollar-a-year firm, Nortel went bankrupt and is shutting down. As of the spring of 2011, Owens now heads the Hong Kong office of Vincent Mai's AEA Investors, and he had been active in China business deals, including with controversial telecoms giant Huawei, where he serves as a consultant.[31]

Politically, Owens has remained true to the Clinton cause. In a surreal event on March 2, 2008, the admiral joined retired general Wes Clark in a conference call with the press to explain why Republican Senator John McCain "doesn't have the right kind of military experience to be Commander-in-Chief" but then-Senator Hillary Rodham Clinton did. Clark pointed to Clinton's travel to more than eighty countries as First Lady, when she was "dealing with the tough issues of national security." Owens chimed in, "I would just say that I agree with Wes on that."[32] Apparently, Senator McCain's military service during the Vietnam War, his torture by Vietnamese communists, and the five and a half years he spent as a prisoner of war did not impress these Democrats.

As of this writing, there have been at least three rounds of meetings of the Sanya Initiative, two in China and one in Hawaii, with travel on to Washington and New York City. At this point, some might look at the Sanya program and say, "So some senior retired American warriors take their wives on all-expense paid junkets to Beijing, a Chinese beach resort, and Hawaii. They go fishing with Chinese communist generals, raise a glass or two, tell some old war stories. Why should anyone care?"

Here's why: First, the American officers, though retired, still have access to the highest levels of the U.S. national security system, a situation exploited by Beijing. At the second Sanya meeting in Hawaii, the Chinese generals and admirals met Admiral Mike Mullen, then chairman of the U.S. Joint Chiefs of Staff, and toured U.S. military facilities in Hawaii. Later Admiral Owens brought the Chinese entourage to Washington, D.C. for a grand tour of the capital. A highlight for the Chinese was a visit and photo session with Secretary of State Hillary Clinton in the James Madison room, the secretary's private dining room. From her smiling countenance in the photo of the event, there is no indication she knows the man standing in front of her, General Xiong, once threatened to nuke Los Angeles or that he is a key figure in Pyongyang's WMD programs.[33] Admiral Owens might not have mentioned that in his introductions of the distinguished Chinese visitors, but Clinton doubtless recalls that Owens endorsed her for president.

Second, the Sanya generals and admirals have respectability based on their military service. At least two of them have been awarded the Silver Star, the third-highest combat decoration behind the Medal of Honor and the service crosses. When they appear on TV, give a speech, or write an op-ed in a major newspaper, the public tends to take their counsel at face value. It's risky criticizing former heroes, even after they've gone over to the Dark Side.

Admiral Owens, for example, has repeatedly called for the United States to abandon Taiwan politically and militarily. His November 2008 opinion piece in the *Financial Times*, entitled "America must start treating China as a friend," revealed his hand with the sentence beginning, "The first step is halting arms sales [to Taiwan]."[34]

Since it was authored by a senior retired officer with exceptionally strong Democratic Party connections, Owens' proposal set off a firestorm among his former colleagues, among them Admiral Eric McVaden, a former U.S. defense attaché in Beijing. In response to Owens' piece, McVaden declared simply, "Taiwan does need weapons to deter an attack by making Beijing realize that the outcome would be uncertain, an attack would be costly, and that Taiwan would not be immediately defenseless and helpless—forced to accept Beijing's terms."[35]

Finally, Sanya's American participants include some of the top opinion leaders among the retired military, people who retain residual influence in the U.S. military establishment and beyond. At the end of the first Sanya session in 2008, the Chinese chose to exploit this by giving their American counterparts two "requests," as they called them: "First, that the American Generals request a delay of a March 3 release of a Department of Defense report on the People's Liberation Army. Second, that the American Generals support repeal of NDA2000, a(n American) law which restricts many avenues for cooperation between the American and Chinese military."[36]

The PLA hates the Pentagon's congressionally mandated annual report on its activities, which they believe undermines their efforts to keep China's massive military build-up secret. The National Defense Authorization Act of FY2000, sponsored by then-Republican Senator Bob Smith, is the prime leverage Congress has to keep the PLA out of America's secret military facilities, a major concern during the Clinton years.

It doesn't take a lot of national security experience to see that China would like to be snooping around in our backyard again.

The Americans had no reciprocal "requests" for their Chinese hosts. Sanya is another one-way street, just as the Chinese have come to expect.

At least one of the American Sanya participants, a member of the Department of Defense (DoD) Defense Policy Board, confronted Secretary of Defense Robert Gates directly at a Defense Policy Board meeting and told Gates of "China's concerns."[37] Another of the American participants called U.S. government officials in a failed effort to postpone the Pentagon's annual PLA report, per the Chinese "request."[38] Unfortunately, all this merely shows how America's defense chief is surrounded by PRC stooges even on his most senior advisory council.

It doesn't take a lot of national security experience to see that China would like to be snooping around in our backyard again.

On their own initiative, Sanya's U.S. generals and admirals set up a series of assignments for themselves. One such task was to begin "writing op-ed pieces to provide a counterpoint to the current writing about China's military, for example that of Bill Gertz of *The Washington Times*."[39] One of the generals was "working ... to arrange a session with Presidential hopeful Senator Barack Obama."[40] We do not know if such a meeting ever took place.

In Chinese, this combination of access, respectability, and influence is called *guanxi*. Looking beyond their DoD connections, the retired generals and admirals fit into an elite social network. One of them is a director of a major U.S. insurance company. Others serve on the boards of directors of major American defense contractors. Another is a frequent commentator on a major U.S. television network. Admiral Owens is an honorary trustee of the Brookings Institution, the premier Washington think tank associated with the Democratic Party. Plugging "William A. Owens" into the Harvard Kennedy School website's search engine returns seventy-seven hits of quotes or other contacts with the school or faculty. It would be a challenge even for Glenn Beck to map out the overlapping connections the Sanya admirals and generals have to the American political, military, business, and academic establishment. Through them, the Chinese Communist Party has access to, and therefore influence on, the United States that no other hostile country has ever achieved.

Extorting Academia, Seeding the Future

China's strategy thus far has sounded like all carrot and no stick. Don't be deceived. Professional China watchers who fail to toe the CCP's line are dealt with accordingly. For example, Harvard University's Dr. Ross Terrill is one of America's foremost China experts. He is the author of definitive biographies of Mao Zedong and his wife Jiang Qing and one of the most widely read books on China, *800,000,000: The Real China*.[41] In the spring of 2009 he told the U.S.–China Economic and Security Review Commission, "In more recent years, it's been individuals including myself who have been denied visas [for China]."[42] This is akin to telling an agronomist that he can no longer visit farms. Coercion and intimidation are part of what Beijing calls "public relations weapons" which it uses to shape what foreigners see, know, and think about China, according to the same-day testimony of Dr. Jacqueline Newmyer, senior fellow at the Foreign Policy Research Institute.

On the carrot side, Newmyer told the commission that American academics who parrot Beijing's line can expect a range of goodies, including "access to archives, research opportunities and interviews" as well as "formerly secret documents." Clearly, "This is very good for their academic careers." It's also good for the pocketbooks of those who use their CCP relationships to open doors in Beijing for U.S. businessmen.

All this can have an enormous impact on the U.S. government's China policy down the road. American academics with China training frequently take important policy positions in the White House or State Department, where they can wield critically important influence. For example, during the Clinton administration, Dr. Susan Shirk of the University of California–San Diego was deputy assistant secretary of state for China and Mongolia while Dr. Kenneth Lieberthal of the University of Michigan had the China account at the National Security Council.

Sometimes CCP stooges don't even try to hide their agendas. The late Dr. Michael Oskenberg of the University of Michigan had the China job on President Jimmy Carter's National Security Council. According to a former staff member of the U.S. Defense Intelligence Agency, during the time he was on the NSC, Oskenberg made no secret of his inclinations, calling himself "a missionary for China," a declaration that some of his colleagues found "disgusting."[43] Notably, while Oskenberg was on the NSC staff, President Carter officially recognized the PRC and relegated Taiwan to the political limbo where it remains today. Taiwan sources have long suggested, in private, that Oskenberg went into the lucrative Beijing door-opening business shortly after he left the Carter White House.

Confucius Institutes

In a bid for the hearts and minds of the next generation of policy makers, the Chinese Communist Party is establishing hundreds of controversial Confucius Institutes at universities around the globe. Here's how it works: an arm of the Chinese Education Ministry comes into an American or other foreign higher institution of learning with an offer of language, literature, culture training, and an opportunity to pair up with a university in China for further exchanges. Chinese money to the American university greases the deal.

Unlike other international educational exchanges, the PRC insists on placing its choice of professors inside the relevant departments of the recipient schools. According to a press report from the summer of 2011, investigators for the University of South Florida found its China-born Confucius Institute director was misrepresenting his authority with the university to help Chinese students and scholars obtain visas for the

United States. He was also accused of unfairly helping Chinese students on exams.[44]

Despite using the Chinese Education Ministry as a front, the Confucius Institutes can't hide the reality that they are a Chinese Communist Party propaganda operation. In fact, Beijing has been careless enough to reveal who is actually in charge. In the fall of 2010, CCP propaganda chief Li Changchun was on hand to announce Beijing's generous financial contribution to the expansion of the Confucius Institute at University College Dublin, one of Ireland's most prestigious universities.[45] Later in his European trip, Li scattered Beijing cash around Confucius Institutes at universities in Eastern Europe. So who is Li Changchun?

- Li ranks fifth on the CCP's Political Bureau (Politburo) Standing Committee, the Communist Party's highest authority, making him the fifth most powerful man in China.[46]
- Li is the CCP's propaganda chief and, unlike most top CCP Politburo officials, he has no official position in the PRC government.
- As noted at the beginning of this chapter, Li is the action officer for the CCP's soft power program abroad.
- Inside China, Li directs the Party's censorship program.
- According to one U.S. State Department cable published by WikiLeaks, Li is accused of having "directed an attack on Google's servers in the United States" in 2009.[47] While reporting on the accusations in the State Department cable, the *New York Times* recorded in an interview with the alleged source of the cable that Li "personally oversaw a campaign against Google's operations in China." As of this writing, it remains unclear whether Li also directed the second round of Chinese attacks on Google in 2011.

In short, Li is a nasty piece of work—just the kind of thug to run Beijing's campaign against undefended colleges and universities around the world in order to make certain the next round of China watchers see China through the red-tinted prism of the Chinese Communist Party.

The money Beijing offers the universities is tempting. First, the Chinese government pays for the Confucius Institutes—$270,000 to the University of Nebraska in 2009, for example.[48] Second, some favored schools cash in on the big money and receive an endowed faculty chair. In 2010, Stanford University proudly announced that a Confucius Institute had been "housed in [Stanford's] Department of East Asian Languages and Cultures" and that there would also be a "Confucius endowed chair."[49] The Chinese may have paid as much as $4 million to get themselves inside Palo Alto.[50]

The academic rumor mill is already working overtime on the Confucius Institutes issue. Did the dean of Stanford's humanities and sciences take the position of head of his Confucius Institute because no member of his own faculty would touch it? Has the head of another well-known West Coast university promised not to be photographed with the Dalai Lama in return for Confucius Institute cash? Was the decision to take a Confucius Institute at a prestigious California university done by the administration while the faculty was away between terms and thus not in position to complain?

For now, these intriguing questions remain rumors. But there is no doubt that faculties in some colleges and universities recognize the clear and present danger and are trying to fight it off. Some of them have even won, but the odds don't favor academic freedom in the long run. Almost every week, news gets out that some university or another has succumbed to the nearly unlimited amounts of money Beijing is willing to shower on those willing to bend. In nearly every case, the conflict over whether to allow a Confucius Institute on campus pits the faculty professors who know subversion and coercion when they see it against the university administrators for whom money talks.

Beijing is too clever to force a university housing a Confucius Institute to put out a "Dalai Lama Not Welcome" sign on the front lawn or officially prohibit discussions of the latest wave of human rights activists arrests in China. Often it is what doesn't happen that is the tip-off. For example, in April 2011 the University of Oregon held a symposium on

China and the information economy without addressing the effects of information technology within China itself. That, you see, would inevitably lead to a discussion of the crackdown on human rights activists who use the internet to exchange information about the latest CCP crimes against the Chinese people.

In the past, our universities have been central arenas for discussing things the CCP doesn't want discussed—Tibet and suppressed democracy in China, just for starters. Given the way Beijing operates, such discussions will diminish slowly but surely over time, and a new generation of American China specialists, nurtured and indoctrinated by the Chinese Communist Party, will take their positions in university faculties and high government positions in Congress and the White House, stamped with Beijing's seal of approval.

Finally, even as the university faculties fight back, sometimes belatedly, Beijing is moving the ball forward. On April 15, 2011, Portland State University in Oregon proudly announced that the Confucius Institutes have advanced into K-12 schools in Oregon—twelve new "Confucius Classrooms" at $30,000 each. Oregon Governor John Kitzhaber personally greeted the Chinese delegation and noted that Oregon "was the first state in the United States to promote the study of Chinese in its classrooms."[51] Kitzhaber has no clue what he just invited into the public schools of his state—Chinese yuan is being used to indoctrinate Oregonian kids in the creed of our enemy.

Uncle Wen Goes to England

Chinese Premier Wen Jiabao, or "Uncle Wen" as he likes to call himself, went to England at the end of June 2011. He posed for a photo-op at the historic MG auto factory where British workers assemble look-alike MG roadsters from made-in-China parts at a Chinese-owned facility and called for more China-UK trade. China, incidentally, runs a healthy three-to-one surplus on its trade with Britain.

During a joint news conference with British Prime Minister David Cameron, Sky News political editor Adam Boulton asked Wen if he thought China needs to make progress on human rights. Uncle Wen angrily scolded the reporter, suggesting he "hadn't taken enough busses in China to make an informed criticism." Boulton told his colleagues by Twitter, "Still recovering from clash with PM Wen says I haven't traveled much in China—pity my last visa [application] was turned down!"[52]

Viewers of Chinese CCN TV never saw the Wen-Boulton exchange. Regime censors must have anticipated trouble, so the news conference was carried on a five-second delay. The moment Boulton began his line of questioning, all the TV screens in China went black and programming didn't resume until the Q&A returned to something less problematic for the Chinese Communist Party.

Around the world there is an enormous soft power battle going on, mostly in secret, between the Chinese Communist Party, assisted by its highly paid agents, and mostly disorganized defenders of liberty, national security, and human rights. Beijing has billions of dollars, the power of coercion, and well-known former public officials on its side. The other side is composed of people the public mostly never heard of—reporters willing to ask tough questions, retired military officers, college professors expert in arcane academic subjects—who are conducting a desperate rear-guard action.

The odds are long, but this is a fight we have to win. So far, Beijing has the upper hand, and that hand is clenched in a menacing fist.

CHAPTER EIGHT

A DAY AND
A NIGHT IN
WASHINGTON

*China will continue to build up democracy with its own
characteristics.*

—Hu Jintao

It was supposed to be a victory lap for the president of the People's
Republic of China. By early 2011, Hu Jintao had served as general
secretary of the Communist Party's Central Committee and thus head
of state for eight years in a 47-year career as a party cadre climbing the
rungs of Mao's political machine.[1] As the PRC's top dog, he was chairman of the Central Military Commission, which directs the armed forces.
In a brutal police state that holds dictatorial control over the lives of
1.3 billion souls, Hu was the police chief. He was the muscle in a massive
country where might is right.

To make matters all the better, China's economy had surpassed rival
Japan's to become second-largest in the world behind America, and it
was closing in on the leader fast. Few people in the world have ever had

as much money and power as Hu had. It's understandable, then, that this accomplished individual wanted to spend the year, expected to be his last as China's leader, seeing the world and enjoying life a bit. At the top of his tour schedule was a January stop in Washington, D.C.—the capital of Beijing's main global competitor and the roadblock to the Communist Party's ambition to become the preeminent power on the planet.

The buildup to Hu's state visit to America was fast and furious. On Friday, three days before Hu's arrival, former Secretary of State Henry Kissinger—who was an architect of Nixon's trip to open relations with Beijing four decades earlier—had a paean published in the *Washington Post* extolling the virtues of "Chinese exceptionalism" and lecturing readers on why it's necessary "to build an emerging world order as a joint [U.S.-Chinese] enterprise."[2] The discussion about the PRC's and America's relative places in the world lasted for weeks. "We can't win or end our wars, balance our budgets or control our borders," bemoaned author Pat Buchanan. "[The Chinese] are eating our lunch, and we sound like losers in a locker room."[3] Talk-show host Charlie Rose asked, "Will China, in 2050, be the most powerful country in the world?" Columnist David Ignatius quipped that "it's hard to imagine Rome giving a state dinner for the marauding Barbarians."[4]

The chattering class was all abuzz about how important this visit was, and the takeaway message was unmistakable: China was coming into its own as a superpower, America was in decline, and here in Washington the two nations—personified by their presidents—would be face to face, toe to toe, discussing bilateral issues for all the world to see with ringside seats. As far as diplomatic stories go, this was as big as it gets, and Hu was riding high.

Across town, in a busy *Washington Times* newsroom, decisions were being made that would trip up Hu's victory lap. Late on Friday, an op-ed article was sent in by William C. Triplett II, a foreign-policy expert and regular contributor whose specialty happens to be the PRC. Angered by Kissinger's puff piece, he could not let the white-washed record on Hu stand uncorrected. The Kissinger article studiously avoided any mention of the PRC's horrific human-rights record or the blood Hu himself had

on his hands. The two nations simply have different values, the old diplomat had averred, and that doesn't mean we can't just all get along.

The problem with Triplett's timing was that it was past the *Times'*
publication deadline and the pages had already been laid out for Monday's edition of the paper. Wrecking a section layout at the end of the day
would mean whole pages would have to be redesigned and re-edited, and
new artwork would have to be created or found somewhere to accom-
pany the new material. It also meant staff would have to stay overtime
at the tail-end of an already killer week of content production. The
company had weathered the rough economic storms the year before, but
not without serious damage to the rigging; more than two-thirds of the
staff had been let go in the previous twelve months, leaving a skeletal
staff to produce the newspaper.

Frank Perley, a wizened editor who had been at the conservative
newspaper since its inception twenty-nine years earlier, immediately
recognized the timely import of Triplett's message. Hu Jintao, who had
presided over the massacre of hundreds of innocent, unarmed Tibetans
when he was party chief in Tibet, was about to be toasted by President
Obama at the White House. Not many in the outside world were aware
of the mass murder perpetrated by the future president of China, and his
official bio distributed by the U.S. State Department neglected to mention
his former post in Tibet at all. As the op-ed put it, Hu has a "red stain he
will never wash off."[5]

The American people had to know the truth; this story had to run
Monday before the communist leader set foot in our nation's capital. But
Perley couldn't make the call on his own. There were too many monetary
and personnel costs to scrapping a lineup and remaking it after deadline.
The *Washington Times* was printed on presses in Baltimore forty miles
away, and at a certain point in the evening the go-ahead had to be given
to crank out the next day's copies. The clock was ticking. The experienced
old inkhorn stopped by the office of David Mastio, the deputy editorial
page editor. Not there. Then he popped in to look for Editorial Page Editor Brett M. Decker. Not there. Running onto the mezzanine overlooking
the shop floor, he scanned the newsroom hoping to catch sight of his

colleagues, with no luck. The *Washington Times* was sitting on a news-breaking story of global importance, but the window for getting the story in the broadsheet was closing rapidly.

Beginning to despair, the newsman gazed out at the snow gently coating the mighty oaks outside. The *Washington Times* newsroom is dominated by three-story windows overlooking the National Arboretum, a 446-acre nature preserve situated in the urban decay of northeast D.C. The peaceful vista outside the windows contrasted with the chaos inside, where phones rang off the hook, reporters barked questions over the phone, competing news programs blared from dozens of TVs, and the incessant sound of fingers clanging on keyboards rattled in the head. Although the Arboretum is one of Washington's hidden jewels, even this sanctuary of nature had been overrun by Beijing as part of a plan to destroy historic azaleas and boxwoods in the Arboretum and use funds for their upkeep to build a 12-acre Chinese garden, which was part of an agreement signed between the PRC and the U.S. Department of Agriculture.[6] The specific spot was in demand because it sat on a hill with a commanding view of the U.S. Capitol, a perch from which visiting Chinese officials could look down on the U.S. government.

That scheme was thwarted by outraged American activists, just like the Hu state visit had to be. If a historically anti-communist publication such as the *Washington Times* couldn't be depended on to play a role in upsetting Hu's sojourn, nobody could, but time was running out. At the last second, as zero hour approached, Perley's coworkers appeared by the elevator next to the *Times*' radio studio. Stop the presses!

After the article was posted, the Sichuan beef really hit the fan. There's a crowd of well-heeled socialites who are regulars on the diplomatic party circuit, and state dinners at the White House are the most prized ticket for this jet set. These types tend to be liberal, at least socially, and wax eloquent about subjects like the environment and human rights. People like Richard Gere and Angelina Jolie are their patron saints. This crowd did not know about Hu's murderous past, and the fact that this visiting dignitary unleashed the dogs of war on pacifist Buddhist monks—the saffron-robed people who developed trendy meditative breathing exercises for housewives everywhere—did not go over well. So many big shots avoided the state dinner that it became a social embarrassment and a protocol problem for the White House. Hu is a major international figure whose country holds one of the five permanent seats on the United Nations Security Council, yet almost everyone in official Washington who wasn't required to meet with him didn't, or at least didn't in public. The terror of Tibet was booed at every stop. Cancellations to Hu events streamed in, and political offices were inundated with calls protesting the visit of the head of the Chinese Communist Party.

The consequences of the *Times* op-ed reverberated even further. The most important warning came in the conclusion: "Reasons of state apply to the executive branch, not the legislative branch. There is no need for anyone in the House or Senate, for example, to be photographed with Mr. Hu or his entourage." This was the shot heard 'round the Capitol.

The truth about Hu Jintao's bloody record had schedulers scrambling to find excuses for politicians to avoid shaking hands or sitting down with the man. House Speaker John Boehner, an Ohio Republican, made headlines by snubbing his invitation to the state dinner,[7] and Senate Minority Leader Mitch McConnell, Kentucky Republican, likewise refused to go.[8] Surprisingly enough, Senate Majority Leader Harry Reid, Nevada Democrat, also stayed away, calling Hu a "dictator,"[9] an honest slip of the tongue that he later hedged. Reid did meet Hu behind closed doors later, but was careful not to have any photographs leak out of the encounter.

The biggest news of all, though, was not who didn't meet with Hu but one important official who did and clearly was not happy about it: Vice President Joseph Biden. As a senator for thirty-six years, Biden had been a reliable liberal northeastern Democratic vote, but he was a solid anti-communist and a strong proponent of human rights in Asia. Radio Free Asia, for example, wouldn't exist were it not for his persistent patronage as chairman of the Foreign Relations Committee. As vice president in the administration that was hosting the communist leader, Biden couldn't get out of appearing in public with Hu, but it was clear by his facial expressions and body language that he would have preferred to be just about anywhere else. In three separate shots from three different angles taken at three different times for three different publications,

Biden is frowning and completely ashen-faced. Joe's a jovial guy whose inappropriate humor frequently gets him into trouble, but there was no joking around during the Hu visit. The vice president's upset visage stood in stark contrast to the conscience-free perma-grin on display by his amoral boss, President Obama.

Slaughtering innocent human beings didn't bother some glitterati, such as washed-up singer Barbra Streisand, kung-fu actor Jackie Chan, jazz pianist Herbie Hancock, Coca-Cola CEO Muhtar Kent, *Vogue* magazine editor Anna Wintour, United Autoworkers President Bob King, Christiane Amanpour of ABC News, and Indiana Senator Dick Lugar, all of whom attended President Obama's boozy dinner honoring Hu.[10] The moral bankruptcy of the modern Democratic Party was reiterated by the happy presence of its three living presidents: Jimmy Carter, Bill Clinton, and Barack Obama. It was especially shameful that Carter and Obama—two Nobel Peace Prize winners—were living it up, eating lobster and toasting the dictator while their fellow Nobel recipient, 2010 laureate Liu Xiaobo, was rotting as a political prisoner in a Chinese dungeon.[11] Still, the protest against Chinese Maoism was successful, transforming what would normally be a star-studded dinner into an embarrassing affair attended mostly by bureaucrats and B-list celebrities.

The *Washington Times* article about the Tibet killings rained on Hu's parade and changed the tenor of his visit to D.C. The perfectly timed piece helped the nation's decision-makers see Hu for the pariah he is. The timeline of official Washington's rejection of Hu is important. There was a great buildup the week before the state visit, culminating in the obsequious Kissinger op-ed; the article about the Tibet massacre warning public officials not to be photographed with Hu hit Monday; Hu arrived in town Tuesday; prominent personages bailed on the dinner Wednesday; and congressional meet-and-greets went down on Thursday, but people on Capitol Hill studiously avoided photo-ops with the Maoist honcho. It was a rare instance of politicians uniformly acting camera-shy.

Setting a good example for America, Vice President Biden's quiet snub reminded us that the U.S.A., the greatest nation in history, doesn't have to kowtow to the PRC, one of history's deadliest regimes. Our national leaders don't have to be toadies to Beijing. President George W. Bush refused to hold a state dinner at the White House when Hu was in Washington in 2006.[12] Even during the 2011 state visit, members of Congress were so cool to Hu that he wasn't invited to appear before a Joint Session of Congress. If anyone is wondering if the People's Republic is really a "strategic partner" as Mr. Obama claims, the lack of a warm reception on Capitol Hill exposes the lie.

The moral of this inside story is that Beijing's evil despots can be beaten. There is no such thing as Chinese Manifest Destiny. The PRC isn't and never will be the greatest nation on earth because it is not a good place, let alone great. Americans should stand up, be heard, question Chinese propaganda, and buy American or buy products from anywhere but China when possible. Feeding the beast only makes it stronger, so starve Beijing and force the communists to learn to behave like a civilized nation. Just as Bill Clinton will always be remembered as the philandering, impeached president, Hu Jintao should go down in history as the Chinese communist leader who was publicly humiliated by Americans during what was intended to be his swan song.

It is not foreordained that Red China will eat our lunch and become the world's preeminent superpower. America needs to muster the determination to manage its economic indiscipline and rally behind its own greatness once again. A United States that believes in itself and stands against evil cannot be challenged by anyone. Barack Obama doesn't believe in American exceptionalism and is thus incapable of restoring U.S. pride in its historical mission as the last, best hope for the world. That's why he should be sent packing into retirement with Hu Jintao in 2012.

The Post-American Myth

The current belief in academic and political salons is that American decline has set in, it is irreversible, and that the United States will inevitably fade into the ash bin of history like all the great empires before it. This pessimistic position, nearly universally held among the smart set, is treated as a fait accompli. White papers, journal articles, and think-tank conferences pound away at what this post-American future will look like, often proffering advice about how U.S. leaders should start to lay the groundwork for our humbled status. If other powers are running the world, then America should start sucking up now, the thinking goes. President Obama is the most prominent spokesman for this view that American exceptionalism has come to an end, if it ever existed in the first place. As Michelle Obama infamously declared in 2008, "For the first time in my adult lifetime, I'm really proud of my country."[13] That new-found national pride, she indicated, stemmed from her husband becoming a leading presidential contender; before that, she wasn't proud of America.

During his 2008 run for the White House, Obama caused a furor when he was photographed carrying Fareed Zakaria's book, *The Post-American World*. In his first chapter, Zakaria writes, "In every other dimension [outside the politico-military level]—industrial, financial, educational, social, cultural—the distribution of power is shifting, moving away from American dominance."[14] His fourth chapter, titled "The Challenger," is about a rising and increasingly assertive China. Zakaria casually mentions that Napoleon was probably speaking apocryphally when he warned, "Let China sleep, for when China awakes, she will shake the world." He goes on to discuss how the future of the world largely depends on whether or not Beijing decides to be a responsible player on the world stage—a "stakeholder," as the George W. Bush administration put it—or continues to devolve into a nationalistic, power-hungry brute rapaciously seizing more resources and territory. "The stability and peace of the post-American world will depend, in large measure, on the balance that China strikes between these forces of integration and disintegration," Zakaria claims.[15] Beijing's choice, then, is between nationalism and globalization—the proffered utopian way forward being for the communists to put down their little red books and join the new world order.

In other words, America doesn't matter anymore; this century is the beginning of the Chinese era, or a world run by a confederation of countries such as the United Nations. In one way, this false choice posits the People's Republic of China as the last great defender of the nation-state.

The PRC is coming into its own and growing in wealth and military might as borders become more porous, the economy becomes more global, and nations become increasingly multi-ethnic. The Chinese want their turn at running the show and thus resist surrendering their sovereignty to international bodies and multilateral treaties. Without a doubt, increasing globalization comes at the expense of national power, and the leaders in Beijing don't want to cede any of their authority to outside forces.

If the communists weren't murderous totalitarian thugs, we would be cheering on this bucking of the global system. In reality, the Chinese Communist Party is not the enemy of globalization because communism is by design a global revolutionary ideology. International bodies like the UN are overwhelmingly leftist, and as such have common cause on most issues with the Marxists in the Middle Kingdom.

The real bulwark to this juggernaut is traditional America and the remnants of Western civilization, which espouse freedom over tyranny, the individual over the state, and faith over ideology. Leftists like the Obamas and Fareed Zakaria might welcome and celebrate a brave, new post-American world because they hate what the traditional world stands for. However, the advent of a post-American world is no fait accompli; Americans are in charge of their own destiny.

It's undeniable that our great country is in a slump, but it is a slump of our own making. America is not getting beaten by any other power; we are beating ourselves through deficit spending to fund wasteful big government. This is within our control. All the doomsday projections that show never-ending U.S. decline and unbroken Chinese growth make assumptions based on static trends in which nothing changes. That's not the real world. Just because China's economy has grown more than 10 percent per year for two decades doesn't mean it can or will maintain that tempo forever. At some point, development slows down.

Some analysts are already refuting the conventional wisdom on China. For example, "World Bank President Robert Zoellick argues that China's export-led growth model is unsustainable over time, because to maintain 8 percent growth would require a doubling of China's share of exports by 2020."[16] Likewise, there is nothing irreversible about American decline. Sometimes, people wake up. In autumn 2011, 88 percent of

Americans said they were dissatisfied with the way things are going, according to Gallup.[17] Such an overwhelming level of dissatisfaction can quickly lead to systemic change. President Obama gutted the U.S. economy and people are hopping mad about it. Now they need to throw him out and undo all the damage "The One" has done. It can happen.

Even the rosiest picture of future American renewal and Chinese mediocrity doesn't mean there won't be conflict between the two nations. At heart, we subscribe to two different worldviews, and we both want to be the biggest guy on the block. As Beijing gains more power and the PRC economy continues to grow, the communists are becoming increasingly hubristic and belligerent toward their neighbors. This bullying has to be contained and managed. In 1956, Soviet Premier Nikita Krushchev thundered, "We will bury you." They didn't. We buried the Soviet Union—and we accomplished this because President Reagan unleashed the entrepreneurial forces of the private sector to create a gangbuster economy that could underwrite an arms race that would bankrupt Russian communism. The stronger system won. The same fate awaits Chinese communism so long as America remembers what makes our nation special and isn't afraid to lead the world from the front again. In short, America's future is in our own hands.

APPENDIX I

The following document is a 2009 cable, published by WikiLeaks, from U.S. Secretary of State Hillary Clinton listing numerous Chinese companies suspected of involvement in missile-related weapons proliferation. As Clinton notes, the United States "received little or no response" after bringing all these cases to China's attention.

P 212230Z JUL 09
FM SECSTATE WASHDC
TO AMEMBASSY BEIJING PRIORITY
INFO MISSILE TECHNOLOGY CONTROL REGIME COLLECTIVE
    PRIORITY

S E C R E T STATE 076155

E.O. 12958: DECL: 07/21/2034

SUBJECT: (S) FOLLOWING UP WITH CHINA ON CASES OF
    PROLIFERATION CONCERN

REF: A. STATE 30007 (BEIJING TIANLIANXING SCIENTIFIC)
     B. BEIJING 861 (BEIJING TIANLIANXING
         SCIENTIFIC/SUZHOU)
     C. STATE 30001 (SUZHOU TESTING INSTRUMENT
         FACTORY)
     D. STATE 25689 (DALIAN SUNNY INDUSTRIES/LIMMT)
     E. BEIJING 728 (DALIAN SUNNY INDUSTRIES/LIMMT)

    F.   STATE 4104 (SHANGHAI YUANSHAN INDUSTRY & TRADE COMPANY)

    G. BEIJING 202 (SHANGHAI YUANSHAN INDUSTRY & TRADE COMPANY)

    H. 08 STATE 113768 (CPMIEC AND CAAA)

    I.   08 BEIJING 4064 (CPMIEC AND CAAA)

    J.   08 STATE 105597 (POLYTECHNOLOGIES INC.)

    K. 08 BEIJING 3854 (POLYTECHNOLOGIES INC.)

    L.   08 STATE 129610 (JFMMRI CNNMIEC BMIEC AND BAMTRI)

    M. 08 BEIJING 4610 (JFMMRI CNNMIEC BMIEC AND BAMTRI)

    N. STATE 4341 (SHENYANG HUALI ECONOMIC TRADING COMPANY)

    O. BEIJING 201 (SHENYANG HUALI ECONOMIC TRADING COMPANY)

    P.   08 STATE 29703 (HONG KONG MOST GROUP CO. LTD.)

    Q. 08 BEIJING 1209 (HONG KONG MOST GROUP CO. LTD.)

    R. 08 STATE 130673 (HONG KONG MOST GROUP CO. LTD.)

    S.   08 BEIJING 4609 (HONG KONG MOST GROUP CO. LTD.)

Classified By: ISN/MTR DIRECTOR PAM DURHAM, REASON: 1.4 (C).

¶1. (U) This is an action request. Embassy Beijing, please see paragraph 3.

¶2. (S) Since March 2008, the U.S. has provided Chinese officials with information regarding a number of cases of missile-related proliferation concern (Refs). In the cases described below, we have received little or no response from China on the status of its investigations or on steps it is taking to address the concerns we have outlined. We therefore want to follow-up with Chinese authorities and request an update on these cases at the earliest possible time.

¶3. (S) Action Request: Request Embassy Beijing approach appropriate host government officials to deliver talking points/non-paper in paragraph 4 below and report response. Talking points also may be provided as a non-paper.

¶4. (S) Begin talking points/non-paper:

(SECRET//REL CHINA)

--Over the past year as well as in the context of our nonproliferation dialogue, we have raised numerous cases of proliferation concern involving Chinese entities. However, we remain concerned as we have not received any substantive response from you on your efforts to investigate these activities.

--We therefore request an update on the status of your investigations or on the steps you have taken to address our concerns in the following cases.

A. Beijing Tianlianxing Scientific Ltd.

-- In March 2009, the U.S. raised with you our concerns that China's Beijing Tianlianxing Scientific Ltd. had offered 1,000 kilograms of specialty steel to Pakistan's Aginel Enterprises, an entity associated with Pakistan's nuclear weapons and missile programs.

--Though not controlled, we noted that this steel has been used to produce components in Pakistan's Ghaznavi short-range ballistic missile, a Missile Technology Control Regime (MTCR) Category I system.

B. Suzhou Testing Instrument Factory

-- In March 2009, the U.S. raised with you our concerns that Pakistan's Intralink Incorporated had sought a quote from the Chinese firm Suzhou Testing Instrument Factory for a vibration test system. Intralink Incorporated appears to be closely associated with the Project Management Organization (PMO), the developer of Pakistan's Ghaznavi short-range ballistic missile.

--As we indicated in our March 2009 demarche, this vibration test system is likely controlled by the MTCR and can be used to simulate the flight vibrations and shocks that rockets and unmanned aerial vehicles (UAVs) experience during launch, stage separation, and normal flight.

C. Dalian Sunny Industries/LIMMT

-- In March 2009, the U.S. reiterated its long-standing serious concerns regarding the proliferation-related trading activities of the Chinese firm Dalian Sunny Industries.

-- As you are aware, for several years we have provided your government information related to Dalian Sunny Industries' supply of components and materials to entities and front companies associated with Iran's ballistic missile programs. In June 2008, the MFA Arms Control and Disarmament Department provided no new information on actions taken against LIMMT, stating only that investigations were "ongoing" and asserting that LIMMT no longer existed as a business entity.

D. Shanghai Yuanshan Industry and Trade Company

-- In January 2009, the U.S. raised with you our concerns that the Syrian entity Industrial Solutions ordered a consignment of 2024-T6 aluminum from the Chinese company Shanghai Yuanshan Industry and Trade Company.

--Industrial Solutions is a cover for the Scientific Studies and Research Center (SSRC), the entity responsible for overseeing Syria's ballistic missile program.

--2024-T6 aluminum can be used to produce structural components in ballistic missiles and in some forms is controlled by the Nuclear Suppliers Group and Wassenaar Arrangement.

E. China Precision Machinery Import/Export Corporation (CPMIEC) and China Academy of Aerospace Aerodynamics (CAAA)

-- In October 2008, the U.S. raised with you our concerns that the China Precision Machinery Import/Export Corporation (CPMIEC) and China Academy of Aerospace Aerodynamics (CAAA) had concluded a contract to supply the Pakistani government with a trisonic wind tunnel.

-- We believe Pakistan may intend to use this wind tunnel, which is controlled by the MTCR, to support missile-related research and development in Pakistan.

F. Polytechnologies Inc.

-- In October 2008, the U.S. raised with you our concerns that the Chinese firm Polytechnologies Inc. had concluded contracts - and used false documentation - to supply a coil winding machine and integrated optical chips to Pakistan's Advanced Engineering and Research Organization (AERO).

-- AERO is a procurement agent and alias for Pakistan's Air Weapons Complex (AWC), which has participated in Pakistan's efforts to develop nuclear weapons delivery systems, cruise missiles, and UAVs.

--We believe this equipment will likely be used by AERO to support missile-related projects in Pakistan.

G. JFMMRI Metal Forming Machinery Engineering Company, Ltd. (JFMMRI), China National Nonferrous Metals Import Export Company (CNNMIEC), Beijing Machinery Import-Export Corporation (BMIEC), and Beijing Aeronautical Manufacturing Technology Research Institute (BAMTRI) Technology and Development Company.

-- Since 2006, the U.S. has raised with China our concerns regarding attempts by Pakistan's missile program to procure ring-rolling and flow forming machines from entities in China.

--These machines may ultimately be destined for Pakistan's National Development Complex (NDC), which is responsible for developing Pakistan's Shaheen series of ballistic missiles.

--In December 2008, we requested an update on activities related to this case, and have not received any response.

H. Shenyang Huali Economic Trading Company

-- In April 2008, the U.S. raised with you our concerns that China-based firm Shenyang Huali Economic Trading Company, working through North Korean intermediaries, was acting as a key source of raw materials and technology for a North Korean ballistic missile development project in Syria.

--In January 2009, we followed up with additional information related to this case.

I. Hong Kong Most Group Co. Ltd.

-- On 24 March 2008, the U.S. raised with you our concerns that the Hong Kong Most Group Co. Ltd. finalized a sales contract to supply the Iranian firm Aluminat Co. with Chinese-origin aluminum plates that can be used to produce a variety of structural components in Scud missiles.

--The specific aluminum being supplied by Hong Kong Most Group to Iran is controlled by the Wassenaar Arrangement. We provided further information to Chinese officials regarding this case in December 2008.

--We appreciate your interest in advancing our mutual nonproliferation goals and look forward to hearing your responses regarding these proliferation cases at the earliest possible time.

End talking points/non-paper

¶5. (U) Washington POC is ISN/MTR Mike Kennedy (Phone: 202-647-3176). Please slug any reporting on this issue for ISN/MTR and EAP/CM.

¶6. (U) A word version of this document will be posted at www.state.sgov.gov/demarche. CLINTON

ACTIVE REGISTERED FOREIGN AGENTS FOR CHINA

Registrant	Registration Date	Foreign Principal
Blank Rome, LLP	7/22/1994	China Shipping Group Company
Hai Tian Development U.S.A., Inc.	12/3/1996	People's Daily Overseas Edition
China National Tourist Office	12/30/1981	China National Tourism Administration (formerly: China International Travel Service)
China Daily Distribution Corporation	4/19/1983	China Daily of Beijing, China
Patton Boggs, LLP	10/9/1969	Embassy of the People's Republic of China
PricewaterhouseCoopers, LLP ("PwC LLP")	8/11/2011	Shenyang Municipal Government (China)
Precision Product, Inc.	6/18/2010	Si Chuan Le Er Kuang Ye Technology, Ltd.
Patton Boggs, LLP	10/9/1969	China Chamber of Commerce for Importers and Exporters of Machinery and Electronic Products
Patton Boggs, LLP	10/9/1969	China Chamber of Commerce for Importers and Exporters of Metals, Minerals & Chemicals
Brown Lloyd James	6/17/2008	China-United States Exchange Foundation
DDB Worldwide Communications Group, Inc.	12/23/2009	Ministry of Commerce of the People's Republic of China

1. List according to U.S. State Department records as of September 17, 2011.

APPENDIX III

SELECTED RECENT CASES OF CHINESE ESPIONAGE[1]

Military Cases

- September 2011: Two professors at a technical university in St. Petersburg, Russia are put on trial, accused of passing state secrets to Chinese spies
- June 2011: Xian Hongwei and Lili plead guilty to attempting to export military microchips to China
- May 2011: U.S. Navy sailor Bryan Minkyu Martin pleads guilty to trying to pass military secrets to China

---

1. These cases are "selected" because we are facing a Niagara of Chinese espionage both at home and abroad. To report on them all would require a book-length production, updated daily. For the same reason, only recent cases have been selected. The term "espionage" is used in the common, not legal sense, as some of these cases have been prosecuted under statutes other than the Espionage Act. Some cases of corporate espionage with defense implications are counted as military cases.

- March 2011: Lian Yang is sentenced for attempting to purchase 300 radiation-hardened military semiconductors for export to China
- January 2011: American citizen Glen Duffie Shriver pleads guilty to attempting to infiltrate the CIA on behalf of Chinese intelligence
- January 2011: Zhen Zhou Wu is sentenced to eight years in prison for exporting American military technology to Chinese military companies
- January 2011: Noshir S. Gowadia, former aerospace engineer, is sentenced to thirty-two years in prison for revealing American B-2 bomber secrets to China
- October 2010: York Yuan Chang and his wife are charged with attempting to export dual-use (civilian and military) electronic technology to China (the case is now pending)
- September 2010: Chi Tong Kuok is sentenced to eight years in prison for attempting to export encryption devices to the PRC via Macao
- February 2010: Boeing engineer Dongfan Chung is sentenced to fifteen years in prison for passing information related to the Delta IV rocket system to China
- January 2010: Pentagon employee James Fondren is sentenced to three years in prison for selling military secrets to China
- August 2009: Tah Wei Chao and Zhi Yong Guo are sentenced for attempting to export advanced thermal imaging cameras to China
- August 2009: William Chi-Wai Tsu is sentenced for exporting military electronics to China
- April 2008: American Defense Department employee Gregg Gergersen pleads guilty to passing weapons sales information to China

Corporate Cases

- September 2011: a former employee of American Semi-conductor Corp is sentenced to three years in prison for passing wind turbine secrets to a Chinese competitor
- February 2011: Dow Chemical employee Huang Kexue is convicted of stealing Dow trade secrets and selling them to China
- November 2010: Ford employee Yu Xiangdong pleads guilty to stealing Ford Motor Co. trade secrets for China
- September 2010: Valspar employee David Yen Lee pleads guilty to stealing Valspar paint and coating formula and selling it to China
- July 2010: GM engineer Du Shanshaw is fired for copying thousands of GM hybrid technology documents and passing them to Chery Automobile Company in China
- June 2010: DuPont engineer Meng Hong pleads guilty to stealing DuPont technology and passing it to China

STATEMENT OF FACTS IN THE CASE OF RONALD MONTAPERTO

The following is the Statement of Facts in the case of Ronald Montaperto, a former Defense Intelligence Agency analyst who admitted to providing classified information to Chinese military attachés.

IN THE UNITED STATES DISTRICT COURT FOR THE EASTERN DISTRICT OF VIRGINIA UNITED STATES OF AMERICA CRIMINAL NO. 1:06cr257

RONALD N. MONTAPERTO
Defendant.

STATEMENT OF FACTS
Should this matter proceed to trial, the United States would prove the following beyond a reasonable doubt:
1. In October 1981, defendant RONALD N. MONTAPERTO began employment with the Defense Intelligence Agency (DIA) in Arlington, Virginia as an intelligence analyst on issues pertaining the People's Republic of

China (PRC). He held a Top Secret security clearance. On October 2, 1981, MONTAPERTO signed a DIA Secrecy Agreement by which he acknowledged that he would never divulge any classified information relating to the national security without prior consent of the Director of the DIA or his designated representative.

MONTAPERTO further acknowledged that he was responsible for ascertaining whether information was classified and who was authorized to receive it. MONTAPERTO acknowledged that he had read and understood the provisions of the Espionage Act, including Title 18, United States Code, Sections 793, 794 and 798.1 expected to cause damage to national security.

2. In 1983, MONTAPERTO was reassigned by the DIA to work as Chief, Current Intelligence, China Branch, at the Pentagon in Arlington. From July 1986 to February 1992, he was assigned by the DIA to work at the Defense Intelligence Analysis Center (DIAC) at Bolling Air Force Base in Washington, D.C.

3. In February 1992, MONTAPERTO began working at the Institute of National Strategic Studies at the National Defense University (NDU) in Washington, D.C. In March 2001, he was hired as the Dean of Academics at the Asia-Pacific Center for Security Studies (APCSS), in Honolulu, Hawaii. APCSS is a Department of Defense (DOD) educational institution in which civilian and military security professionals from the various nations of the Asia-Pacific Region and the United States study issues and problems related to Asian security.

4. As part of his responsibilities as a PRC analyst at the DIA, MONTAPERTO was among five or six DIA analysts selected in 1982 to participate in a pilot program initiated by the DIA to foster social and professional interaction between DIA's PRC experts and the PRC military attachés assigned to the PRC Embassy in Washington, D.C. All contacts between DIA participants and the PRC military attachés were to be documented. None of the DIA participants was authorized to disseminate classified information to the PRC military attachés. By 1984, when MONTAPERTO was working at the Pentagon, all the other participants in the pilot program had either retired or transferred. MONTAPERTO continued to maintain contact with the PRC military attachés as part of his official responsibilities, yet failed to execute contact reports after each meeting as required by DIA regulations. He did file an official "assessment" of each of the two PRC military attachés with whom he was primarily meeting–one was filed in October 1983, the other in May 1987. He only filed these two assessments after being directed to do

so by DIA security. He then submitted additional assessments in 1988. On occasion, MONTAPERTO discussed with his superiors his meetings with the military attachés, and, by early 1989, he was directed by his immediate supervisor to discontinue his meetings with the military attachés altogether.

5. In 1988, MONTAPERTO applied for a position as a DIA analyst detailed to the Central Intelligence Agency (CIA). During security processing in January 1989, MONTAPERTO made the following admissions: a) in 1982, he separately showed both his father and his wife (neither of whom held a security clearance) a classified document (level unknown); b) in 1982, he removed a Confidential U.S. government document from its proper place of storage and brought it home; c) in 1987, he invited into the DIAC, without authorization, a private researcher (who, further investigation revealed, was uncleared and had been given access to classified information by Montaperto); and d) in 1988, he removed and brought home a Secret document. He also admitted to maintaining contact with PRC military attaché Yu Zenghe and his predecessor. MONTAPERTO was not able to successfully complete security processing at the CIA and was not offered the position he was seeking at that agency. However, his DIA clearances remained in place and no effort was made to restrict his access to classified information.

6. On January 29, February 6, February 13, and February 20, 1991, FBI agents interviewed MONTAPERTO about his relationship with the PRC attachés. MONTAPERTO stated that he had developed close relationships with at least two of the attachés–Senior Colonels Yang Qiming and Yu Zenghe. Investigation by the FBI has determined that both men were intelligence officers for the PRC during the time of MONTAPERTO's association with them. MONTAPERTO admitted to verbally providing these attachés a considerable amount of information that was useful to them, including classified information. However, MONTAPERTO stated he could not recall specifically what classified information he had disclosed to the attachés, and the investigation was closed by the FBI without referral for a prosecutive opinion.

7. In August 2001, a joint Naval Criminal Investigative Service (NCIS) and FBI investigation was initiated on MONTAPERTO in Honolulu, Hawaii. As part of the investigation, a ruse was established in which a U.S. military representative approached MONTAPERTO in July 2003 and asked him whether he would be interested in working on a sensitive project on China. In accordance with the ruse, MONTAPERTO was told that he would have to submit to a counterintelligence polygraph examination administered by

the NCIS as a prerequisite to working on this special project. MONTAP-
ERTO volunteered to do so.

8. In two pre-polygraph interviews conducted by NCIS agents in October
2003, MONTAPERTO admitted the following: a) he met with PRC military
attachés Yang Qiming and Yu Zenghe, individually, from 1983 to 1990; b)
he knew when he met with the two attachés that both were trained intelligence officers; c) he would often discuss classified issues with the attachés by
talking "around" the information; and d) he had verbally disclosed to Yu
Zenghe information classified by the U.S. government at the Secret and Top
Secret levels (although he stated he could not recall specifically what classified
information he had disclosed to Yu Zenghe). Additionally, MONTAPERTO
stated that he might have a document either at his residence or his office in
Honolulu, Hawaii, or at his townhouse in Springfield, Virginia, which
MONTAPERTO had written based on a conversation he had had with Yang
Qiming.

MONTAPERTO stated that this document pertained to relations between
the United States government and the PRC and that he believed he had placed
the document in question in a book. He provided the NCIS with consent to
search his residence, vehicle, and office in Hawaii, as well as his residence in
Springfield. Consequently, after the October interviews were completed,
NCIS agents conducted searches of the locations in Honolulu. No document
of the sort described by MONTAPERTO was found.

9. When NCIS agents arrived at MONTAPERTO's Springfield, Virginia
townhouse on November 12, 2003 to conduct a search, MONTAPERTO's
wife directed the agents to a large bookshelf containing numerous books in
a second floor office. The agents did not find any document of the sort
described by MONTAPERTO or any other related evidence during the search
of those books.

10. On November 19, 2003, NCIS agents conducted a third pre-polygraph
examination interview of MONTAPERTO in Honolulu. MONTAPERTO
stated that during the late 1980's, he had two discussions with Yu Zenghe
involving Top Secret information. One disclosure dealt with the sale of
military equipment by the PRC to a Middle Eastern country.

MONTAPERTO identified the specific type of equipment and the country
that purchased the equipment. The second Top Secret discussion dealt with
the sale of missiles from the PRC to another Middle Eastern country.
MONTAPERTO stated he could not recall specifically what he had

disclosed to Yu Zenghe with respect to these sales. Although some information about these sales was officially available to the public, MONTAPERTO's knowledge on this topic was derived from highly classified sources and sensitive compartmented information. Pursuant to his secrecy agreement with the government, MONTAPERTO had a legal duty to confirm that any such derived information was releasable, yet he failed to do so.

11. On December 3, 2003, the FBI conducted a final interview of MONTAPERTO in Honolulu. During this interview, MONTAPERTO elaborated on admissions he had made in previous interviews about having disclosed classified information to PRC military attachés in the 1980's. He also stated that from 1989 to 2001 he continued to meet with PRC military attachés from the PRC Embassy. MONTAPERTO named several attachés, all of whom were determined by the FBI to be PRC intelligence officers who worked within the United States.

MONTAPERTO admitted he may have orally disclosed classified information that he recollected from his previous position to PRC military attachés as late as 2001. However, during this interview, MONTAPERTO stated he could not recall specifically what classified information he had disclosed to the attachés.

12. On February 4, 2004, FBI agents executed a search warrant issued by the U.S. District Court for the Eastern District of Virginia at MONTAPERTO's residence at 7936 Birchtree Court, Springfield, Virginia. At this time, MONTAPERTO had stored within a file cabinet drawer in his basement a number of classified documents, six of which contained national defense information classified at the Secret level and clearly marked as such. These documents consisted of: three February 1984 DIA memoranda regarding "Future PRC Relationship," "Future DIA-PRC Relationship,"and "A Plan for DIA-PRC Relationship;" a February 1984 DOD cable regarding "The Maturing US/PRC Military Relationship;" and two July 1988 DIA memoranda regarding "Policy Regarding Contact with Chinese Nationals."

MONTAPERTO had previously removed these documents from their proper place of storage within the DOD. As MONTAPERTO well knew, he was not authorized to store or retain classified materials at his residence.

13. A July 2005 paragraph-by-paragraph analysis by the DIA of the previouslydescribed Secret documents seized from MONTAPERTO's townhouse determined that all of these documents were properly classified at the time they were created and that all retained their Secret classification at the time of this analysis.

14. At all times during the above-described incidents, defendant MONTAPERTO acted unlawfully and knowingly and not by mistake or other innocent reason.

Respectfully submitted,

Chuck Rosenberg
United States Attorney
By: _____
W. Neil Hammerstrom, Jr.
Assistant United States Attorney

_____
Stephen M. Campbell
Assistant United States Attorney

_____
Renate D. Staley
Trial Attorney
U. S. Department of Justice

After consulting with my attorney and pursuant to the plea agreement entered into this day between the defendant, RONALD N. MONTAPERTO, and the United States, I hereby stipulate that the above Statement of Facts is true and accurate, and that had the matter proceeded to trial, the United States would have proved the same beyond a reasonable doubt.

_____
Ronald N. Montaperto
Defendant

I am RONALD N. MONTAPERTO's attorney. I have carefully reviewed the above Statement of Facts with him. To my knowledge, his decision to stipulate to these facts is an informed and voluntary one.

_____
Stephen P. Anthony
Counsel for Defendant

_____
Hope Hamilton
Counsel for Defendant

NOTES

Chapter One

1. "Chief Justice Leads Obama to Stumble Presidential Oath," Agence France Presse, January 20, 2009.
2. "Obama retakes oath of office after Roberts' mistake," CNN, January 21, 2009, http://articles.cnn.com/2009-01-21/politics/obama.oath_1_oath-president-obama-chief-justice-john-roberts?_s=PM:POLITICS.
3. President Barack Hussein Obama, "Inaugural Address," January 20, 2009, www.whitehouse.gov/blog/inaugural-address/.
4. Editorial Board, "Obama's Third World America," *Washington Times*, April 15, 2011.
5. "Obama Acknowledges Decline of U.S. Dominance," *Times of India*, November 8, 2010.

6. Lee Ross, "Greenspan Says Obama Admin Is Too 'Active' in Economy," Fox News, March 15, 2011, http://politics.blogs.foxnews.com/2011/03/15/greenspan-says-obama-admin-too-active-economy.

7. Mark Knoller, "National debt has increased $4 trillion under Obama," CBS News, August 22, 2011, http://www.cbsnews.com/8301-503544_162-20095704-503544.html.

8. Anya Strzemien, "Michelle Obama's China State Dinner Dress By Alexander McQueen," *Huffington Post*, January 21, 2011, http://www.huffingtonpost.com/2011/01/19/michelle-obama-china-dress-state-dinner_n_811320.html#226583.

9. Dr. Lillian Glass, "Does Obama's Body Language Bow to Chinese Leader Hu Jintao Weaken His Image Among Americans and Worldwide?" The Body Language Blog, January 18, 2011, http://drlillianglassbodylanguageblog.wordpress.com/2011/01/18/does-obama%E2%80%99s-body-language-bow-to-chinese-leader-hu-jintao-weaken-his-image-among-americans-and-worldwide/.

10. Ibid.

11. Aaron L. Friedberg, "Hegemony with Chinese Characteristics," *The National Interest*, June 21, 2011.

12. Amy Svitak, "China Viewed as Potential U.S. Partner in Future Mars Exploration," *Space News*, May 4, 2011, http://www.spacenews.com/policy/110504-china-partner-mars-exploration.html.

13. Jay Branegan, "Bush's Big Test: A Blue Team Blocks Beijing," *TIME*, April 16, 2001.

14. Ibid.

15. Gustav Niebuhr, "Lieberman Is Asked to Stop Invoking Faith in Campaign," *New York Times*, August 29, 2000, http://www.nytimes.com/2000/08/29/us/2000-campaign-religion-issue-lieberman-asked-stop-invoking-faith-campaign.html?src=pm.

Chapter Two

1. "Nobel Jury Concerned About Lack of Updates About Chinese Peace Prize Winner," Associated Press, March 24, 2011.

2. Andrew Jacobs and Jonathan Ansfield, "Nobel Peace Prize Given to Jailed Chinese Dissident," *New York Times*, October 8, 2010.

3. Peter Foster, "Nobel Laureate in Jail," *London Daily Telegraph*, December 10, 2010.

4. As quoted by Andrew Jacobs and Alan Cowell, "Nobel Winner's Absence May Delay Awarding of Prize," *New York Times*, November 18, 2010.

5. Richard M. Nixon, "Remarks at Andrews Air Force base on Returning From the People's Republic of China," February 28, 1972.

6. "Trade in Goods (Imports, Exports and Trade Balance) with China: 1985-2011," U.S. Census Bureau, Foreign Trade Division, Data Dissemination Branch, Washington D.C., http://www.census.gov/foreign-trade/balance/c5700.html.

7. "Milk Activist Told 'Be Quiet or Go Back to Jail,'" *South China Morning Post*, April 8, 2011.

8. "China milk activist 'force-fed on hunger strike,'" Agence France Presse, April 7, 2011; and "Milk Activist Told 'Be Quiet or Go Back to Jail,'" op. cit.

9. Tania Branigan, "China Media Condemn 'Unruly' Ai Weiwei," *Manchester Guardian*, April 6, 2011.

10. Eunice Yoon, "Chinese Artist Ai Weiwei: Economic Criminal?" CNN.com, April 8, 2011, http://business.blogs.cnn.com/2011/04/08/chinese-artist-ai-weiwei-economic-criminal/.

11. "Law Will Not Concede before maverick," *Global Times*, April 6, 2011.

12. Clifford Coonan, "Shanghai Cancels St. Patrick's Day Parade Over Fears of Revolt," *Irish Times*, March 7, 2011.

13. Ian Johnson, "Calls for a 'Jasmine Revolution' in China Persist," *New York Times*, February 23, 2011.

14. Austin Ramzy, "State Stamps Out Small 'Jasmine' Protests in China," *TIME*, February 21, 2011.

15. "China Hushes Up Olympic Deaths," *Times of London*, January 20, 2008.

16. Kent Ewing, "Chinese Prisons: Horror and Reform," *Asia Times*, March 24, 2009.

17. Geoff Dyer, "Nervous China Puts Security Apparatus Into Overdrive," *Financial Times*, February 23, 2011.

18. "The Death Penalty in 2009," A Report by Amnesty International, http://www.amnesty.org/en/death-penalty/death-sentences-and-executions-in-2009.

19. "Death Sentences and Executions in 2010," A Report by Amnesty International, PDF available at http://www.amnesty.org/en/library/info/ACT50/001/2011/en.

20. Olga Craig, "The Butchers of Beijing," *Sunday Telegraph of London*, March 1, 1998.

21. Ibid.

22. Robin Munro, "Political Bedlam: China's Judicial Psychiatry," *Asian Wall Street Journal*, February 19, 2001.

23. Kent Ewing, "Chinese Prisons: Horror and Reform," *Asia Times*, March 24, 2009.

24. RWZ and AEF, "Ministry of Public Security Notice Reveals Police Brutality and Corruption," Chinascope, March 22, 2011, http://chinascope.org/main/content/view/3412/109/.

25. "Brother Turns Self in For Evading Expressway Tolls in Case That Intrigues Controversies in China," Xinhua, January 16, 2011, http://news.xinhua net.com/english2010/china/2011-01/16/c_13692495.htm.

26. Joshua Rosenzweig, "China Abandons the Law: The Nation Is Reverting to a Primitive Type of Dictatorship," *Wall Street Journal*, March 24, 2011.

27. June Teufel Dreyer, *China's Political System: Modernization and Tradition* (Glenview, IL: Longman, 2012).

28. Sui-Lee Wee, "China Detains Rights Lawyer, Sends Man to Labor Camp," Reuters, April 15, 2011.

29. Martin Hickman, "Shop until they drop: UK stores shocked by conditions in their Chinese factories," *The Independent*, January 14, 2006; Macworld staff, "Inside Apple's iPod factories," Macworld, June 12, 2006; He Hui-feng, "40 children rescued from Shenzhen plant; Teenagers aged 12 to 14 found working at electronics factory were paid 5 yuan an hour," *South China Morning Post*, March 26, 2011.

30. "Uighur Website Editor Sentenced in Secret in China," The Committee to Protect Journalists, March 10, 2011, http://www.cpj.org/2011/03/uighur-website-editor-sentenced-in-secret-in-china.php.

31. Part of this subchapter appeared in Brett M. Decker, "Beijing's Fear of Faith: Death of Catholic Bishop Has Communist on Red Alert," which appeared in the *Washington Times* on March 14, 2011.

32. Blog Editor, "In China, Christ is living out his Passion," RomeReports.com, May 18, 2011, http://www.romereports.com/palio/benedict-xvi-in-china-christ-is-living-out-his-passion-english-4166.html.

33. Pope Benedict XVI, "Letter of the Holy Father to the Bishops, Priests, Consecrated Persons and Lay Faithful of the Catholic Church in the People's Republic of China," The Vatican, May 27, 2007.

34. See: *2010 Annual Report: Chinese Government Persecution of Christians and Churches in Mainland China*, Midland, TX, ChinaAid, March 2011.

35. Alexa Olesen, "Beijing Police Halt Unapproved Church Service," Associated Press, April 10, 2011.

36. David Aikman, *Jesus in Beijing* (Washington: Regnery Publishing, 2003).

37. David Aikman, "China's Diocletian," blog post on ChinaAid.org, December 21, 2010, http://www.chinaaid.org/2010/12/chinas-diocletian.html.

38. Edward Wong, "Tibetan Who Set Himself Afire Dies," *New York Times*, March 18, 2011.

39. "Tibetan Monk Self-immolates in Freedom Protest," Xinhua, March 18, 2011.

40. Michael Bristow, "China confirms Tibetan executions," BBC News, October 27, 2009, http://news.bbc.co.uk/2/hi/8327347.stm.

41. William C. Triplett II, "Who is Hu Jintao? Official niceties obscure his bloody record," *Washington Times*, January 14, 2011.

42. Chen Jia, "Birth Defects Soar Due to Pollution," *China Daily*, January 31, 2009.

43. Anonymous, "China pollution 'threatens growth,'" BBC News, February 28, 2011, http://www.bbc.co.uk/news/world-asia-pacific-12595872.

44. David Edwards, "China's Poor Treated to Fake Rice Made From Plastic," *The Raw Story*, February 8, 2011, http://www.rawstory.com/rs/2011/02/08/report-china-fake-rice-plastic/.

45. Gong Jing, "Heavy Metals Tainting China's Rice Bowls," Caixin Online, February 13, 2011, http://english.caing.com/2011-02-13/100224762.html.

46. Choi Chi-yuk, "Tainted Bean Sprouts Seized in Police Raids," *South China Morning Post*, April 20, 2011.

47. Peter Foster, "Top 10 Chinese Food Scandals," *London Daily Telegraph*, April 27, 2011.

48. Private correspondence.

49. This fairy tale was passed by word of mouth for generations and exists today in many different forms. Another version, "The Rainmakers," appears in: Cyril Birch, ed., *Tales from China* (Oxford: Oxford University Press, 2000), pp. 97–105.

Chapter Three

1. "GDP per capita (current US$), The World Bank, http://data.worldbank. org/indicator/NY.GDP.PCAP.CD.

2. Cheng Li, "China's Midterm Jockeying: Gearing Up for 2012 (Cabinet Ministers)," *China Leadership Monitor*, No. 32.

3. Ibid.

4. Michael Forsythe, "Wen Jiabao Sees Billionaires in Congress as Wealth Gap Widens," Bloomberg, March 3, 2011.

5. Cheng Li, "China's Midterm Jockeying: Gearing Up for 2012 (Top Leaders of Major State-Owned Enterprises)," *China Leadership Monitor*, No. 34.

6. John Garnaut, "Children of the Revolution," *Sydney Morning Herald*, February 13, 2010.

7. Editor, "New Horizon Capital to Set Up $1 Billion Private Equity Fund," *China Economic Review*, February 1, 2010.

8. Rick Carew, "China's Princelings and the PE," *Wall Street Journal*, February 1, 2010.

9. Michael Sheridan, "China Snaps At Its Junior Princelings," *Times of London*, June 6, 2010.

10. "CDB Posts Impressive Results for 2010," Press Release from China Development Bank, January 27, 2011.

11. "China Development Bank Announces Earnings Results for the Year of 2010," *Business Week*, January 31, 2011.

12. Erica S. Downs, "Inside China, Inc.: China Development Bank's Cross-Border Energy Deals," The Brookings Institution, March 21, 2011.

13. "China's 'going out' strategy," *The Economist*, July 21, 2009.

14. Ibid.

15. Jamil Anderlini, "On Good Terms: Chinese Banks Fuel 'Going Global' Drive," *Financial Times*, April 5, 2011.

16. Eric Fox, "Introduction to the Chinese Banking System," *San Francisco Chronicle*, April 8, 2011.

17. John Garnaut, "Bank Chief Just the Man to Show You the Money," *Sydney Morning Herald*, April 12, 2011.

18. Jamil Anderlini, "The Courting of China's Powerful Princelings," *Financial Times*, November 15, 2010.

19. Paul Eckert, "Cables Show U.S. Sizing Up China's Next Leader," Reuters, February 17, 2011.

20. "Former Shanghai Party Chief Gets 18-Year Term for Bribery," Xinhua, April 11, 2008.

21. Joseph Kahn, "Shanghai Party Boss Held for Corruption," *New York Times*, September 25, 2006.

22. Yang Weihan, "9,633 Officials of County or Division Level and Above 'Unseated' During past Three Years," Xinhua, June 29, 2006.

23. Wang Guanqun, "Highlights of work report of China's Supreme People's Procuratorate," Xinhua, March 11, 2011.

24. Dan Martin, "China News Blackout Linked to President's Son," Agence France Presse, July 22, 2009.

25. Kirby Chien and David Holmes, "CDB Vice President Wang Yi Sacked," Reuters, February 4, 2009.

26. Wang Jingqiong, "Bank's Former VP Found Guilty of Taking 12 Million Yuan in Bribes," *China Daily*, April 16, 2010.

27. James Mulvenon, "So Crooked They have to Screw Their Pants On: New Trends in Chinese Military Corruption," *China Leadership Monitor*, No. 19.

28. Cheng Li, "China's Midterm Jockeying: Gearing Up for 2012 (Military Leaders)," *China Leadership Monitor*, No. 33.

29. "Crackdown in Response to Calls for jasmine Revolution," *China Reform Monitor*: No. 884; The American Foreign Policy Council, March 11, 2011.

30. A version of this section appeared in Brett M. Decker, "Co-opted by Commies in China," which appeared in the *Washington Times* on February 17, 2011.

31. Teresa Wright, *Accepting Authoritarianism: State-Society Relations in China's Reform Era* (Stanford University Press, 2010).

32. Brett M. Decker, "Co-opted by Commies in China," op. cit.

33. Wang Dan, "China's Party of Princelings," *Wall Street Journal*, April 12, 2011.

34. Boye Lafayette de Mente, *The Chinese Mind: Understanding Traditional Chinese Beliefs and Their Influence on Contemporary Culture* (Tokyo: Tuttle Publishing, 2009), p. 46.

Chapter Four

1.   Kiyoshi Takenaka, "Japan wary of rise in China's maritime activities," Reuters, August 2, 2011, http://www.reuters.com/article/2011/08/02/us-japan-military-china-idUSTRE7711DO20110802.

2.   Yoree Koh, "Japan Sharpens Rhetoric on China, Calling It 'Assertive' for First Time," *Wall Street Journal*, August 3, 2011.

3.   Online reporter, "China says it will boost its defence budget in 2011," BBC, March 4, 2011, http://www.bbc.co.uk/news/business-12631357.

4.   International Institute for Strategic Studies, *The Military Balance 2010*, ed. James Hackett (London: Routledge, 2010).

5.   Bill Gertz, "Beijing Develops Pulse Weapons; Blasts Thwart All Electronics," *Washington Times*, July 22, 2011.

6.   U.S. defense analysts, *Military and Security Developments Involving the People's Republic of China* (Washington, D.C.: Department of Defense, 2010).

7.   Wire reporter, "China's First Aircraft Carrier Starts Sea Trial," Agence France Presse, August 9, 2011.

8.   Philip Dorling, "Chinese 'hiding military build-up,'" *The Age (Australia)*, January 7, 2011.

9.   Desy Nurhayati, "Japan concerned about Chinese military buildup," *Jakarta Post*, July 23, 2011.

10. Richard Weitz, "China's Military Buildup Stokes Regional Arms Race," *World Politics Review*, March 16, 2010.

11. Ibid.

12. Tom Donnelly and Gary Schmitt, "China's military buildup could push U.S. out of Asia," *Washington Examiner*, March 12, 2011.

13. Emily Miller, "Debt deal encircles Pentagon," *Washington Times*, August 2, 2011.

14. David E. Sanger, "U.S. Said to Stop North Korea Missile Shipment," *New York Times*, June 12, 2011; William Wan and Craig Whitlock, "North Korean Cargo Ship Turned Back by U. S. Navy," *Washington Post*, June 13, 2011; and Evan Ramstad, "North Korea Keeps Silent on Ship's Turnaround," *Wall Street Journal,* June 14, 2011.

15. "US Denied Request to Board N. Korean Ship Suspected of Carrying Illegal Weapons," *The Maritime Executive* (online) June 14, 2011, http://www.maritime-executive.com article/u-s-denied-request-to- board-ship-suspected-of-carrying-illegal-weapons.

16. "New theory on N Korea rail blast," BBC News, April 23, 2004, http://news.bbc.co.uk/2/hi/asia-pacific/3651705.stm.

17. "Red Cross: North Korea site flattened," *China Daily*, April 25, 2004.

18. Ibid.

19. "New theory on N Korea rail blast," op. cit.

20. Hamish McDonald, "North Korea rejects blast aid," *The Age*, April 27, 2004, http://www.theage.com.au/articles/2004/04/26/1082831497107.html.

21. Ibid.

22. "Red Cross: North Korea site flattened," op. cit.

23. Bruce E. Bechtol Jr., "The Impact of North Korea's WMD Programs on Regional Security and the ROK-US Alliance," Air Command and Staff College, *International Journal of Korean Studies*, Fall/Winter 2004 vol. IIX, no. 1, p. 139.

24. Takahashi Arimoto, "Ten Iranian Missile Engineers Visited N. Korea," *Sankei Shinbun*, June 30, 2006.

25. Carol Giacomo, "US says Iran witnessed N. Korean missile tests," Reuters, July 21, 2006; and Simon Tisdall, "China pressed over Iran and North Korea's nuclear trade," *The Guardian*, November 28, 2010.

26. David E. Sanger and William J. Broad, "Watchdog Finds That Iran Worked on Nuclear Triggers," *New York Times*, May 25, 2011.

27. Press Release, "Treasury Designates Iranian Proliferation Network and Identifies New Aliases," U.S. Department of the Treasury, June 13, 2006.

28. "North Korea: U.S. Policy Options," Hearing before the Committee on Foreign Relations, United States Senate, July 20, 2006, http://foreign.senate.gov/hearings/hearing/?id=cf6062ed-fc31-7f70-1bda-9b7d9ca6b2a3, at p. 20.

29. Simon Tisdall, "China pressed over Iran and North Korea's nuclear trade," op. cit.

30. Louis Charbonneau, "Exclusive—N. Korea, Iran trade missile technology," Reuters, May 14, 2011, http://in.reuters.com/article/2011/05/14/idINIndia-57017820110514.

31. Daniel Halper, "The U.N. Report on North Korea that China Doesn't Want You to See," *Weekly Standard*, May 19, 2011.

32. "Report of the Panel of Experts established pursuant to Resolution 1874, (2009)," The United Nations, May 2011, http://www.nkeconwatch.com/nk-uploads/UN-Panel-of-Experts-NORK-Report-May-2011.pdf, Paragraph 14, p. 9.

33. Ibid., Paragraph 129, p. 40.

34. Ibid., Paragraph 71, p. 25.

35. Shinichi Nishiwaki, "North Korea Dispatches Over 200 Engineers to Iran to Transfer Technology for Iran's Nuclear, Missile Development," *Mainichi*, May 16, 2011.

36. Clemens Wergin, "Dangerous Alliance-Iranian Missile Base on Venezuelan Drawing Boards," Berlin *Welt-Online*, May 13, 2011.

37. For a further comparison of life in North Korea for the haves and the have-nots, see William C. Triplett II, *Rogue State* (Washington, D.C.: Regnery, 2004).

38. "Jong-un's birthday gift train derailed," *JoongAng Daily*, December 28, 2010, http://koreajoongangdaily.joinsmsn.com/news/article/article.aspx?aid=2930202.

39. Hanan Greenberg, "Officers reprimanded over Hanit vessel incident," YNetNews.com, January 1, 2007, http://www.ynetnews.com/articles/0,7340,L-3347191,00.html.

40. Barbara Opall-Rome, "Israel Navy Faults Humans, Not Technology, for Ship Attack," *Defense News,* January 1, 2007.

41. Amos Harel, "Soldier killed, 3 missing after navy vessel hit off Beirut coast," *Haaretz*, July 15, 2006.

42. Hanan Greenberg, "Officers reprimanded over Hanit vessel incident," op. cit.

43. Frank Gardner, "Hezbollah missile threat assessed," BBC News, August 3, 2006, http://news.bbc.co.uk/2/hi/5242566.stm; Amos Harel, "Soldier killed, 3 missing after navy vessel hit off Beirut coast," op. cit.

44. Hanan Greenberg, "Officers reprimanded over Hanit vessel incident," op. cit.

45. Ibid.

46. Tom Zeller, "Psssst...Can I Get A Bomb Trigger?" *New York Times*, September 15, 2002.

47. Joby Warrick and Peter Slevin, "Libyan Arms Designs Traced Back to China," *Washington Post,* February 15, 2004, p. A01.

48. Joseph Cirincione, Jon Wolfsthal, and Miriam Rajkumar, *Deadly Arsenals: Nuclear, Biological, and Chemical Threats*, Second Edition, Revised and Expanded (Washington, D.C.: Carnegie Endowment for International Peace, 2005).

49. Carol Giacomo, "China Helping Iran, N Korea With Weapons," op. cit.; Henry Sikolski, "China and Nuclear Proliferation: Rethinking the Link," Testimony before the US-China Economic and Security Review Commis-

sion, May 20, 2008, http://www.uscc.gov/hearings/2008hearings/tran scripts/08_05_20_trans/sokolski.pdf, p. 1 of written testimony.

50. For expertise on this issue we particularly recommend the Wisconsin Project on Nuclear Arms Control and the Nonproliferation Policy Education Center, both in Washington, D.C.

51. Richard Weitz, "China's Proliferation Problem," *The Diplomat*, May 24, 2011.

52. With Triplett, fall 1988.

53. For a more complete discussion of this event, see William C. Triplett II, "China's Weapons Mafia," *Washington Post*, October 27, 1991; and William C. Triplett, II, "Nuke Crux: 'Clans,'" *Washington Post*, October 27, 1991.

54. Conversation with William C. Triplett II.

55. Chris Buckley, "China PLA officer urges challenging U.S. dominance," Reuters, February 28, 2010, http://www.reuters.com/article/2010/03/01/us-china-usa-military-exclusive-idUSTRE6200P620100301.

56. Joseph Kahn, "Chinese General Threatens Use of A-Bombs if U.S. Intrudes," *New York Times*, July 15, 2005.

57. Marc Erikson, "China, Japan and General Xiong," *Asia Times*, May 10, 2003.

58. Damian Grammaticas, "Aircraft carrier symbol of China's Naval Ambitions," BBC News, June 8, 2011, http://www.bbc.co.uk/news/world-asia-pacific-13693495.

59. James Grubel, "South China Sea disputes could lead to Asian war: think tank," Reuters, June 28, 2011, http://www.reuters.com/article/2011/06/28/us-southchinasea-idUSTRE75R0C820110628.

60. "China's dependency on foreign oil exceeds 55%," *People's Daily*, August 11, 2011.

61. Ryan Dezember, "Diamond Offshore To Move U.S. Rig From Gulf Of Mexico To Vietnam," *Dow-Jones Newswires*, June 15, 2011.

62. Jim Gomez, "China to neighbors: Stop oil search in Spratlys," Associated Press, June 9, 2011.

63. Staff reporter, "China aims to beat rivals to deep sea oil and gas fields," WantChinaTimes online, May 24, 2011, http://www.wantchinatimes.com/news-subclass-cnt.aspx?id=20110524000085&cid=1102&MainCatID=11.

64. "Country Analysis Briefs, South China Sea," Energy Information Administration, March 2008, p. 4.

65. Richard D. Fisher Jr., *China's Military Modernization: Building for Regional and Global Reach* (Praeger Security International, 2008).
66. (State 076155)
67. Joby Warrick and Peter Slevin, "Libyan Arms Designs Traced Back to China," op. cit.
68. William J. Broad and David E. Sanger, "As Nuclear Secrets Emerge in Khan Inquiry, More Are Suspected," *The New York Times*, December 26, 2004.
69. Mathew Godsey, "Chinese Companies Evade U. S. Trade Ban," The Wisconsin Project on Nuclear Arms Control, p. 1.
70. Jim Mann, *The China Fantasy* (Viking: 2007), p. 60.
71. Ibid., p. 59.

Chapter Five

1. Pauline Arrillaga. "America's New Threat: China's Spies," Associated Press, May 7, 2011.
2. Confidential interview with one of the authors.
3. Pauline Arrillaga, "China's spying seeks secret US info," Associated Press, May 7, 2011.
4. "2 Chinese nationals pleaded guilty to illegally attempting to export radiation-hardened microchips to the PRC," Department of Justice News Release, June 1, 2011.
5. For example, see Richard D. Fisher, "...And Races Into Space," originally published in the *Wall Street Journal Asia*, January 3, 2008, available on the International Assessment and Strategy Center website, http://www.strategycenter.net/research/pubID.175/pub_detail.asp.
6. "Ex-Space Shuttle Engineer Sentenced for China Spying," Bloomberg, February 8, 2010.
7. FBI Honolulu Division Press Release, "Hawaii Man Sentenced to 32 Years in Prison for Providing Defense Information and Services to the People's Republic of China," January 25, 2011, http://www.justice.gov/opa/pr/2011/January/11-nsd-104.html.
8. Lee Tae-hoon, "Probe into Shanghai scandal faces hurdles," *Korea Times*, March 11, 2011.
9. Kim Willsher, "Leaked French intelligence reports accuse China of industrial espionage," *The Guardian*, February 1, 2011.

10. John F. Burns, "Britain Warned Businesses of Threat of Chinese Spying," *New York Times,* February 1, 2011.

11. Mari Yamaguchi, "Japanese Officer Arrested in alleged Aegis Leak," Associated Press, December 13, 2007.

12. Private correspondence.

13. Malcolm Moore, "China opens string of spy schools," *Telegraph,* June 24, 2011.

14. "Ex-Pentagon Official sentenced to 3 years in China spy case," AFP, January 22, 2010.

15. Wire reporter, "Retired AF officer on Trial in China Spy Case," Associated Press, September 22, 2009.

16. Jerry Markon, "Defense Department official sentenced in spy case," *Washington Post,* January 23, 2010.

17. CNN Wire Staff, "Man gets 4 years in jail for attempt to spy for China," CNN Justice, January 21, 2011, http://articles.cnn.com/2011-01-21/justice/us.china.spying.sentence_1_china-chinese-president-hu-jintao-chinese-intelligence?_s=PM:CRIME.

18. Steve Kroft, "Cyber War: Sabotaging the System," *60 Minutes,* June 15, 2010, http://www.cbsnews.com/stories/2009/11/06/60minutes/main5555565.shtml.

19. CBS News Transcripts, Steve Kroft, "Cyber War; Weakness of Military and Civilian Computer Systems In the United States Against Outside Computer Hackers," *60 Minutes,* April 9, 2000.

20. "Cyberwar; Weakness of Military and Civilian Computer Systems in the United States Against Outside Computer Hackers," *60 Minutes,* April 9, 2000.

21. Robert McMillan, "Siemens: Stuxnet worm hit industrial systems," Computerworld, September 14, 2010, http://www.computerworld.com/s/article/9185419/Siemens_Stuxnet_worm_hit_industrial_systems.

22. Deputy Secretary of Defense William J. Lynn, III, "Remarks at the 28th Annual International Workshop on Global Security," Paris, France, June 16, 2011.

23. Raphael G. Satter, "US Shut Down Q's Refineries- Project Cyber Dawn," Associated Press, June 16, 2011.

24. Pierre Thomas, "Experts prepare for 'an electronic Pearl Harbor,'" CNN November 7, 1997, http://www.cnn.com/US/9711/07/terrorism.infrastructure/.

25. Representative Curt Weldon (R-Pa) quoting Mr. Hamre, in John Donnelly and Vincent Crawley, "Hamre to Hill: 'We're in a Cyberwar,'" *Defense News*, March 1, 1999, p.1.
26. Steve Kroft, "Cyber War: Sabotaging the System," op. cit.
27. Richard A. Clarke, "China's Cyberassault on America," *Wall Street Journal*, June 15, 2011, p. A15.
28. On September 11, 2001, Richard Clarke was the National Security Council official with responsibility for counter-terrorism. In both his 9-11 Commission testimony and his subsequent book, he blamed President Bush and his National Security Advisor Condoleezza Rice for failing to take Osama Bin Laden and al Qaeda seriously. See his book *Against All Enemies: Inside America's War on Terror* (Free Press, 2004).
29. William J. Lynn, "Remarks at the 28th Annual International Workshop on Global Security," op. cit.
30. Siobhan Gorman, "Computer spies Breach Fighter-Jet Project," *Wall Street Journal*, April 21, 2010.
31. Christopher Williams, "Google Gmail cyber attack: 'Chinese spies had months of access,'" *Telegraph*, June 2, 2011.
32. Bill Gertz, "Chinese Hackers Prompt Navy College Site Closure," *Washington Times*, November 30, 2006.
33. Richard Behar, "World Bank Under Cyber Siege in 'Unprecedented Crisis,'" Fox News, October 10, 2008.
34. Howard Schneider and Ellen Nakashima, "IMF Investigates suspected attack on its computers," *Washington Post*, June 11, 2011.
35. "China Believed to be behind cyber spy network," Associated Press, March 29, 2009.
36. Dr. Adam Segal, "Curbing Chinese cyber espionage," CNN, May 9, 2011, http://globalpublicsquare.blogs.cnn.com/2011/05/09/curbing-chinese-cyber-espionage/.
37. Nathan Hodge and Adam Entous, "Oil Firms Hit by Hackers from China," *Wall Street Journal*, February 10, 2011.
38. Nathan Olivarez-Giles, "McAfee says 'one state actor' behind international hacking spree," *Los Angeles Times*, August 2, 2011.
39. John Markoff, "China Link Suspected in Lab Hacking," *New York Times*, December 9, 2007.
40. Brian Grow and Mark Hosenball, "In cyberspy vs cyberspy, China has the edge," Reuters, April 14, 2011, http://www.reuters.com/article/2011/04/14/us-china-usa-cyberespionage-idUSTRE73D24220110414.

41. Demetri Sevastopulo, "Chinese hacked into Pentagon," *Financial Times*, September 3, 2007.

42. Steve Kroft, "Cyber War: Sabotaging the System," op. cit.

43. Jeffrey Carr, "Huawei Investigated for Bribery in Obtaining Telekom Austria Contracts," *Digital Dao* blog, April 6, 2011, http://jeffreycarr. blogspot.com/2011/04/huawei-investigated-for-bribery-in.html.

44. "China's Telecom Industry on the Move; Domestic Competition, Global Ambition and Leadership Transition," *China Leadership Monitor*, No. 19, Hoover Institution, October 24, 2006.

45. Evan S. Medeiros, Roger Cliff, Keith Crane, and James Mulvenon, "A New Direction for China's Defense Industry," A RAND monograph, 2005, p. 246.

46. Economic and Commercial Counselor's Office of the Embassy of China in the Islamic Republic of Iran. "Huawei Plans Takeover of Iran's Telecom Market," August 17, 2009, quoted in an August 18, 2010 letter from Senators Jon Kyl (R-AZ), Christopher Bond (R-MO) and others to Secretary of the Treasury Timothy Geithner and others.

47. Doug Palmer, "U.S. must confront China export advantages—Eximbank," Reuters, June 15, 2011, http://www.reuters.com/article/2011/06/15/usa-china-financing-idUSN159870520110615.

48. Margaret Kane, "Cisco sues Huawei over Patents," ZDNet UK, January 23, 2003, http://news.cnet.com/Cisco-sues-Huawei-over-patents/2100-1033_3-981811.html.

49. John Markoff and David Barboza, "Chinese Telecom Giant in Push for U.S. Market," *New York Times*, October 25, 2010.

50. Bruce Einhorn, "A Huawei Story Lost in Translation," *BusinessWeek*, August 3, 2004.

51. Phil Harvey and Peter Heywood, "Huawei in Spying Flap," *Light Reading*, June 24, 2004, http://www.lightreading.com/document.asp?doc_id=55172&site=supercomm; Phil Harvey and Peter Heywood, "Huawei Fires Supercomm Snooper," *Light Reading*, August 17, 2004, http://www.lightreading.com/document.asp?doc_id=57888.

52. Peter Borrows, "Huawei Isn't in the Clear Yet," *BusinessWeek*, July 30, 2004.

53. Steven R. Weisman, "Sale of 3Com to Huawei is derailed by U. S. security concerns," *New York Times*, February 28, 2008.

54. August 18, 2010, from Senators Jon Kyl (R-AZ), Christopher Bond (R-MO) and others to Treasury Secretary Timothy Geithner and others.

55. Press Release, Senator Jim Webb, February 10, 2011, http://webb.senate.
gov/newsroom/pressreleases/02-10-2011-01.cfm.

56. David Barboza, "China Telecom Giant, Thwarted in U.S. Deals, Seeks
Inquiry to Clear Name," *New York Times*, February 25, 2011.

57. "Capability of the People's Republic of China to Conduct Cyber Warfare
and Computer Network Exploitation," Northrop Grumman, prepared
for the U.S.–China Economic and Security Review Commission, October
9, 2009, p. 58.

58. Bill Gertz, "Ex-DIA Analyst Admits Passing Secrets to China," *Washington
Times*, June 23, 2006.

59. See Bill Gertz, *The China Threat* (Regnery, 2000), pp. 34–38.

60. Statement of Facts, Paragraph 10.

61. Bill Gertz, "Leak Cost U.S. Spy Links to Chinese Arms Sales," *Washington
Times*, September 15, 2006.

62. Ibid.

63. Triplett, 1992.

64. "US Treasury Secretary Tim Geithner blasts China for 'systematically
stealing' US intellectual property," the *Telegraph*, September 30, 2011.

65. "The National Intelligence Strategy of the United States, of America,"
August 2009, p 3.

66. "Transcript Of President Obama's Jobs Speech," September 8, 2011, NPR,
http://www.npr.org/2011/09/08/140320022/transcript-of-president-
obamas-jobs-speech.

67. Pauline Arrillaga, "China's spying seeks Secret U.S. info," Associated Press,
May 5, 2011. Ms Van Cleave and Mr. Brenner's formal title was "National
Counterintelligence Executive."

68. Bill Gertz, "China removed as top priority for spies," *Washington Times*,
January 20, 2010.

69. Prepared Statement of I. C. Smith, hearing before the U.S.–China Economic
and Security Commission, "China's Espionage and Intelligence Operations
Directed Against the United States," April 30, 2009.

70. Ibid., p. 118.

71. Press Release, "International Student Enrollments Rose Modestly in
2009/10, led by Strong Increase in Students from China," Institute of
International Education, November 15, 2010.

Chapter Six

1. "Trade in Goods (Imports, Exports and Trade Balance) with China: 1985-2011," U.S. Census Bureau, Foreign Trade Division, Data Dissemination Branch, Washington D.C., http://www.census.gov/foreign-trade/balance/c5700.html.

2. Staff economists, "World Development Indicators," The World Bank, 2011, http://data.worldbank.org/data-catalog/world-development-indicators.

3. Anonymous, *The World Fact Book*, The Central Intelligence Agency, 2011, https://www.cia.gov/library/publications/the-world-factbook/fields/2011.html.

4. Brett Arends, "IMF bombshell: Age of America nears end," *MarketWatch*, April 25, 2011, http://www.marketwatch.com/story/imf-bombshell-age-of-america-about-to-end-2011-04-25.

5. Angus K. Ross, "It's Not Rocket Science ... But It Won't Be Easy Either," *The Bridge*, May 2011, p. 10.

6. Editorial board, "President Pumps Politics," *Washington Times*, March 30, 2011.

7. *See*: "What is ANWR and Where Is the Coastal Plain?" http://www.anwr.org/backgrnd/where.htm, and George Berkin, "Drill, Baby, Drill—in Alaska's ANWR," *New Jersey Star-Ledger*, May 16, 2011.

8. Paritosh Bansal and Farah Master, "Chesapeake, CNOOC strike second shale deal for $1.3 billion," Reuters, January 30, 2011, http://www.reuters.com/article/2011/01/31/us-cnooc-chesapeake-idUSTRE70U0JE20110131.

9. David Winning and Jing Yang, "Cnooc, Chesapeake Agree on Deal," *Wall Street Journal*, January 31, 2011.

10. Alison Tudor, "China Is Paying Up in Push to Join the Shale-Gas Boom," *Wall Street Journal*, February 14, 2011.

11. *Gweilo* is the Chinese word for "white demon," a common epithet used to denigrate Westerners, especially British subjects and Americans who historically were seen as foreign Imperial invaders.

12. Paritosh Bansal and Farah Master, "Chesapeake, CNOOC strike second shale deal for $1.3 billion," op. cit.

13. *See*: www.uscc.gov/hearings/2009hearings/transcripts/09_04_30_trans/09_04_30_trans.pdf.

14. Daniel Golden, "China's Test Prep Juggernaut," *BusinessWeek*, May 5, 2011.

15. Wire service reporter, "New Oriental School's compensation to ETS reduced," Xinhua, February 6, 2005.

16. Daniel Golden, "China's Test Prep Juggernaut," op. cit.

17. Matthew Robertson, "Fellowes, American Stationary Giant, Brought to Its Knees in China," *Epoch Times*, April 23, 2011.

18. John Bussey, "U.S. Firms, China Are Locked in Major War Over Technology," *Wall Street Journal*, February 2, 2011.

19. John Bussey, "U.S. Technology Firms, China Tangle Again Over Contracts," *Wall Street Journal*, April 18, 2011.

20. Wire service reporter, "ETS and New Oriental Enter Into Strategic Agreement," Xinhua, November 26, 2007.

21. "Cisco Files Suit Against China's Huawei Technologies," Reuters, January 23, 2003.

22. Press release, "Former Dow Research Scientist Convicted of Stealing Trade Secrets and Perjury," U.S. Department of Justice, February 7, 2011.

23. *See*: "2010 U.S. Intellectual Property Enforcement Coordinator Annual Report on Intellectual Property Enforcement," February 2011, http://www. justice.gov/criminal/cybercrime/ipecreport2010.pdf.

24. Sylvia Cochran, "China Criticizes Buy American Stimulus Provision; Demands Buy Chinese," Associated Content, 2011, http://www.associat edcontent.com/article/1854203/china_criticizes_buy_american_stimulus. html.

25. Speech by Robert Agostinelli, Newport, Rhode Island, U.S. Naval War College, February 15, 2011.

26. Staff blogger, "Funding United States Stimulus Package with Chinese Investment in U.S. Treasuries," CM Capital Market Research, March 15, 2009, http://www.cmcapitalmarketresearch.com/blog/?p=1555.

27. Belinda Cao and Judy Chen, "China Will Fund U.S. Debt," Bloomberg, February 11, 2009.

28. Ibid.

29. Min Ye, "China's Massive Stimulus and U.S. Steel Companies," *Hemscott News*, July 30, 2009.

30. Mike Tarsala, "At Least the Chinese Stimulus Works for the American Economy," 24/7WallSt.com, July 22, 2009, http://247wallst. com/2009/07/22/at-least-the-chinese-stimulus-works-for-the-american- economy/.

31. Staff reporter, "World Markets Buoyed by Massive Chinese Stimulus Plan," Xinhua, November 11, 2008.

32. Simon Montlake, "China's Stimulus Working—Perhaps Too Well," *Christian Science Monitor*, August 12, 2009.

33. Staff blogger, "No Chinese Stimulus Plan, Alcoa Falls," MarketMinute. com, Stock News, March 5, 2009, http://blog.marketminute.com/finan cial_stock_news/2009/03/no-chinese-stimulus-plan-alcoa.html.

34. Henny Sender, "China to Stick with U.S. Bonds," *Financial Times*, February 11, 2009.

35. Jonathan Adams, "American Jobs vs. China's Currency: Is the Yuan Too High?" *Christian Science Monitor*, April 13, 2010.

36. Staff editorial writers, "Talking to China," *New York Times*, May 7, 2011.

37. Thea M. Lee, "China's Industrial, Investment and Exchange-Rate Policies: Impact on the U.S.," Testimony Before the Commission on U.S.–China Economic and Security Review, September 25, 2003.

38. Representative Duncan Hunter, May 6, 2007.

39. Jonathan Rothwell, "Are U.S. Financial Markets Sending Manufacturing Jobs to China?" *The New Republic*, January 19, 2011.

40. Ian Katz, "China Must Let Yuan Rise Faster, Treasury Tells Congress," Bloomberg-*BusinessWeek*, May 27, 2011.

41. Glenn Somerville, "Treasury's Geithner Says China Needs faster Yuan Rise," Reuters, January 12, 2011.

42. Mark Drajem and Rebecca Christie, "Geithner Warning on Yuan May Renew U.S.–China Tension," Bloomberg, January 23, 2009.

43. Unsigned editorial, "Handle China Carefully," *The Augusta Chronicle*, January 24, 2011.

44. Mike McGraw, "Stimulus? U.S. to buy Chinese condoms, ending Alabama jobs," *Kansas City Star*, November 24, 2010.

45. "Made in America: Could College Dorm Rooms Hold the Key to Half a Million New U.S. Jobs?" ABC News, http://abcnews.go.com/Business/ MadeInAmerica/made-america-back-school/story?id=14428881.

46. Pete Engardio, "Can the U.S. Bring Jobs Back from China?" *BusinessWeek*, June 19, 2008.

47. Roy Nersesian, "Globalization Creates Jobs for China and Not for U.S.," NewJerseyNewsroom.com, December 26, 2010, http://www.newjer seynewsroom.com/commentary/globalization-creates-jobs-for-china-and-not-for-us.

48. Suzanne Goldenberg, "Obama Focuses on Green Economy in Speech Before Congress," *Manchester Guardian*, February 25, 2009.

49. Wire reporter, "Green Jobs Going to China: Avg. Wage Is $141 Mo," Bloomberg, February 4, 2010.

50. Stacy Feldman, "China Winning Race for Green Jobs," *Manchester Guardian*, October 7, 2010.

51. "Want a Green Job? Move to China," *The Independent*, October 12, 2010, and Wire reporter. "China's Global Dominance in Green Jobs Growing," *China Daily*, October 8, 2010.

52. Derrick Z. Jackson, "A Green Loss Here Is a Win for China," *Boston Globe*, January 15, 2011.

53. Seth Leitman, "BP Solar Cuts U.S. Jobs, Moved to China," *The Daily Green*, July 14, 2010.

54. Mike Elk, "GE Moves Green Jobs To China," OurFuture.org, July 23, 2009, http://www.ourfuture.org/node/40003.

55. Peter Whoriskey, "Light Bulb Factory Closes; End of Era for U.S. Means More Jobs Overseas," *Washington Post*, September 8, 2010.

56. Christopher Martin and Jim Efstathiou Jr., "China's Labor Edge Overpowers Obama's 'Green' Jobs Initiatives," Bloomberg, February 4, 2010.

57. Jonathon M. Seidl, "Dems Helping Chinese Get $450 Million in Stimulus Money," *The Blaze*, December 9, 2010.

58. Keith Bradsher, "Union Accuses China of Illegal Clean Energy Subsidies," *New York Times*, September 9, 2010.

59. *See:* http://www.census.gov/popest/archives/pre-1980.

60. Mortimer B. Zuckerman, "Why the Jobs Situation Is Worse Than It Looks," *U.S. News & World Report*, June 20, 2011.

61. "Import Refusal Report," U.S. Food and Drug Administration Import Refusal Reports for OASIS, U.S. Department of Health and Human Services, January 26, 2011, http://www.accessdata.fda.gov/scripts/importrefusals/.

62. Josh Goldstein, "Jefferson Emergency Doctors Discover Lead Danger in Philly's Chinatown … and Beyond," The Daily Dose, February 18, 2011, http://www.jeffersonhospital.org/The-Daily-Dose/jefferson-emergency-doctors-discover-lead-danger-in-phillys-chinatown-and-beyond.aspx.

63. Online producer, "Zhu Zhu Hamsters May Pose Health Risk," CBS News, December 7, 2009, http://www.cbsnews.com/stories/2009/12/05/health/main5902520.shtml.

64. Justin Pritchard, "Tween Brands to Limit Toxic Cadmium in Its Jewelry," Associated Press, March 22, 2011.

65. Wire-service reporter, "Toxic Cadmium Found in Chinese Toys," Associated Press, January 12, 2010.

66. Nancy Shute, "A Fresh Look in China's Toxic Toy Chest," *U.S. News & World Report*, August 19, 2007.

67. Susannah Nesmith, "Whole Foods Lawsuit Over Chinese Frozen Vegetables Can proceed in Florida," *Bloomberg News*, April 21, 2011.

68. Carey Alexander, "Chinese Poison Train Declared Unstoppable: Next Stop, You!" *The Consumerist*, May 21, 2007, http://consumerist.com/2007/05/chinese-poison-train-declared-unstoppable-next-stop-you.html.

69. Rick Weiss, "Tainted Chinese Imports Common," *Washington Post*, May 20, 2007.

70. Michael Maiello, "Martha Stewart's Exploding Tables," Forbes, June 20, 2008.

71. Wenonah Hauter, executive director, "A Decade of Dangerous Food Exports from China," Washington: Food & Water Watch, 2011, http://documents.foodandwaterwatch.org/DecadeofDangerousImports.pdf.

72. "China detains manager at heart of U.S. pet food recall," CNN, May 8, 2007, http://articles.cnn.com/2007-05-08/world/china.petfood_1_rice-protein-wheat-gluten-commissioner-for-food-protection?_s=PM:WORLD.

73. "U.S. holds 20 million chickens because of melamine-tainted feed," CBC News, May 7, 2007, http://www.cbc.ca/news/story/2007/05/07/feed-assessment.html?ref=rss.

74. Martin Jacques, *When China Rules the World: The End of the Western World and the Birth of a New Global Order* (New York: Penguin Press, 2009).

75. Cary Huang, "Obama Hails China as Strategic Partner," Reuters, November 11, 2009.

76. Private correspondence.

Chapter Seven

1. Joseph S. Nye, Jr., *The Future of Power* (New York: PublicAffairs, 2011), p. 4.

2. Pat Choate, *Agents of Influence: How Japan's Lobbyists in the United States Manipulate America's Political and Economic System* (New York: Knopf, 1990), p. vii.

3. Joseph S. Nye, Jr., *Soft Power: The Means to Success in World Politics* (New York: PublicAffairs, 2004), p. x.

4. John Pomfret, "China's $6.6 billion global media strategy includes AM station in Galveston," *Washington Post,* April 25, 2010.

5.   "Beyond Beijing: WILD becomes CRI's window on the world," *Boston Radio Watch* blog, June 1, 2011, http://bostonradiowatch.blogspot.com/2011/06/beyond-bejing-wild-becomes-cris-window.html.

6.   Fourteen years ago, reporter and editor John Judis pointed out that carrying water for Beijing in Washington was mostly being done by Republicans. He was right, but times have changed. See "Chinatown" by John B. Judis, *The New Republic*, March 10, 1997.

7.   Department of Justice, Supplemental Statement of Patton Boggs LLP for the period ending June 30, 2008. Attachment D- Section III, #12.

8.   Department of Justice records.

9.   Akin Gump China Practice on-line.

10.   J. Bennett Johnston FARA filing, August 7, 2002, Exhibit "B".

11.   Marina Walker Guevara and Bob Williams, "China Steps Up its Lobbying Game," The Center for Public Integrity, September 13, 2005, http://projects.publicintegrity.org/lobby/report.aspx?aid=734.

12.   The lawyer signing this "CONFIDENTIAL" contract for Hale Boggs in 2010 was Mark D. Cowan, a significant contributor to Republican causes. The previous contracts in 2007 and 2005, also signed by Cowan, did not mention Boggs by name and indicated the account was handled by Cowan and others. A later Justice Department document (not the Hale Boggs contract with the PRC embassy), signed by Boggs but not dated by him, reveals that he has been rendering services to the PRC embassy for some unknown length of time. One might reasonably speculate that Boggs was explicitly named the team leader on the 2010 contract with the PRC embassy in order to justify the huge increase in retainer, or that the PRC insisted on his name in the contract. Source: Department of Justice.

13.   China Chamber of Commerce for Importers and Exporters of Metals, Minerals and Chemicals; and China Chamber of Commerce for Importers and Exporters of Machinery and Electronic Products. Department of Justice records and Hale Boggs online China practice areas.

14.   Dr. Ho, as he likes to call himself after his honorary title, was extensively covered in Edward P. Timperlake and William C. Triplett, II, *Year of the Rat* (Regnery, 1998).

15.   Department of Justice, Patton Boggs FARA filing for January 1, 2008–June 30, 2008, Attachment C-Section III #11.

16.   C. H. Tung, "In China, There's a lot to Celebrate," *Washington Post*, October 31, 2009.

17.   Ambassador James R. Lilley (1928–2009).

18. Jim gave a version of this explanation to journalist John Judis, Senior Editor of *The New Republic* in the late 1990s ("Chinatown," by John Judis, *The New Republic*, March 10, 1997).

19. Henry Kissinger, "Turmoil on Top," Los Angeles Times, July 30, 1989 Part 5, p. 1.

20. Joanna Slater, "Kissinger 'still a bit of a rock star' in world affairs, focusing on China," *The Toronto Globe and Mail*, June 10, 2011.

21. Leslie Gelb, "Kissinger Means Business," *New York Times*, April 20, 1986.

22. Henry Kissinger, *On China* (The Penguin Press, 2011).

23. *Report of the Special Examination of Fannie Mae conducted by the Office of Housing Enterprise Oversight,* May 2006.

24. Ibid., p. 305.

25. As of May 7, 2011, the taxpayer was already on the hook for $86 billion for Fannie Mae, which still had an additional $206 billion in delinquent loans on its books. See Nick Timiraos, "Fannie Mae Falls Back Into the Loss Column," *Wall Street Journal*, May 7, 2011.

26. David Brooks, "Who is James Johnson?" *New York Times*, June 17, 2011, p. A31.

27. *Report of the Special Examination of Fannie Mae conducted by the Office of Housing Enterprise Oversight*, May, 2006 p. 58.

28. Jason Horowitz, "Obama campaign visits shunned NYC home in search for Clinton's Wall Street cash," *Washington Post*, May 25, 2011 p. C-1.

29. See William C. Triplett, II, *Rogue State* (Regnery, 2004), p. 163.

30. Former Commander of the U.S. Pacific Command Admiral Timothy Keating, former AF chief of staff General Ronald R. Fogleman, former vice chief of staff of the U.S. Army General John M. Keane, and Marine General Charles E. Wilhelm.

31. Eli Lake, "Beijing Spying Feared in Telecom Proposal," Washington Times, October 20, 2010.

32. Byron York, "Wes Clark: McCain Doesn't Have the Right Kind of Military Experience to be Commander-in-Chief," National Review Online, *The Corner,* March 2, 2008, http://www.nationalreview.com/corner/159750/wes-clark-mccain-doesnt-have-right-kind-military-experience-be-commander-chief/byron-y.

33. See William C. Triplett, II, *Rogue State*, p. 163.

34. Bill Owens, "America must start treating China as a friend," *Financial Times*, November 17, 2009.

35. *The Nelson Report*, November 2008.

36. "Sanya Initiative: Key Outcomes & Summary Report," March 2008, p. 2.
37. Ibid.
38. "A Briefing on the Sanya Initiative," Center for Strategic and International Studies, June 8, 2008.
39. "Sanya Initiative: Key Outcomes & Summary Report," p. 3.
40. Ibid.
41. Dr. Ross Terrill, *800,000,000 The Real China* (Boston: Little Brown and Company, 1973).
42. Testimony of April 30, 2009. In an email response of May 9, 2011, Dr. Terrill reports [private correspondence] that he has been able to get a "tourist" visa but not a working visa.
43. Private correspondence.
44. Kim Wilmath, "USF Professor is impugned, but employed," *St. Petersburg Times*, June 5, 2011.
45. Mary Minihan, "China will co-finance new institute building at UCB, says Taoiseach," *The Irish Times,* September 28, 2010.
46. Dan Sabbagh, "Google attacks ordered by Li Changchun," The Guardian, December 5, 2010.
47. James Glanz and John Markoff, "Vast Hacking by China Fearful of the Web," New York Times, March 10, 2010.
48. Mary Beth Marklein, "A Culture Clash over Confucius Institutes," *USA Today*, December 7, 2009.
49. Stanford University, Center for East Asian Studies, *Horizons*, 2010, p. 1.
50. private correspondence from American academic.
51. Portland State University Press Release.
52. Catherine Mayer, "China Pandas to Public Opinion in Britain," *TIME*, June 27, 2011, http://globalspin.blogs.time.com/2011/06/27/china-pandas-to-public-opinion-in-britain/.

Chapter Eight

1. Hu Jintao biography, *People's Daily*, http://english.peopledaily.com.cn/data/people/hujintao.shtml.
2. Henry A. Kissinger, "Avoiding a U.S.–China cold war," *Washington Post*, January 14, 2011.
3. Patrick J. Buchanan, "How the Chinese Must See Us," *Townhall*, January 21, 2011.

4. David Ignatius, "Amid the wining and dining of Hu Jintao, a display of American 'smart power,'" *Washington Post*, January 21, 2011.

5. William C. Triplett II, "Who Is Hu Jintao? Official niceties obscure his bloody record," *Washington Times*, January 17, 2011.

6. Don Hyatt, "Arboretum Update: $1 Million Donation," American Rhododendron Society, Potomac Valley Chapter, *Spring Newsletter,* March 2011.

7. Amie Parnes and Karin Tanabe, "Boehner Declines State Dinner Invite," *Politico*, January 17, 2011.

8. Darlene Superville and Nancy Benac, "A Jazzy All-American state dinner for China's Hu," *MSNBC*, January 19, 2011, http://www.msnbc.msn.com/id/41161688/ns/politics-white_house/t/jazzy-all-american-state-dinner-chinas-hu/#.ToHk7ez64rU.

9. Scott Wong, "Reid calls Chinese leader Hu Jintao 'dictator,'" *Politico*, January 19, 2011.

10. The White House: Guest List for State Dinner for Hu Jintao of China, January 19, 2011.

11. YC Dhardhowa, "Nobel Laureates Liu in Prison, Obama Hosts State Dinner for Hu," *Tibet Post*, January 21, 2011.

12. Sheryl Gay Stolberg, "Diplomatic Dangers Lurk in the State Dinner," *New York Times*, January 18, 2011.

13. Mosheh Oinounou and Bonney Kapp, "Michelle Obama Takes Heat for Saying She's 'Proud of My Country' for the First Time," Fox News, February 19, 2008, http://www.foxnews.com/story/0,2933,331288,00.html.

14. Fareed Zakaria, *The Post-American World* (New York: Norton, 2008), p. 5.

15. Ibid., p. 88.

16. Joseph S. Nye, Jr., *The Future of Power* (New York: PublicAffairs, 2011), p. 182.

17. "Gallup Poll Social Series: Work and Education," Gallup News Service, August 11–14, 2011.

INDEX